THE PSALMS

Volume 1

G. A. F. KNIGHT

THE SAINT ANDREW PRESS
EDINBURGH

THE WESTMINSTER PRESS
PHILADELPHIA

Published by
The Saint Andrew Press
Edinburgh, Scotland
and
The Westminster Press ®
Philadelphia, Pennsylvania

Printed and bound in Great Britain.
by Thomson Litho Ltd., East Kilbride, Scotland

ISBN (Great Britain) 0 7152 0520 X

THE DAILY STUDY BIBLE

(OLD TESTAMENT)

General Editor: John C.L. Gibson

THE PSALMS

GENERAL PREFACE

The series of Old Testament commentaries to which this volume by Dr. Knight belongs has been planned as a companion series to the much-acclaimed New Testament series of the late Professor William Barclay. As with that series, each volume is arranged in successive headed portions suitable for daily study. The Biblical text followed is that of the Revised Standard Version or Common Bible. Eleven contributors share the work, each being responsible for from one to three volumes. The series is issued in the hope that it will do for the Old Testament what Professor Barclay's series succeeded so splendidly in doing for the New Testament—make it come alive for the Christian believer in the twentieth century.

Its two-fold aim is the same as his. Firstly, it is intended to introduce the reader to some of the more important results and fascinating insights of modern Old Testament scholarship. Most of the contributors are already established experts in the field with many publications to their credit. Some are younger scholars who have yet to make their names but who in my judgment as General Editor are now ready to be tested. I can assure those who use these commentaries that they are in the hands of competent teachers who know what is of real consequence in their subject and are able to present it in a form that will appeal to the general public.

The primary purpose of the series, however, is *not* an academic one. Professor Barclay summed it up for his New Testament series in the words of Richard of Chichester's prayer—to enable men and women "to know Jesus Christ more clearly, to love Him more dearly, and to follow Him more nearly." In the case of the Old Testament we have to be a little more circumspect than that. The Old Testament was completed long before the time of Our Lord, and it was (as it still is) the sole Bible of the Jews, God's first people, before it became part of the Christian Bible. We must take this fact seriously.

Yet in its strangely compelling way, sometimes dimly and sometimes directly, sometimes charmingly and sometimes embarrassingly, it holds up before us the things of Christ. It should not be forgotten that Jesus Himself was raised on this Book, that He based His whole ministry on what it says, and that He approached His death with its words on His lips. Christian men and women have in this ancient collection of Jewish writings a uniquely illuminating avenue not only into the will and purposes of God the Father, but into the mind and heart of Him who is named God's Son, who was Himself born a Jew but went on through the Cross and Resurrection to become the Saviour of the world. Read reverently and imaginatively the Old Testament can become a living and relevant force in their everyday lives.

It is the prayer of myself and my colleagues that this series may be used by its readers and blessed by God to that end.

New College
Edinburgh

JOHN C.L. GIBSON
General Editor

CONTENTS

CONTENTS

ABBREVIATIONS

AV   Authorized, or King James, Version of the Bible.
ftn. Footnote to a verse in the RSV.
LXX The Septuagint or Greek Version of the OT.
NAB New American Bible.
NEB New English Bible.
NIV New International Version.
NT   New Testament.
OT   Old Testament.
RSV Revised Standard Version of the Bible.
RV   Revised Version, 1885.
TEV Today's English Version, or Good News Bible.

INTRODUCTION

"To open the book of Psalms is to open the door into the worship of all believers in all countries of the world in all centuries from 1,000 B.C. till the present time." This is a challenging statement when we remember how there are wide differences both in structure and in theological emphasis between the Churches today. Yet we all have the book of Psalms in common. One Church may chant the Psalms in prose, another may sing them in metrical form. A congregation here may read them aloud verse about with the minister; a congregation there may listen to a powerful interpretation given by a talented choir. But over and above whatever use we make of the Psalms in public worship, we all know the value of reading the Psalms quietly in the privacy of our own homes.

The word *psalm* in the original Hebrew means just *song*. It did not mean originally anything specially "religious", because to the Hebrews the whole of life belonged to God who gave it. Yet all the Psalms are either addressed to God or speak about the loving will and purpose of God. Some are complaints from the heart spoken directly to God. Others are very personal confessions of sin, which the speaker knows has separated him from God. Others are shouts of praise made in wonder when the psalmist feels overwhelmed by grace. Some seem to have been composed on a sick-bed, others even at the approach of death. Some are congregational hymns that can be set alongside our modern form of hymn-writing. Some look back upon the long story of God's loving handling of his people Israel, right back over the centuries. They thus lead the singers to a confident declaration of faith about the future. Others centre round the person of the king, who takes a very special place in Israel's thoughts and in God's plans for his people. Others again exult in the beauty and significance of the holy city of Jerusalem from which the divinely chosen king reigns, and from which, one day, he will reign over all the earth. Others rejoice in God's gift of the Law, seeing it as a light to the path of the individual believer. Others stand in awe before the mystery of nature, of the thunderstorm, the earthquake, the migration of birds, the majesty of the mighty cedars of Lebanon; but these psalms always acknowledge that the strange forces of nature remain in the hand of God.

GRACE COMES FIRST

The Psalms, in short, express a deep awareness of the grace of God. Every psalm writer is conscious that what he is, what he thinks and feels and believes, depends entirely on the God who has acted first in his life. He is aware that God has revealed himself to Israel by what he "did" in days of old, in all those activities that we read about in the early books of the OT. It was for humanity that God had created the heavens and the earth, that God had revealed himself and his loving plan to Abraham, Isaac and Jacob. Thus now in later centuries the psalmist could look back and call his God "the God of the Fathers". God had rescued the psalmist's ancestors from slavery in Egypt under the hand of Moses. He had brought them through the perils of the Red Sea and the dangers inherent in the Wilderness Wanderings. God had given them for their own the land in which they now dwelt. Through Moses, moreover, God had given Israel the Law. This word is *Torah* in the Psalms, and means basically Teaching. But since it refers to God's teaching it also naturally means Revelation, revelation of the mind and purpose of God. The psalmists are deeply grateful for all that God has called upon them to do and to be through *Torah*.

But more; God had chosen Israel out of all the nations of the earth to be his own special people. Following upon the Covenant which God made with Abraham (Gen. 17:1–8), God had made a Covenant with the whole people of Israel at the foot of Mount Sinai (Exod. 19:3–6): "You will be my people, and I will be your God," he had declared. The name that God used about himself to Moses when he revealed himself at that time was *Yahweh*. This purely Hebrew name was never pronounced by the Jewish caretakers of the OT, out of reverence for "The Name". In its place they spoke of the "The Lord"; and so today, in the RSV translation of the Psalms that we are using in our Daily Study Bible it is that word which occurs when *Yahweh* is written. The form *Jehovah* is only the spelling of *Yahweh* produced by the first printers of the Bible in English six hundred years ago; it is now known to be inaccurate and should not be perpetuated.

THE COVENANT GOD

Because the *Lord* is the Covenant God, there occurs language in the Psalms that can only be understood as "covenant language". The idea of covenant has been clarified recently when scholars noted that in Moses' day conquering kings were in the habit of imposing a covenant agreement upon their subject peoples. Moses' "covenant" was thus something that the ancient Near East fully understood. Yet the Lord's Covenant with Israel was wholly different from that imposed by, say, a Babylonian monarch upon a small-time princeling. Its *content* was something completely new in the world's history. If we think of the Covenant as a kind of treaty that God made with Israel, then we can picture it in terms of a coconut. The hard shell of the nut is the covenant agreement, like the agreement a couple sign on their wedding day. But it is the edible portion inside which is important, just as are the promises the couple make: "For richer for poorer, in sickness and health ... till death us do part."

The Hebrew word *hesed* is used in the OT to describe the *content* of the Lord's Covenant, that which God is *doing* for Israel, and in and through Israel for the world. Moreover, it is what God expects Israel to do for him in return, *in covenant*. The translators of the old KJV of 1611 had little idea that they were handling a covenantal term when they met with this word *hesed*. So they were unable to penetrate to its essential meaning. They used up to forty-five different English words to render it, many of which occur in the Psalms, such as mercy, goodness, love, loving-kindness, and so on. Not that we need boast that we have put our finger on its exact meaning either. For it is a word that seeks to express, not an idea humanity has thought up, but God's gracious love and unspeakable loyalty within the bonds of the Covenant that he himself has laid upon Israel, so that the fulness of it is beyond our human understanding. We shall watch for this word then, as we meet with it later from psalm to psalm.

Then there are other covenant terms which keep recurring and which we shall try to translate in their context; but again we shall find that no one English word is fit to do so. These are words such as *righteousness, salvation, goodness* and more. One problem in regard to the first two of these words is that in the Psalms they appear in both a masculine and a feminine form. Translators right up till recently could not fathom wherein lies the difference between the two, especially as the two forms can occur within the one sentence. But today we believe we know the difference between them; for we have noticed how Isaiah made a clear distinction between them when he used them as covenant terms. But again we must humbly say that since they describe aspects of the unspeakable grace and goodness of the living God, we can only fumble for words as we try to express what God is doing through his use of them to reveal aspects of his amazing grace to us now in the twentieth century.

In the world of the Old Testament period objects and ideas connected with the sky above were regarded as masculine while the earth below was feminine. (Only the Egyptians reversed this way of thinking.) That is why the supreme god is always masculine, and why the earth is always feminine. Thus we have *erets* in Hebrew, *ge* in Greek, *terra* in Latin. The Near East always thought of the earth as being the Earth Mother. That then is why the nouns that describe God's *righteousness* and *salvation*, which he pours upon us from above, are shown in the masculine. Isa.45:8 makes this clear. It runs:

Shower, O heavens (masculine), from above
    and let the skies (masculine) rain down righteousness
        (masculine, *tsedeq*);

let the earth (feminine) open, that they (people) may bear
  the fruit of (God's) salvation (masculine),
  and let it cause righteousness (feminine, *tsedaqah*) to
    spring up also (this time out of the ground, or out of the
    human heart);
I the Lord have created it.

The psalm writers use the same two forms as Isaiah. They
use both the masculine and the feminine forms for the words
salvation and *righteousness*. The masculine noun for the first
(*yesha*) describes what God does or has done for us. He *saves* us
"from above", that is to say, out of sheer grace; consequently,
we junior partners in God's covenant love and grace are now
called to bear the fruit of (God's) saving love, (still masculine).
But as a result of that, something happens to us. As Genesis 1:26
puts it, the Creator God made us in his own image, meaning
that we are created to do what God does, and so be creators
also. God's *yesha*, then, now rooted in our hearts, empowers us
to show *yeshu'ah* (the feminine word), "saving love" to other
people. For love is not a mere sentiment. Love is an activity.
The whole new way of life that God offers us when "he puts us
right" with himself (the verb *tsadaq*) is called by the second
masculine noun *tsedeq*, translated in the RSV only too often,
unfortunately, as *righteous(ness)*. Having been given this new
life of love, however, we who are in the covenant are empowered to pass it on as *tsedaqah* (feminine) to other people, and so
to be God's instrument in putting other people *right with God*.
This is not done by force, or persuasion, or by might. It is done
by means of *yeshu'ah* (feminine), compassionate, creative love
that a human being can show towards his neighbour, and which
is a gift of God, by means of which he can bring his neighbour
out of the chaotic power of sin into the joy and peace of God.
Those who thus *recreate* their neighbours have earned the right,
as Jesus puts it, to be called children of God.

As Jesus put it at Matt.5:9: "Blessed are the *shalom* creators.
For by their creative love which is able to recreate the lives of
other people they show themselves to be the children of God".

The word *good*. In the Psalms we find this word used of God.

Modern man immediately thinks of its use in terms of morals. Of course it may mean morally good in certain circumstances, but notice in the first chapter of Genesis how, after each creative act, we read: "And God saw that it was good." Such a phrase excludes the idea of morality. For of course *good* here means "*good for* God's creative purpose". Or again, we read at Exod.2:2 that when the baby Moses was born, his mother "saw that he was good". The RSV does the forbidden thing at this point, for it reads into the Hebrew text what it thinks ought to be there. There is no "goodly child" in the original. No, like the Virgin Mary in the New Testament, this mother realizes that her child was going to be *good for* God's plan for the redemption of Israel. So, when we read the Psalms, we are to let ourselves discover God's creative purpose pressing through at all levels of human life.

Finally, the word *mercy*. This noun derives from the word for "womb". It expresses the "existential" overpowering and compassionate love, which only a mother can know, for the baby who has come forth from her womb. Again we see it illustrated in a passage from the great Second Isaiah. At Isa.49:14–15 we read:

> But Zion said, "The Lord has forsaken me,
>   my Lord has forgotten me."
> "Can a woman forget her sucking child,
>   that she should have no compassion on the son of her
>   womb?
> Even these may forget,
>   yet I will not forget you."

In the Old Testament the love of God is shown to be just as much the love of the divine Mother as it is of the divine Father. But at Luke 1:50 Mary makes the same claim for God's mercy as does the Old Testament and the book of Psalms in it.

But whatever words we are forced to employ to translate such Hebrew terms, we discover that the basic and essential truth about the meaning of grace is that God has acted first. God has already *saved* his people, before they could even cry to him for salvation. No psalmist, we note, cries to God for salvation. What he does do frequently is to cry to be forgiven, for rebelling (that is another covenantal term we shall meet with) against God's loving purpose for him and for this people whom he has already saved. So he cries for faith, or for hope, or for more awareness of God's grace. When he shouts with gratitude and love, particularly in public worship, he does so remembering *what God has already done for him*. Moreover, he is glad to make use of the whole sacrificial system which God has ordained for Israel's use, not in order to gain God's good will, for he already has that, but in order to help him stay loyal to God and grateful to him *for what God has already done*. Yet even as they worshipped, those very human psalm writers discovered that the sacrifices of bulls and goats had only been given them by God to educate them to the true meaning of sacrifice, which must be an act of the heart and the will in response to the strangeness of human life that must be lived out in a world of disease, earthquake and war.

THE GAP IN TIME AND CULTURE

There are great differences in thinking between the ancient Psalter and ourselves today. The psalms are anything up to 3,000 years old. Thus it is difficult to translate some of them word for word into English, or Swahili, or Chinese, for that matter. Look at this simple case of translation between two modern languages of closely related cultures. *"La plume de ma tante"* does not mean merely "My aunt's pen". Language uses pictorial ideas that arise out of the culture into which they form a kind of window. The Frenchman's picture, when he says "plume", is that of a bird's feather. But mine is of a fountain-pen! Whereas my son, of a later generation, envisages a ball-point pen! The Frenchman has an intuition that his feather-quill is feminine. We wonder what there is in his culture to make him think that way (see what we said before about the two words for "salvation", one of them being feminine). Then he has a mental picture of his dear aunt sitting on a beach at Nice lunching on frogs' legs and a bottle of wine; yet the word "aunt" may convey to me a picture of a stern old lady in her cold climate enjoying porridge and tea for her breakfast. So too even the seemingly straightforward words king, priest, house, love, etc., do not always mean to the Hebrew what they mean to us.

THE AUTHORSHIP OF THE PSALMS

The language of the Psalter has its roots in the ancient poems of the Hebrew people. A good example is the Song of Deborah, to be found at Judg.5, or the so-called Song of Moses (Deut.32). The Canaanites too wrote poems which remind us in many ways of the Hebrew Psalms.

The name most commonly associated with the Psalms is that of David, and there seems little reason to doubt that his influence was crucial in the rise of Hebrew psalmody. But that does not mean that he personally wrote them all. It is now recognized that the *headings of the Psalms* were added only in later centuries, and are not original. But even if we accord them a high credence as reflecting the tradition of the temple priests and singers, only about half of them contain the words "of David". Moreover, there is considerable argument about what this phrase exactly denotes. The preposition *of* (*le* in Hebrew), can mean more than one thing. It can mean (a) composed *by* David, as we would expect; and doubtless some psalms were. But it can also mean (b) composed *for* David; and a number of psalms were clearly written by someone else in honour of David. But (c) the *le* can also equal the French *à la*, meaning "in the manner of David", David having set the pattern, so to speak.

Many crockery jars have been turned up by the spade of the archaeologist in the Palestine region, with the word *le-melek* incised on them, meaning "(belonging) to the king", or "royal property". And so we may have in this a *fourth* possible meaning, "authorized by" or the like. Various collections of "songs" were made as the centuries went by, to be used by the temple choirs. One would be known as the Davidic collection, and would contain all those headed "of David". Others were collected by the Sons of Asaph (Ps.50) or the Sons of Korah

(Ps.84). These "sons of . . ." were evidently groups of temple functionaries responsible for the music at public worship. I know of a female-voice choir today called similarly "The Daughters of Saint Cecilia". The Second Book of Chronicles, which was written some seven hundred years after the time of David, preserves memories of the choirs and of their music. By then it would seem that David, as "responsible" for the largest collection, had become what we might call the patron saint of Israel's psalmody.

We should note finally, that "David" does not necessarily mean only the great king of that name. For one thing, public worship in his day must have been quite rudimentary in form, for it was only his son, Solomon, who built the temple, and who set up the choirs and music which we associate with that building. Moreover we learn from 2 Sam.7 that, through the prophet Nathan, God called not just David, but the whole line of David's descendants to be in a special relationship to himself as his "son". And so, a couple of centuries later, the reigning monarch, whoever he might be, could still be known as "David, son of God". The heading "of David" may sometimes have to be interpreted in that sense.

It is in fact impossible now to date the Psalms with any certainty. All we can be sure of is that the book as a whole reached its present form quite late. Some psalms evidently arose — and of course nobody knows who wrote them — during the Babylonian exile (586–539 B.C.); for example, the one which tells us how their foreign masters called upon the forlorn Israelites to "sing for their supper". We have their reply: "How shall we sing the Lord's song in a foreign land?" (Ps. 137). The long 119th Psalm probably comes from the period after the temple had been rebuilt (see Ezra 3:5 6), and after worship had been re-established by the returning community. The presence of such psalms suggests that it was from that period onwards that the Psalter as we know it was edited. Our present 150 psalms are contained in five collections or books—see the endings of Psalms 41, 72, 89, 106, and 150. Perhaps the five collections were authorized to be used in public worship in parallel with the "Five Books of Moses", as they were called, Genesis, Exodus, Leviticus, Numbers and Deuteronomy, for these were also put in their final form from about this time. Then too the elaborate orders of priests, the many sacrifices, the orchestras and choirs, came to full development only after 515 B.C., the year the Second Temple was dedicated, thus providing the form of temple worship that Jesus met with when, as a twelve-year-old boy, he first went up from Galilee to Jerusalem to attend one of the great festivals.

THE THEOLOGY OF THE PSALMS

There is too much to say on this matter to include in a short Introduction. We shall note what the writers have to say about God and his plan for the world as we reach each psalm in turn. However, we can say here that the Psalter, being the heart of the OT, so to speak, sums up and expresses the theology of the OT as a whole.

It is important to realize that the theology of the Psalms is quite unaffected by Greek thinking, even if some psalms were revised and updated as late as the period of Socrates, Plato, and Aristotle. These men had a great influence on the Mediterranean peoples as a whole, but absolutely none on Israel. Thus it is clearly inadmissible for us today with our cultural heritage in good part rooted in Greece, to read back into the Psalms philosophical ideas that we have learned from Plato. All Greek thought, despite its many variations, was dualistic. That is, it cut every aspect of life in two. It separated between heaven and earth, between the world of ideas or ideals and the world of scientific facts, between time and eternity, body and soul, love and sex, this world and the next world, town and country, Greeks and all other peoples (all of whom were known as barbarians), politics and religion, and so on.

The Hebraic philosophy of life that the psalm writers naturally accepted was, on the contrary, a unified one. Jeremiah spoke of creation as being *ha-kol*, "the whole". Of course one could speak of heaven, and then speak of earth. But the two were like the two sides of a coin. You could speak of and even describe and discuss each of the two sides in turn, and thus handle the question of a man's soul and of his body. But for the psalmists a human being is not a soul living temporarily in a body, as "the Greeks" maintained, or as the eastern religions do today. A person is one *nephesh* (AV "soul"), a word for which we have no English equivalent, for it describes not just what we think of as an individual, but a person all tied up in his relationships with other people, his mother, father, boss, employee, and so on. It is this whole *nephesh* then that is the object of God's love. Thus we must not read into the Psalms such Greek, secular ideas as that of "saving souls" or "the immortality of the soul".

A consequence of this view of the human *nephesh* as we find it in the Psalms is that it was natural for Israel to develop a representative form of government quite unlike that of Greece. Greek "democracy" is the direct ancestor of the apartheid philosophy of South Africa, for it was the domain of the top level of society only, and women and workers were excluded from taking part. In Israel each village elected its "judge", or "elder". This person sat at the gate of the village or small town to administer justice, and he had to do so even-handedly, to men, women, resident foreigners and slave-workers alike (and remember that a man worked as a slave for only six years and then was set free with a large bonus)—how unlike the Greek and Roman empires! This elder came up to Jerusalem, the capital city, three times a year at the three great festivals. On those occasions he sat with all his fellow-elders in a kind of parliament that advised the king on what justice for the ordinary villager meant in the changing circumstances of the times. If the king did not listen to these "MPs" it was not the fault of the system. We read that a very large number of these elders came back from exile in Babylon, and so we can presume that they had acted as representatives of their people even there where there was no king. This all means that when we read in the Psalms of the administration of justice through the king, we are to envisage behind it a "democratic" form of representative government that involved each level of responsibility in society.

Yet the psalmists were vividly aware of a dividing line, not a dividing line like that between matter and spirit, but one that cuts right through this one world of heaven and earth. It is the dividing line that exists between good and evil. There are modern "Greeks" who deny the very existence of such a distinction, and so of the existence of sin. They declare that what this world needs to put things right is a scientific education, political planning, environmental balance, and so on. The psalmists are occupied, on the contrary, with the fact that God is at war with the powers of evil, and so they even depict him as a warrior. To reach God's goal, the redemption of all mankind, blood must necessarily be shed. It is shed in the animal world, where we observe "nature red in tooth and claw". And so God's people too must be prepared to share with God in the dangers of this war, and to recognize that if they are unwilling to shoulder their share of the world's pain and sorrow, then, acting as one partner within the Covenant, God will himself lay that share upon their hearts, minds and bodies that they ought to have taken up willingly for themselves. For it is only *out of* pain and sorrow, borne in creative love and compassion, that "the Kingdom can come on earth even as it is in heaven". Because of this truth, God is hailed in the Psalms not only as Creator, but also as Saviour.

HOW TO READ THE PSALMS

In our days there are at least three ways of reading the Psalms:

(1) They may be read as ancient literature, as interesting poems coming from a period when an ancient people was emerging from the Bronze Age. A study of them thus helps us today to learn something about the civilization of their writers and their development of thought.

(2) They may be read by people whose background is the Synagogue. It is not for the Christian, however, to dictate to the Jew how he should understand the Psalms. But it would be a good exercise in his own appreciation of them to keep wondering what the Jew might make of each of them, and keep asking himself why he himself would interpret them differently.

(3) They may be read by the Christian, for whom the person of Christ has opened up a new range of revelation. In consequence of this he recognizes that the Church today must necessarily discover more in the Psalms than either their original writers intended, or anyone not a Christian can find. He reads the Psalms in the consciousness that both Jesus and Paul quoted from them, and that Jesus even quoted the 22nd Psalm when suffering the agony of his crucifixion. Was he not therefore showing how that particular psalm had something to say that was relevant to his passion?

It seems then that we are to read the Psalms in a number of ways at once!

(1) We are to remember that they have come out of a particular historical period, and are conditioned by the way that period expressed itself. Consequently we cannot really know what they are saying till we get a picture in our mind of ancient Jerusalem, of the walls of Zion, of the enthronement festival of a descendant of David, of the crowds clamouring to get through the gates of the city to worship in the temple courts, of cruel kings like Nebuchadnezzar, of Israelites as miserable displaced persons in far-off Babylon, longing to get home and live in fellowship again with the God who had chosen Jerusalem as his abode—and so on.

(2) We are to remember that these poems were written by people who had already discovered the wonders of the goodness of God in his making covenant with them, a covenant of love and loyalty. The Psalms were not written by our pagan Anglo-Saxon or Teutonic or Slav or Celtic ancestors, but by the People of God.

(3) We are to remember that the Psalms, being part of the Word of God, are more than mere dead print. They are alive with the Spirit of God that leads us into all truth. So they are alive not only for us *forwards* in time to our day. The NT writers believe that Christ is the Word of God both forward and *backwards* in time, because he is the same, yesterday, today and for ever. "Before Abraham was, I am." As we have noted above, the psalmists were aware that God had already redeemed them,

just as we know that we have already been redeemed by the Cross of Christ. The psalmists naturally did not know *how* God had redeemed them, except that they had been given a sacramental sign of his redemptive act at the crossing of the Red Sea. So in this regard we can understand and perceive more than they could do in their day. Thus the Christian is justified in finding in these ancient poems more about the grace and loving purpose of God than their writers knew. In fact, reading the Psalms is no less than a glorious and exciting experience.

PSALMS

THE TWO WAYS

Psalm 1:1–6

1 Blessed is the man
    who walks not in the counsel of the wicked,
  nor stands in the way of sinners,
    nor sits in the seat of scoffers;
2 but his delight is in the law of the Lord,
    and on his law he meditates day and night.
3 He is like a tree
    planted by streams of water,
  that yields its fruit in its season,
    and its leaf does not wither
  In all that he does, he prospers.

4 The wicked are not so,
    but are like chaff which the wind drives away.
5 Therefore the wicked will not stand in the judgment,
    nor sinners in the congregation of the righteous;
6 for the Lord knows the way of the righteous,
    but the way of the wicked will perish.

Our very first word, *blessed*, reminds us of the Beatitudes in the Sermon on the Mount (Matt. 5:3–12). There at verse 2 we read, by way of introduction, that Jesus sat and taught people. Jesus was thus carrying on the teaching ways of those parts of the OT which we call by the name of *Wisdom Literature*. It includes Proverbs, Ecclesiastes, Job, several of the Psalms and some passages in the Prophets. "Wisdom" means, of course, the teaching of God about the true way of life. Wisdom, which is a feminine noun in Hebrew, is thought of as a Daughter of God (as in Prov. 9). The schoolmaster seeks to pass on this divine Wisdom to "my son", as he delights to call his student, a phrase we find in the first verse of each of chapters 2–7 in Proverbs.

King David, in his long reign in Jerusalem, turned the little citadel of Jebus into his capital city. Solomon, his son, consolidated his work. He built the temple, his own palace, and palaces for members of the royal family, and many public buildings also. In order to run his quite extensive empire he had to have many young men trained and educated for the task of administration. So he established at least one school for such young men alongside the temple building in Jerusalem. By so doing he showed these young men that *Wisdom* and *Religion* were inseparable in the sight of God, in fact, that true religion was in reality *the Wisdom of God*.

The editor of this our first collection of Psalms placed this significant one at the head of the whole collection of 150 psalms. He did so for the same reason that Matthew places the Beatitudes at the beginning of Jesus' teaching. It is as if he were saying: "You should read all the psalms that follow in the light of this one." For life lived in the fellowship of God and in humble obedience to him is the real way of life. As Micah 6:8 puts it:

What does the Lord require of you
but to do justice, and to love kindness,
and to walk humbly with your God?

Or, as Psalm 25:12 puts it:

Who is the man that fears the Lord?
Him will be instruct in the way that he should choose.

Here then are those young administrators, attending worship at the temple, and singing about what they have learned at school. Jeremiah seems to have done the same thing when he echoes this psalm in his own writings (Jer. 17:5–8). How easy it would be, our young man realizes, to let his moral convictions slide, and so to accept a bribe (just a wee one!) and go off drinking with those who think the very moral plans for the ruling of Israel prescribed by Solomon and Solomon's successors were a mere joke. Those hard-liners had been around. They had seen the toughness and cruelty of the administration that was the accepted way of life in the surrounding nations. As they sneered at this "Mosaic" way of life that showed love and compassion for the poor and needy, our young civil servant has his answer ready, one that would keep him loyal to God's revealed Word. For what he is trying to put into practice is not the teaching of either Moses or Solomon, but of the Lord.

The word *law* is the Hebrew word *Torah*, and that word means both teaching and revelation. It is the name given to the first five books of the OT. Of course much of the Pentateuch (its scholarly name) had not yet come into being. But in the days of the kings the stories in Genesis, for one thing, would be taught in this school, along with those about God's covenant with Noah, God's covenant with Abraham, and how God had kept covenant with all his descendants after him according to his promise. Then there was the great story of Moses and of God's rescuing Israel from the power of Egypt; then of his making covenant with all Israel at Mount Sinai; then he learned the Ten Commandments and some of the legislation we now find attributed to Moses; and, finally, he would be told of God's amazing grace in giving to his people this land of theirs flowing with milk and honey. And now this young man had the honour of helping to administer it, including the city of Jerusalem, the *City of God*! No wonder our young civil servant delighted in the *Torah* of the Lord, and now went about his tasks with a quiet and contented heart. He *meditated*, or perhaps "recited into himself", as the word may mean, bits from the *Torah* he had learned at school. For he had recognized that the whole gracious and kindly community way of life that God had revealed to Israel through the *Torah*, in comparision with the ferocity and cruelty of the Canaanites, was the only hope for the future of human society.

What God *says* is always effective (Isa. 55:10–11). The word *prospers* carries this idea. In all he does in obedience to God he finds himself to be an effective and efficient workman of God. A well-irrigated tree will certainly be productive. Perhaps the word *planted* means "transplanted", so that this young man is like an adopted son now growing up in a happy home (cf. John

15:16). How often in the Bible is water used as the symbol of the giving of new life!

That then is the one way. But there are two ways that covenantal man, "the remaining descendants of Joseph" as Amos 5:14–15 calls the People of God, can choose from (see Deut. 30:15–18). Those who have put their feet on this other way are not rooted and grounded in the will of God like a tree, and so they are not effective people. They and their work are like chaff that the wind blows away. Chaff is no use for feeding the hungry. Thus, in the judgment of the congregation they don't have a leg to *stand* on. God does not have to destroy them, their way of life destroys itself—they just blow away.

What a comfort it is, however, for those who honestly try to be obedient to God's revealed Way of life to go about their work aware that the Lord *knows the way they are going*, and knowing it, loves and cares for this son or daughter of his who delights in doing his will. But those who opt out of the Covenant are useless, hollow, empty people.

We read at Acts 11:26: "In Antioch the disciples were for the first time called Christians"—yes, by other people. But it was not their own name for themselves. They had already given their new movement the name of "The Way" (Acts 9:2; 19:9,23; 22:4).

DAVID'S UNIVERSAL DOMINION

Psalm 2:1–12

1   Why do the nations conspire,
        and the peoples plot in vain?
2   The kings of the earth set themselves,
        and the rulers take counsel together,
        against the Lord and his anointed, saying,
3   "Let us burst their bonds asunder,
        and cast their cords from us."

4   He who sits in the heavens laughs;
        the Lord has them in derision.

5 Then he will speak to them in his wrath,
     and terrify them in his fury, saying,
6 "I have set my king
     on Zion, my holy hill."

7 I will tell of the decree of the Lord:
   He said to me, "You are my son,
     today I have begotten you.
8 Ask of me, and I will make the nations your heritage,
     and the ends of the earth your possession.
9 You shall break them with a rod of iron,
     and dash them in pieces like a potter's vessel."

10 Now therefore, O kings, be wise;
      be warned, O rulers of the earth.
11 Serve the Lord with fear,
      with trembling kiss his feet,
12 lest he be angry, and you perish in the way;
      for his wrath is quickly kindled.

   Blessed are all who take refuge in him.

Another of God's gifts to Israel was the person of its king. We read in 2 Sam. 7 how the young King David discovered through his court chaplain Nathan that God had specially chosen him to guide and shepherd his covenant people. David had wanted to build a "house" for God, that is to say, a temple-building, even as all the kings of the nations round about had temples for their gods. But Nathan goes on to use this word in another sense. For one thing, he wanted David to see that God does not need temples to dwell in. Solomon, who *did* build one when he took over the kingship, declares in his prayer of dedication: "Behold, heaven and the highest heaven cannot contain thee, how much less this house which I have built!" (1 Kings 8:27). Israel's understanding of God was meant to be quite different from that of all the surrounding nations. Israel was destined to discover the abiding presence of God, not in a building, but in a human being. So Nathan explains: "The Lord declares to you that the Lord will make you a house" (verse 11). That "house" was to be the dynasty of kings from David onwards. Nathan was punning here. For the verb "to build" can also mean "to have children". In this way, each "son" of the Davidic line would become God's "son" in a special way (verse 14).

So here we have still another of God's covenants (see Ps. 89:3), one now made with the line of David. God promised to be eternally faithful to that line. "I will not take my *steadfast love* from him . . . and your house and your kingdom shall be *made sure* before me . . . for ever" (verse 15).

Both of these double words in italics are "covenantal" terms. Steadfast love is the one Hebrew word *hesed*, a word we shall find recurring throughout the Psalms, being used to describe the loyalty and reliability of God's love, in fact, a "love that wilt not let me go". In the old AV or KJV this word was translated by many different English words, such as mercy, kindness, loving-kindness, goodness, to name only a few. But the RSV, by using the two words *steadfast love* that it regularly employs, is trying to bring out the *kind* of love that it meant for Israel within the Covenant. It is not just a general kindness or mercy, nor is it like the natural love of a mother for her baby. It is the loyal love of the partner in the covenant-agreement which God has bestowed upon his people. Then, *made sure* is the word we know in English as *Amen*. God himself is the *Amen*; he is the answer "yes" to all the doubts and questions and problems of humanity. God is I AM (Exod. 3:14), therefore nothing can be stronger than his promised love. *Amen* means *sure*, solid, immovable. We recognize that a stone temple could have a sure, solid, immovable foundation, provided it were built upon a rock. Similarly the dynastic *house* of David was to have a *sure* and certain foundation, for it was to be built upon God, the Rock himself (Ps. 18:2).

From David in 1,000 B.C. till the destruction of Jerusalem in 587 B.C. each *son* of David ascended the throne on the occasion of his enthronement with a great ceremony at which "all the people" were present—that is, as many as could find it possible to leave their homes in their villages and go on the long climb to their capital city of Jerusalem upon its high hill. The important moment of what must have been a colourful ceremony, however, was when the court chaplain hailed the new monarch, not just as *son of David*, but, in accordance with 2 Sam. 7, actually as *son of God*!

This poem may have been used again and again for each of Israel's kings in turn. Moreover, in all probability, there took place some kind of acted drama at the time of the coronation. Notice how each of the verses we have before us could be both spoken and acted by the temple choir and various groups of priests—the kings of the earth in conclave (verse 2), the snapping of a rope (verse 3), God laughing in heaven (verse 4), then a shout as a priest says "Then . . ." and points to the new king on the throne of Zion standing on its temple hill (verse 6), the recital of verses from 2 Sam. 7 by another priest (verses 7–9), with *God* saying "It is *I* who have set *my* king on Zion"; and then the drama of people dressed as foreign kings kissing the feet of the new monarch on his throne (verses 10–11). This last act would be introduced by the dramatic shout of "And now . . . !" with the action recorded at 2 Kings 11:12. What an exciting moment it must have been for the whole People of God to experience!

YOU ARE MY SON

Psalm 2:1–12 *(cont'd)*

What were the ordinary folk learning from all this colourful activity?

(1) They were being reminded that, when a great king who had conquered many people came to die, other kings everywhere *set themselves*, made themselves ready, for battle in order to overthrow his successor. But now we see that it was ludicrous for heathen kings to *conspire* and *plot* against this son of David; for they were planning to make war actually against God! The power of this verse may come home to us better if we sing over to ourselves the great line in Handel's *Messiah*: "Why do the heathen so furiously rage together?"

(2) The heathen supposed that the purposes of God through his anointed king would lead in fact to their slavery. What they wanted was freedom. But all men and women have got to learn—usually the hard way—that *liberation* is not an end in itself, whether it be Women's Lib., freedom from colonial domination, or freedom from all moral restraints. Liberation means being set free to a new obedience, in this case obedience to the loving plan for the whole world of God the King that he had already revealed.

(3) The worshippers learned that God knows the End from the Beginning, and so knows what will be the outcome of all human selfishness and rebellion. It is for this reason that God in heaven can laugh.

(4) They learned that there is no true love without *wrath*. God expresses his *fury* at sinners, simply because he knows their inner hearts. It is only because he knows *all*, therefore, that he can forgive *all*, and be able to speak to them as persons. God is not a remote deity dwelling in the high heavens. He is actually concerned with the life of humanity, and to that end he uses his vice-regent, David, to act for him.

(5) They learned that God had told the whole world of persons his secret plan, his *decree*, the announcement made by the King of kings that was *absolute*. All Israel was of course the *son of God* (Exod. 4:22). This meant that God had chosen Israel for his own grand purpose of the redemption of the world. God's purpose was not meant to work out through Shiva in India, or Buddha in Ceylon, or through Confucius in China. It was to be through the specially chosen people with the peculiar name of Yisrael (i.e. "He who has wrestled with God and won the bout"! (Gen. 32:27–32)) although they were sinners all. Now, enthroned at the pinnacle of the communal life of this chosen son of God, just one man, viz. David, seated there by God's choice, was being *anointed* to lead and shepherd the People of God for all time. Incidentally, an Israelite king, it seemed, did not become king by conquering his enemies, but by the choice of the living God.

(6) This chosen son of God, however, must of his own free

will, *ask* to be allowed to be used by God. Only then would God make him ruler over all the nations of the earth.

(7) All rulers, kings, prime ministers, dictators, presidents, are commanded by God to bow in awe before the strange fact that they are being given, at this moment in history, a glimpse of the purpose and plan of the living God. We possess today a wall relief picturing conquered Elamite nobles kissing the feet of the king of Nineveh in Assyria. Our psalmist knew that the people of Jerusalem would be aware of this custom. "Now therefore O kings, be wise; be warned, O rulers of the earth. Serve the Lord with fear"—and, as the LXX, the Greek version of the OT puts it, "with trembling rejoice in him"!

(8) But some of the worshipping throng were people of insight and spirituality. These may have had grave misgivings as they looked at the young man on his throne, and wondered how such a sinful individual could ever be in any way the *son of God* to lead their own sinful people, Israel, who, considered as a whole, we recall, were also known as the *son of God*. If the enthronement ceremony in question was that of one of the kings reigning a couple of centuries after David was dead, there would be reason for this anxiety. What a succession of self-centred violent men we read of in the Second Book of Kings. Some, of course, were sincere, but others were perverse through and through. If it were such a one now sitting up there, then what were the worshippers to make of the promises of God?

Yet the very fact of the sinfulness of this line of kings taught Israel something very deep about the nature of God. We are to remember that the Bible is not "pietistic" like some of its readers. It does not draw a veil over the wickedness of the human race, even over God's chosen servants. This is because the Bible is not about man, but about God and his love for this humanity whom he has created.

The key, then, to the agonizing question in the mind of our Israelite worshipper is to be found in the word *anointed* (verse 2). The word in Hebrew is *mashiach*, which we render by the word Messiah. When the new king was anointed with oil, as the word implies, to be the son of God, the action itself became a promise for the future, that God would be loyal to his covenant with David. So the ceremony, for those who could accept it, had turned into a sacramental revelation, we could say, of the purposes of God who keeps his promises, even when sinners seem to block their outcome. Our thoughtful villager could now go back home in the sure and certain faith that, *one day*, a real son would appear, one who could truly say to God "My Father", who would sit on the throne, not just of Israel, but of all nations (see Ps. 89:24–29; Acts 13:33).

This powerful liturgy for the enthronement of a son of David ends with words sung by the whole congregation of God's believing people: "Blessed are all [echoing the first verse of Psalm 1?] who take refuge", not in a son of David, but "in God himself".

OUR TRUSTWORTHY GOD

Psalm 3:1–8

A Psalm of David, when he fled from Absalom his son.

1 O Lord, how many are my foes!
     Many are rising against me;
2 many are saying of me,
     there is no help for him in God.   *Selah*

3 But thou, O Lord, art a shield about me,
     my glory, and the lifter of my head.
4 I cry aloud to the Lord,
     and he answers me from his holy hill.   *Selah*

5 I lie down and sleep;
     I wake again, for the Lord sustains me.
6 I am not afraid of ten thousands of people
     who have set themselves against me round about.

7 Arise, O Lord!
     Deliver me, O my God!
   For thou dost smite all my enemies on the cheek,
     thou dost break the teeth of the wicked.
8 Deliverance belongs to the Lord;
     thy blessing be upon thy people!   *Selah*

This is a psalm of David. There are many more in this first part of the Psalter. Some 700 years after David, the editors of the Psalter placed headings on some of them, but not on others. The tradition they worked on may not be very accurate. Sometimes the psalm in question seems to fit with an event in David's life; oftener than not, though, it does not. Because of such doubt neither the NEB nor the TEV includes such headings in the text.

The greatness of the Psalms, however, lies in their having a universal and all-time message. Even if this psalm did fit with a particular experience in David's life, it also fitted in the life of Paul, when he was flogged, of Martin Luther when he was in prison, of Martin Luther King when he was persecuted to death—and of myself today at many moments in my life.

Three times in it we meet with the Hebrew word *Selah*. What it means exactly we do not know. But it was evidently a musical direction to be used when the psalm was sung by the congregation. It probably meant "Pause here, and make a loud noise with the cymbals and other instruments". Notice how that joyous sound leads, in the words that follow, to a joyous expression of trust and a new emphasis on faith.

But to flee from your own son must be a terrible and heart-rending experience. We read of David's grief in 2 Sam. 15:30. Moreover, It was when he was "in hell" that he had to acccept as well without retort the curses of Shimei (2 Sam. 16:5–14). This experience of David, then, can help us all in all ages to find new faith in our own particular situation.

Since all men are sinners, all men and women are our enemies, as we are to them. It is a terrible thing to realize this fact. And since we are born this way, we only too easily put the blame for it on God. Moreover, "God does not intervene", we all cry. I feel the same way, exclaims the psalmist, and yet I cling to what faith I have left. But people, being sinners all, laugh at me for my simplistic, childlike dependence upon God. It is a terrible mark of the self-righteousness that can creep into the hearts even of believers when one can exclaim about another: "There is no help for him in God. He has not been born again of the Spirit like me. Thank you for being trustworthy to me."

God himself gives this poet the answer of faith, as against the logic of sinners who say that God is not interested. So why not shout it out loud? "The answer is", he says, "God himself, not the degree of faith I may have." Since our life is a continual warfare, God sets within our imagination the picture of himself as a kind of five-foot high shield a man carried in front of himself in battle (cf. Gen. 15:1; Deut. 33:29). But the person whose language was Hebrew made use here of a *double entendre*. For the word can mean both shield and sovereign lord!

But God is much more than that. For God is the God of grace. As a king lifts up by the chin the suppliant who has prostrated himself before his throne, and thus shows him favour, so does God do to me. I cry to God, hoping he will hear me in heaven. I don't really need to do so, however, for he answers me *at once and where I am*, when I meet with him in worship at the sanctuary.

In place of sorrow and grief he gives absolute assurance of his love and care. Since our poet now knows that God is already present in tomorrow (a great gift from God), he can go to sleep in peace, certain that that peace will still be there when he wakes in the morning. "I lay down and fell into a natural sleep. I awoke, naturally, because the Lord was holding me." So (back to the picture of warfare) I don't need to worry whatsoever, he reminds himself, no matter how great an army is arrayed against me—even if I am in a minority of one!

"Arise, O Lord!" These words echo the cry of Israel's ancestors in the days of the Wilderness Wanderings, when they claimed the aid of the Lord (see Num. 10:35). But in later centuries they became the cry to God to rise up in his glory and majesty, as the sun does daily in the east. And so the poet clamours to God to do for him what he cannot do for himself, that is, to rid him of his enemies. Is it right, we may ask, to be so cheeky to God? Jesus does not seem to think so. We remember his story of the importunate widow who kept harassing her local judge till she got her way (Luke 18:1–8).

"Enemies", of course, were not just soldiers with their weapons of war. Our personal enemies, in their thousands, may in fact be those evil thoughts, decadent and destructive, that crowd in upon our minds, thoughts of meanness, jealousy and greed, of lasciviousness and self-justification, even while we say our prayers. How many a painting by a medieval artist shows a believer in prayer surrounded by hosts of little demons, all prodding him with their forks. Such evil thoughts may actually crowd us out of the Kingdom, out of the fellowship of God. How desperately we need the power of God to save us from what once were called demons, but which today may be more pointedly described in psychological terms. But by whatever name we call them, these thoughts are terribly real, as every one of us knows.

So it was for a very good purpose that the poet importuned God in this way: "Smack those evil thoughts of mine in the teeth," he shouted in despair. "Only you can do it; I can't do it myself." Yet (and here comes the mystery of faith) this is all in a poem meant to be sung, a poem about fear and despair! But then, singing about how God destroys those forces that prevent me from loving and serving my neighbours is indeed something to sing about!

Finally, the whole congregation joins in with a response of deepest faith, and with a cry for the blessing of God himself.

A DIALOGUE WITH GOD

Psalm 4:1–8

To the choirmaster: with stringed instruments.
A Psalm of David.

1 Answer me when I call, O God of my right!
   Thou hast given me room when I was in distress.
   Be gracious to me, and hear my prayer.

2 O men, how long shall my honour suffer shame?
   How long will you love vain words, and seek after lies? *Selah*

3 But know that the Lord has set apart the godly for himself;
   the Lord hears when I call to him.

4 Be angry, but sin not;
   commune with your own hearts on your beds, and be
   silent.   *Selah*
5 Offer right sacrifices,
   and put your trust in the Lord.

6 There are many who say, "O that we might see some good!
   Lift up the light of thy countenance upon us, O Lord!"
7 Thou hast put more joy in my heart
   than they have when their grain and wine abound.

8 In peace I will both lie down and sleep;
   for thou alone, O Lord, makest me dwell in safety.

The heading probably means: "Belonging to the choirmaster's collection; A Psalm à la David" (see Introduction). There were store-rooms built on to the outer walls of the temple, in which were housed the various accoutrements for the many and various types of sacrifices. Undoubtedly some space was given as well to the needs of the various choirs and orchestral instruments.

The psalmist speaks: You alone can put me right with yourself. I have already experienced your grace. You have already given me room to stand up and be myself when I was hemmed in from all sides. (This is an important element in the Polynesian understanding of the biblical faith.) So, more grace, please, God!

God replies: O you poor human beings, why don't you trust *me*? There you go, putting your trust in what is emptiness and even vicious, things like (could we say today?) astrology, witchcraft, yoga, superstition, science, politics. (Clash go the cymbals!)

The psalmist speaks: Let us accept the fact, then, that the Lord has already made us his covenant people (this is what "godly" means), and consequently is bound to answer our cry when we call upon him—at least I have always found this to be so! We note that the word "godly" comes from the noun *hesed* that we have looked at, the word which describes God's *steadfast love*, as the RSV usually translates it. The godly are those who experience this love. In the NT, the translation of this word becomes "saints", as at Acts 9:32; Phil. 1:1. We might translate it today simply by "church members"!

The Lord replies: Since you are my covenant people you have a right to be angry at those things I am angry at; but don't sin against your fellow man. (Paul quotes this verse at Eph. 4:26.) Think such things through in bed at night and don't speak out of turn, saying, "*I* think this, and *I* think that." Discover rather what *God* thinks. That is the important thing (and so clash go the cymbals!). So then, turn away from what is negative to what is positive. Keep in touch with me through your sacramental worship, and just go on *believing*. We might add, as the old hymn puts it: "Trust and obey, there is no other way."

The psalmist responds, in tune with the father in the NT incident, who said, "I believe, help my unbelief!" (Mark 9:24). We can't make much sense of the ways of Providence. We've thought plenty about it on our beds at night, such as, Why does God allow evil to continue to flourish, when, as the Almighty, he could so easily squash it all with one hand? Rather let the Aaronic blessing (Num. 6:22–27) have real meaning for us, for we remember that a blessing from God is *effective*.

And so God acts. The psalmist receives his blessing. There was an old lady who consistently arrived at morning worship five minutes before the end of the service. When asked why she did so, she replied, "Well, you see, I feel all right if I just receive the blessing." The blessing here is "the light of God's face". How exciting it is to realize that..

No wonder our poet knows a joy that is not of this world. For it comes from God. A Palestinian peasant reaped two separate harvests each year, the grain harvest and the grape harvest. What a deep sense of satisfaction he would feel when all was safely gathered in; for now he could face the winter with equanimity (see Isa. 9:3). But the joy of the Lord is even greater than that.

This joy is not the same as the human word *happiness*. Happiness is something we can enjoy; then it evaporates and leaves us empty. The word *happiness* has been built into the

American Constitution. But *joy* is built into the revelation of the grace of God; for joy never evaporates, since joy belongs to God, and God is always with us.

Does verse 8 follow from knowing this joy of the Lord? Or, as in so many psalms, is this last verse the response of the whole congregation as it takes God's reply to itself and says "Amen" to the wondrous grace of their covenant Lord? For God's gift is the possession of peace of mind right in the midst of this wicked world. "You alone, Lord, keep me perfectly safe" (TEV), in fact *eternally* safe, for sleep is the sacramental image of death that God gives us *nightly*, to show us we need never have any fear at all.

I NEED YOU, LORD

Psalm 5:1–6

To the choirmaster: for the flutes.
A Psalm of David.

1 Give ear to my words, O Lord;
     give heed to my groaning.
2 Hearken to the sound of my cry,
     my King and my God,
     for to thee do I pray.
3 O Lord, in the morning thou dost hear my voice;
     in the morning I prepare a sacrifice for thee, and watch.

4 For thou art not a God who delights in wickedness;
     evil may not sojourn with thee.
5 The boastful may not stand before thy eyes;
     thou hatest all evildoers.
6 Thou destroyest those who speak lies;
     the Lord abhors bloodthirsty and deceitful men.

This psalm has been used down the centuries as a morning hymn, particularly on entering the sanctuary (see verse 7). It is composed in the Davidic style, comes from the temple choirmaster's music collection, and so is intended to be accompanied by an orchestra of flutes. 1 Chron. 15:16 tells us that David appointed singers and players even before his son, Solomon, built the temple. See also 1 Chron. 6:31–33; 25:1–8; and for the Second Temple, see Ezra 3:10–11; Neh. 12:45–46.

Straightaway we should note that this psalmist takes the wrath of God for granted, as did Jesus. There are moderns, however, who are shocked at the idea, and who consequently try to produce new sects which omit from their creed any reference to the wrath of God. Here God's wrath is, of course, regarded as a mark of his love. For he employs it to cleanse and preserve the people of his Covenant. These he has already redeemed. But now they have rebelled against his loving purpose for their lives.

"Remember, O Lord," he says, "that I am a weak creature, in great distress of soul. Remember the difference between us. I need you desperately, Lord. After all, you are my King and my God! And I know that you hear my voice whether I think you hear it or not." There is no actual word for *sacrifice* in the Hebrew of verse 3. *Prepare* means to set things in order, even to set a table for a meal. So the verb was used for making ready all that was required for a morning sacrifice (see Lev. 1). But in later years it was used for preparing one's own self to do that most awesome thing, speak in prayer to the living God! The Muslim shares this sense of awe with the Jew and the Christian. One hears as dawn breaks the call of the muezzin from every minaret in every town and village: "In the name of God, the merciful and the compassionate . . . on him we rely."

At school we learn about the antics of the gods of ancient Greece. Many of these, both male and female, simply delighted in wickedness. *Evil may not sojourn with thee*, however, or, as we would say, it is impossible to associate the very idea of evil with Israel's God. Consequently *persons* who are evil are hateful and abhorrent to the Lord (see Deut. 32:21–22).

We must be careful to learn to distinguish between the various words for sin, which we shall do as we proceed. But in the original they all show that sin, in some way, is an *action*, and therefore it is something that people *do*. Sin is not a *thing* that one can purchase and bring into the sanctuary and lay upon

God's altar. In the final analysis, there is no such thing as sin.
But there are certainly sinners. And it is evil-minded *sinners*
whom God is concerned to redeem. That is why, as Jesus
declares, God goes on and on sending the rain on sinners, just as
much as he does upon the redeemed, in order to keep on
exhibiting his patient, redeeming love, even when, as we read,
"Thou *hatest* all evildoers".

We shall never be able to understand the Cross of Christ until
we glimpse the reality that the God of love must hate sinners.

LEAD ME, LORD

Psalm 5:7–12

7 But I through the abundance of thy steadfast love
    will enter thy house,
 I will worship toward thy holy temple in the fear of thee.
8 Lead me, O Lord, in thy righteousness
    because of my enemies;
    make thy way straight before me.

9 For there is no truth in their mouth;
    their heart is destruction,
 their throat is an open sepulchre,
    they flatter with their tongue.
10 Make them bear their guilt, O God;
    let them fall by their own counsels;
 because of their many transgressions cast them out,
    for they have rebelled against thee.

11 But let all who take refuge in thee rejoice,
    let them ever sing for joy;
 and do thou defend them,
    that those who love thy name may exult in thee.
12 For thou dost bless the righteous, O Lord;
    thou dost cover him with favour as with a shield.

Steadfast love in verse 7 is the word *hesed*, which as we have
already noted, means the content of the Covenant God has

made with Israel (see the Introduction). So, says our poet, because of it I can enter the sanctuary in total assurance that I shall be welcome there, since my presence depends, not on me, nor on my quality of life, but upon God and his unconditional promise. Yet, in consequence, I dare not be cocksure in my approach to him, as Paul argues at Rom. 6:1. I must approach the Lord in awe and reverence. So he prays, "Lead me, Lord, from ahead of me, even as a shepherd leads his sheep. For you alone know the way."

In the Introduction we also noted that some "covenantal" terms need careful thought when we translate them into the words we use in our modern society. The word *righteousness* (verse 8) has two forms in Hebrew, one masculine, one feminine. All the psalm writers take for granted the distinction between the two (which doesn't show itself in English), the distinction that Isaiah made.

As a result of God's saving, creative love, something happens in man's heart. A new righteousness springs up as a result, as wheat springs out of the soil—but still God has *created* even that. The word *create*, as here, is never used of humanity, but only of God. So human *righteousness* is something that God has to create, and does not exist apart from God, just as the creative love that a man receives from God and which he bestows upon his neighbours is not of his own devising.

This, then, is what verse 8 is about. *Thy righteousness* (feminine) is the creative concern I can show to other people, because I have received it from God already (masculine). Such then is God's *Way* for me, just as we discovered in the 1st Psalm. So we can translate: "Lead me, Lord, by that way of love for others you demanded of me, and which I have already received from you, because I am now face to face with enemies, not friends" (cf. Matt. 5:44).

Even if people just think evil thoughts, that is enough to turn them into evil persons. For example, if we foster lustful thoughts, we gradually develop a split personality. We find it impossible to be faithful to the one we love in marriage. An evil breath, like the smell of a stinking corpse, then rises in a person's throat, for *sepulchre* here is a pun in Hebrew upon the word heart or stomach.

Our psalmist has by now learned at least part of God's ways. He asks God to cure his enemies with their own medicine. Their *many transgressions* means the many times that they have *rebelled* (the real meaning of the word) against God's loving covenant. Rebellion, is, of course, an action. So here we see one aspect of what it means to be a sinner; it is to reject God's love and grace and to despise one's election. We should think about this when we repeat the Lord's Prayer, where the word is rendered "trespasses".

But those who live within the fellowship and love of the Covenant can actually *exult* (verse 11) with joy—endlessly. This is because God has *already put them right with himself.* Moreover, this is something that God will never undo. Therefore they will *ever* sing for joy, which means, we would claim from the Hebrew, "for all eternity". To *crown* that assertion (the word *cover* means this) we notice that the word translated *favour* means more than the English does. God's favour is his will, his plan for the life of his beloved. And God will *crown* him with such favour! What a triumphant ending to a psalm that begins with a cry for help. Before he has finished his prayer, our psalmist has received complete assurance of God's *unending* care. That is what God's *blessing* means.

Before the battle of Edgehill in England's Civil War, on October 23, 1642, Sir Jacob Astley, who must surely have known this psalm by heart, reveals his complete confidence in God when he prays, "O Lord, thou knowest how busy I must be this day. If I forget thee, do not thou forget me."

O LORD, HOW LONG?

Psalm 6:1-10

To the choirmaster: with stringed instruments; according to the Sheminith. A Psalm of David.

1   O Lord, rebuke me not in thy anger,
      nor chasten me in thy wrath.

2 Be gracious to me, O Lord, for I am languishing;
       O Lord, heal me, for my bones are troubled.
3 My soul also is sorely troubled.
       But thou, O Lord—how long?

4 Turn, O Lord, save my life;
       deliver me for the sake of thy steadfast love.
5 For in death there is no remembrance of thee;
       in Sheol who can give thee praise?

6 I am weary with my moaning;
       every night I flood my bed with tears;
       I drench my couch with my weeping.
7 My eye wastes away because of grief,
       it grows weak because of all my foes.

8 Depart from me, all you workers of evil;
       for the Lord has heard the sound of my weeping.
9 The Lord has heard my supplication;
       the Lord accepts my prayer.
10 All my enemies shall be ashamed and sorely troubled;
       they shall turn back, and be put to shame in a moment

The word *Sheminith* in the heading means "eighth". We use
eight notes to an octave, but we do not know if the ancients did
likewise. In fact we don't know what it really means. Then,
whoever wrote this psalm must have done so in retrospect when
all was calm again, not in the midst of the agonizing experiences
he speaks of at verse 8. If the writer was David, was he now
down in the wild, forested Jordan valley, with Absalom at his
heels (2 Sam. 17:21–22)? David's enemies were flesh and blood
soldiers. But in its present form, this psalmist's enemies seem to
be as much within his own heart as outside it. Moreover, he
believes that his oppression of spirit is the Lord's doing, and so
he begs God to put an end to it all. Since oppression of spirit can
result from sickness of the body, he asks also how long he must
suffer the pain that is racking him. His sickness then seems to be
a combination of pain, weariness, pessimism, boredom and just
sheer weakness. In a word, he was a very sick man. So he cries
(or she cries) *Turn, O Lord,* or better, "Return, come back, just

as you would expect me to do to you. I appeal to your covenant love, your *hesed*."

In verse 3 he speaks of *my soul* as being troubled. Then in the next verse he pleads, "Save *my life*." In Hebrew, however, soul and life are the same word, the word *nephesh*. We saw in the Introduction that no psalmist would do what Socrates and Plato took for granted, suppose that the soul was something separate from the body. When Jesus cured the sick man whom his friends let down through the roof, he drew no line between curing the body and forgiving a sinner.

That too is why OT man found it so difficult to believe in life after death. His logic told him that when man, a whole *nephesh*, died, then the whole of him was dead (verse 5). It is quite amazing to realize that Israel was the only nation in the Near East to have no conception of the immortality of the soul. Moses had brought their ancestors out of Egypt. The whole religious life of that great people was aimed at preparing the soul for its journey beyond death. The mighty pyramids that still stand for us to see, and which were there in Moses' day, testify to this belief. All India today believes in the immortality of the soul, just as did the ancient Greek philosophers. Only Israel, by God's grace did not—else we would never have known the Resurrection of Christ. For one thing, a doctrine of the immortality of the soul tends to put the stress on the *after* life (like "pie in the sky") to the neglect of that social righteousness in *this* life which the great prophets so emphasized. In reality, the Law of Moses went in just the opposite direction. It taught Israel that *this* life is what is important, on the grounds that God made it, and made it to be good. Or, as Paul was to make a like stress later, "*Now* is the day of salvation", not in the hereafter. How Israel thought through, under the pressure of the grace of God, the relationship between the wholeness and oneness of the human *nephesh* and life after death is something we can actually see taking place as we read the Psalms.

The scholarly studies of the last couple of generations lead us today to believe that there were, attached to the temple and its worship, not only priests and Levites, but also another category of "employees". Just as Nathan was, as we would call him, the royal chaplain, whose task it was to interpret to the king the mind and teaching of Israel's King, the Lord, so there seem to have been prophets attached to the temple to help the people too to know the mind of God. Scholars call them "cultic prophets"; we might best picture them under the name of "minister"; for, like the great Isaiah, they seem to have regularly preached sermons that accompanied, interpreted and explained the sacrifices and celebrations of the great festivals. In fact it may be that most of our OT prophets were ministers in this sense. But between periods of worship it seems that the individual Israelite could go and consult the temple minister about his own spiritual problems, just as he might do today.

Note how the whole tone of the psalm changes at verse 8. Has the psalmist had an interview in private with his minister in this way? And has this temple prophet led the poor man or woman back out of the depths to a renewal of faith and courage? It would seem that the minister and this individual had now prayed together (verse 9). For up he or she jumps, completely sure now that God has heard the prayer, completely sure that the Lord, not he himself, will overcome all his enemies—whether they be flesh and blood, or the awful oppression of mind, spirit and body which he has been undergoing, and that God will do it now, in a moment, suddenly! And so, when this individual sings his song before his fellow worshippers, they all learn, as one corporate Body, to share in the rich grace of the living God. But this last word *moment* employs a pun. It is a name also for the underworld of death. And so the poet is saying that the power of God covers the whole of both life and death, both this world and what is beyond the grave.

When Martin Luther was shut up in Wartburg Castle he knew such periods of depression. So what did he do? On one occasion he threw his ink-pot at the devil, and then suddenly all was well. At other times he shouted aloud "Baptizatus sum", "I have been baptized"—and then all the devils of depression and fear were helpless. The poet Cowper put it differently. Like John Wesley he knew the power of song. And so he wrote:

"Sometimes a light surprises the Christian while he sings." But whatever happens to each individual, the *sudden* change of heart is an act, not of man, but of God.

APPEAL TO THE HIGHEST COURT

Psalm 7:1–17

A Shiggaion of David, which he sang to the Lord concerning Cush a Benjaminite.

1 O Lord my God, in thee do I take refuge;
  save me from all my pursuers, and deliver me,
2 lest like a lion they rend me,
  dragging me away, with none to rescue.

3 O Lord my God, if I have done this,
  if there is wrong in my hands,
4 if I have requited my friend with evil
  or plundered my enemy without cause,
5 let the enemy pursue me and overtake me,
  and let him trample my life to the ground,
  and lay my soul in the dust.   *Selah*

6 Arise, O Lord, in thy anger,
  lift thyself up against the fury of my enemies;
  awake, O my God; thou hast appointed a judgment.
7 Let the assembly of the peoples be gathered about thee;
  and over it take thy seat on high.
8 The Lord judges the peoples;
  judge me, O Lord, according to my righteousness
  and according to the integrity that is in me.

9 O let the evil of the wicked come to an end,
  but establish thou the righteous,
  thou who triest the minds and hearts,
  thou righteous God.
10 My shield is with God,
  who saves the upright in heart.
11 God is a righteous judge,
  and a God who has indignation every day.

12 If a man does not repent, God will whet his sword;
        he has bent and strung his bow;
13 he has prepared his deadly weapons,
        making his arrows fiery shafts.
14 Behold, the wicked man conceives evil,
        and is pregnant with mischief,
        and brings forth lies.
15 He makes a pit, digging it out,
        and falls into the hole which he has made.
16 His mischief returns upon his own head,
        and on his own pate his violence descends.

17 I will give to the Lord the thanks due to his righteousness,
        and I will sing praise to the name of the Lord, the Most High.

Shiggaion is another musical term that leaves us puzzled today.
The root of the word means "to wander". So suggestions like
arpeggio-like music, emotional, wild, storm-tossed, have all
been suggested. The name *Cush* may refer to someone from the
Sudan, and so, perhaps, to a black man. If this is correct, then
he was evidently accepted quite happily as one of the tribe of
Benjamin. The Hebrews seem to have been completely free of
colour-consciousness.

If we today are living in a peaceful, civilized community, we
may find it difficult to identify with this psalmist. So let one or
two instances from history show us how real this psalm can be.
Only a century ago brave Salvation Army lassies by the score
had to take refuge from their *pursuers, lest like a lion they rend
me*, in the streets of "civilized" London. Night after night the
mob were whipped into a frenzy against these young women,
even in some cases by the local clergy. They were brutally
assaulted and the Army's buildings were wrecked, while the
police stood by and watched. Or again, Spain, which has had a
turbulent history, has produced the saying: "He who would be a
Christ must expect crucifixion." The horror of Hitler's "Final
Solution" of the Jews of Europe will never be eradicated from
human memory. The Ku Klux Klan, up till the time of Martin
Luther King, produced this terrible fear, which we read of here,
in the hearts of thousands. The fact is that violence such as this

lies only just beneath the surface of all unredeemed mankind, even of children. This has been frighteningly depicted in William Golding's novel *Lord of the Flies*. Even today many people live in terror of the mugger, the loan shark, the political assassin, the kidnapper, and so on.

Granted that such violence is a fact of human life, the poet cries, Why should I, a believer in you, Lord, have to suffer at the hands of such people? I have never done anything like this myself. If I had done so, then I ought now to be a victim of violence myself; "Let him then trample my vitals in Sheol; let him cause my liver to dwell in the mud," as M.J. Dahood, a specialist in the languages of Canaan, has translated verse 5. It is only gradually, of course, that the People of God came to discover the answer to this very human question of suffering. In fact, if all humanity must suffer, even as all nature does, as Paul says at Rom. 8:22, and if, as it was said of Jesus, even he *must suffer* then it is a sheer impertinence for any believer to cry, "Why should this happen to me?" For, of course, it is *out of* pain and suffering that the Kingdom of God arrives.

But our psalmist is very human. He challenges God to set up his court, his high court of justice, and to call all nations to its bar, including himself. He knows that he will get off all right, "because of my integrity". "I belong among the *righteous*," he exclaims.

So we return to this word *righteous* that we met with in Psalm 5. It is used (a) in the first place of God. The righteous God is he who *puts his people right with himself*, and then gives them *power* (an important element in his love) to live in fellowship with himself, that is, in a *right* relationship with God. Then it is used (b) of God's people. To say that they are now *righteous* does not mean that they are *self-righteous*, annoyingly aware of how good they are. God's *righteous* ones are his forgiven ones, whom God has brought home, perhaps, if they had wandered away and got lost. Then finally (c) the feminine form of the word (not used in this verse) describes the creative love that God puts in the heart of his *righteous* people, the love that gives them power to do for others what God has first done for them.

At verse 12 the psalmist takes up this issue from another angle. We must never forget, he says, that God is the God of judgment. Consequently, he so orders things that evil men destroy themselves. "Be sure your sin will find you out," we say today. Evil is self-destructive. And since evil comes from the heart of evil *persons*, then the judgment is upon those persons.

But finally the *chorus*, or the congregation singing together, hail the Lord (Yahweh) not just by that name, the name of the God of the Covenant, but also by the name *The Most High*. This was the name Abraham used, learning it from Melchizedek (this name means "My God is *righteous*"), when he visited him at Salem. This was the citadel which David captured later on from the Jebusites, and which he made into his capital city, Jeru-*shalom* (Gen. 14:17–20). The inference drawn is that the Lord is the Judge of all the nations of men, in India, China, and the U.S.S.R. equally with Israel. So the psalm ends with the people giving thanks to God that he is what he is, the God of justice and not a capricious deity like the gods of men· "As flies to wanton boys, are we to the gods; They kill us for their sport," wrote Shakespeare in *King Lear*.

HOW GREAT THOU ART!

Psalm 8:1–4

> *To the choirmaster: according to the Gittith.*
> *A Psalm of David.*

1 O Lord, our Lord,
  how majestic is thy name in all the earth!

2 Thou whose glory above the heavens is chanted
   by the mouth of babes and infants,
  thou hast founded a bulwark because of thy foes,
   to still the enemy and the avenger.

3 When I look at thy heavens, the work of thy fingers,
   the moon and the stars which thou hast established;
4 what is man that thou art mindful of him,
   and the son of man that thou dost care for him?

One of the marks of true religion is a sense of awe and wonder, wonder at the mystery of this vast universe; but even a sense of awe as one ruminates on what kind of a creature one is oneself.

We remember how Sir William Booth, founder of the Salvation Army, declared that the devil should not have all the good tunes. It is recommended here that this great psalm should be sung to the tune "The Young Lady from Gath"! Yet Gath was a city of the enemy, of the Philistines, against whom David had to fight aplenty!

It begins emphatically by declaring "O Lord!", not "O how beautiful Nature is!" Then next it claims the God of creation by using the title of the God of the Covenant made with Israel alone, "Our Lord!" The story told by Chaucer's Prioress, one of the Canterbury Tales, begins with a Prologue which repeats these very words: "'O Lord, our Lord, thy name, how marvellous/ Is in this large world y-spread', quod she."

God's glory is that part of God's being that, the Bible dares to say, is visible to the eyes of faith. This is so, even though (as Solomon puts it at 1 Kings 8:27), his glory is *above* the heavens. *Yet*, this God accepts the praise of innocent little children. No wonder Jesus could say, "Suffer the little children to come unto me, for of such is the Kingdom of God." Evidently it is just *that* simplicity of faith, and not the big guns and lethal weapons of sophisticated adults, that can stop the *avenger* in his tracks.

This is the paradox of revelation. You can't argue with a baby, nor can you shut the mouth of the small boy who tells the truth when grown men will not dare to do so, as we recall from the story known as *The Emperor's Clothing*, by Hans Christian Andersen. In the same way, you can't understand the miracle of grace through human reason; you can only accept it as a little child accepts. How different all this is from the words of the Soviet poet: "Enough of the sky and the strangeness of things! Give us more plain nails!"

Fortunately, poetry is not meant to be taken literally, for in its imagery it can penetrate depths of truth that prose, especially scientific prose, can never probe. But then the poet too is like a child. He stands in awe before the majesty of God. He recognizes this, though, only when he has shed his egotism and has had the courage to look beyond his own self-centred desires to the creation around him.

Today we are inclined to feel superior to biblical man, because we believe we take an objective and scientific view of creation. We believe that biblical man held a "three-decker" view of the universe. European medieval man certainly did so. Poor Galileo learned this to his sorrow; for the medieval Church condemned him for rejecting the notion of a flat earth, and of the earth being at the centre of the universe, with heaven above and hell beneath. We have newly quoted Solomon's prayer; so now we may quote verse 1 of this psalm to show that Hebrew man did *not* think of heaven as being "up there". What he did think was that *the heavens*, that is, the sky, was in fact up there. Nor did he believe that hell was "down below"; for in the Psalms Sheol is spoken of in parallel with the grave, and a grave is only six feet deep! For of course Sheol and the grave were merely picture-terms to describe the fact of death.

The place of Man in all this vast universe then is even stranger both for the psalmist and for us than if this were just a three-decker universe. Pagan man in OT times put the top-deck even a little lower than medieval man. He put the abode of the gods just on the tops of the mountains! Yet in our day the space projects we indulge in are no further forward than our psalmist in establishing the existence of living beings anywhere else in the vastness of the universe other than here on earth. But our psalmist adds a further statement to this mystery. It is that this planet is the only one that God has actually *visited!*

Verse 4 speaks of God being *mindful* of man. This means that God never lets man slip out of his thoughts as he weaves his plan for the whole of the universe. But the word for *man* here is not the usual *adam*. We can claim that the psalmist's word was taken from Gen. 4:26, because the fourth chapter of Genesis was available to Israel at least by the time of Solomon, and would be learned in the school we discussed at Psalm 1. In that chapter we have in poetry a theological picture of fallen man becoming ever more sophisticated in the egocentricity of his ways as the generations succeed each other. Cain kills merely one man. His descendant Lamech boasts of taking vengeance seventy-seven times merely for an injury sustained. But immediately following that account the author shows how God has created another type of humanity as well as the boastful brute. His name is Enosh; "and at that time men began to call upon the name of the Lord." Enosh is this other word for man or men, the word that the psalmist uses here. Thus Enosh refers to the human being, man or woman, who lives his or her life aware of the mystery of God's loving care for his world, frail man, mortal man, man living in awareness of the mystery of human life.

This word for man is then immediately paralleled with the title *son of man, ben adam.* Literally, this means a descendant of Adam. But the words "son of . . . " have two meanings in biblical Hebrew. The first is the literal one. So and so is the son of his parents. But in both Testaments we are presented with another usage as well. The bully boys of a village, its "Lamechs", were known as "sons of Belial", as their title is literally translated in the AV. We read of them at Judg. 19:22; 1 Sam. 2:12; 2 Sam. 20:1, and often again. Belial was a mythical god, a useless being, as the origin of the word implies, whose *sons* therefore were chips off the old block. Like father, like son. So "son of . . . " could mean "one who represents the spirit of . . . ", in this case, a god with a horrid nature. That is why Paul can say, "What accord has Christ with Belial?" (2 Cor. 6:15). In the second Testament Jesus wittily calls his dear James and John *Sons of Thunder.* Perhaps they had liked to take part in, or even organize, noisy street demonstrations against—what? The cruelty of the Roman police? The greed of the money-lenders? The avarice of people like Matthew the tax-farmer? We can only guess.

THE SON OF MAN

Psalm 8:5–9

5   Yet thou has made him little less than God,
      and dost crown him with glory and honour.

6 Thou has given him dominion over the works of thy hands;
    thou hast put all things under his feet,
7 all sheep and oxen,
    and also the beasts of the field,
8 the birds of the air, and the fish of the sea,
    whatever passes along the paths of the sea.

9 O Lord, our Lord,
    how majestic is thy name in all the earth!

Three important theological issues depend upon the meaning of
the title Son of Man, or Son of Adam.

(1) God created Adam in his own image, we read at Gen. 1:27,
and so a *son of Adam* is one who, in opposition to a *son of
Belial*, continues to do what God does ceaselessly, in whose
image he has been created, viz., live a creatively loving life. He
creates order out of the chaos of the jungle by turning Eden into
a Garden—with God's help; for God provides the raw material,
the soil, and the rivers, and God gives the growth. But a *son of
Adam* acknowledges this to be so, and remains, even though he
is always a sinner, a son of God.

(2) But we must complete the sentence at Gen. 1:27. "God
created Adam, *man*, male and female created he them." In both
the Hebrew of the OT and the Greek of the NT there are two
words for *man*. One means male as distinct from female. The
other means mankind, humanity, made up of both male and
female. This, then, is what Adam means originally, *humanity*.
The story in the next chapter of Genesis which tells of the two
personalities, Adam and Eve, yet both of whom are *man*,
humanity, is dealing with the reality that God has created *man*
in two sexes. So it is also with the NT. In Christ, says Paul,
there is the *new man*, neither male nor female.

(3) The NT offers the amazing number of over fifty different
titles that people gave to Jesus—all but one. There is one title
that no one gave him, that of Son of Man. He alone called
himself by that title, no one else did. And it is this very title that
we find here at verse 4. So we see that Jesus must have meant at
least two things by his choice of this name: (a) He represented

not only the male sex, but also the female. (b) He knew himself to be the very essence of humanity, the one who, as Son, *par excellence*, does what his Father does, that is, creates a new humanity, even, as the NT goes on to say, a new heaven and a new earth.

The poet's astonished exclamation continues: "Yet thou hast made him little less than God!" The reason why the old AV had *angels* here and not *God* is because it used the LXX, the Greek translation of the OT that was made a couple of centuries before Christ. The Greek translators were shocked to find the word *God* here, and the translators of the English Bible in 1611 followed them in being shocked! This is a good instance of human beings thinking they know better than the Word of God!

In Gen. 1:27 we read that God made man to be "godlike", that is, God gave man the power to do what God does, but now, adds our psalmist, in doing so, God also granted man the power to reflect his own glory! God has assigned to man the fantastic responsibility of carrying forward his creative activity. Yet with shame we remember what man has done to the game of the African steppes, and to the millions of bison that once roamed the plains of North America. What ruination might we have caused to the birds of the air, if we had understood the mystery of their migration, or to the eel and the salmon if we had understood what happens to them as they *pass along the paths of the sea* (verse 8)?

He still continues with the revelation given us at Gen. 1:27-28. For there we read that God has put "all creatures great and small" into the hands and care of man. We add, "and care", because that is the meaning of the word *dominion*. We get it wrong if we think of man's dominion over nature as being the right to exploit it as he sees fit. This word, found at Gen. 1:28, is parallel with the word that occurs at Gen. 1:16-18, where God bade the sun, moon and stars *regulate* (*not* have dominion over) the seasons, and certainly not *exploit* them. Rather, the heavenly bodies were to control them and keep them occurring in the cycle of the year. Yet the seasons mentioned here at verse 14 were not spring, summer, autumn, winter, but the religious convocations held three times a year at Jerusalem, periods when all Israel gathered to praise and glorify the God who had called them into service of love and compassion for all creation.

Having heard this great poem of faith recited in their ears, the whole congregation, at verse 9, then exclaims in one voice the glory with which the poem began. It does so with a deep sense of excitement and satisfaction, for the psalmist has just told the congregation *who they are* in God's great scheme of things! And he has told them what they are called to do and be. Under God, a son of man is he who is obedient to the creative purposes of God. And so the praise goes up, not to man "the measure of all things" as the Greeks loved to say, but to God, the Creator of the ends of the earth.

A LESSON ABOUT GOD

Psalm 9:1–10

> *To the choirmaster: according to Muth-labben.*
> *A Psalm of David.*

1 I will give thanks to the Lord with my whole heart;
   I will tell of all thy wonderful deeds.
2 I will be glad and exult in thee,
   I will sing praise to thy name, O Most High.

3 When my enemies turned back,
   they stumbled and perished before thee.
4 For thou has maintained my just cause;
   thou hast sat on the throne giving righteous judgment.

5 Thou has rebuked the nations, thou hast destroyed the wicked;
   thou has blotted out their name for ever and ever.
6 The enemy have vanished in everlasting ruins;
   their cities thou hast rooted out;
   the very memory of them has perished.

7 But the Lord sits enthroned for ever,
   he has established his throne for judgment;
8 and he judges the world with righteousness,
   he judges the peoples with equity.

9 The Lord is a stronghold for the oppressed,
 a stronghold in times of trouble.
10 And those who know thy name put their trust in thee,
 for thou, O Lord, hast not forsaken those who seek thee.

There are twenty-two letters in the Hebrew alphabet. Psalms 9 and 10 are alphabetic, that is to say, each second verse begins with a different letter of the alphabet. The first half of the alphabet occurs in Psalm 9, the second half in Psalm 10. Probably, therefore, the two psalms were composed originally as one, even as they are found to be now in the Greek translation, the LXX. This supposition is reinforced when we note that Psalm 10 has no heading.

Together, the two psalms form a careful work of art. We might compare their structure with the complexity of composition seen in an English sonnet. We remember that Psalm 1 was probably intended for the use of the older student, so this one may well have been meant for the edification of the school child. Perhaps he learned it by heart, the class then recited it, and the master then discussed and elucidated it, using the old question and answer method. The title of the music chosen for it is a solemn one. *Muth-labben* means "The Death of the Son". A youthful member of the class may have died, to the great grief of the rest of the class. This would have given the master the opportunity to raise with the children questions about the meaning of life and death, and show them why we should trust in God at all times. Someone later on thought that this master's poem was worthy of including in Israel's "hymn book".

1–2 *Aleph*. The Lord has done so much for me, the teacher says, that I always keep on *thanking him with my whole heart*, the whole of my being. God's acts on our behalf, he explains to his class, are so *wonderful* (a word meaning strange, other-wordly, inexplicable, beyond scientific analysis) that he can only be astonished. This particular noun, by the way, is reserved in the OT to describe acts of God alone, and never of man. (See Psalm 72:18.) Then notice how, as a thankful believer, no sooner does he begin to talk *about* God than he finds himself speaking *to* God, even in front of his class of boys! This kind of religious education must have been experienced by the present-day writer who declared: "He was alive as a child to the simple aspects of the world."

3-4 *Beth*. The teacher lets his charges see that they all belong together as one fellowship in God's covenant love. When he says "My enemies", therefore, he gets the class to repeat the words after him in one voice. See, for example, the way that Joshua speaks at Josh. 7:6; or how, when messengers from Moses asked the king of Edom to allow Israel to pass through his territory, the king replied: *"Thou* shalt not pass through *me."* The messengers answered that refusal with: "Let *me* only pass through on foot, nothing more" (Num. 20:14–21). So the students were invited to look back over their history to see how God had maintained Israel's cause ever since, as one people, they had escaped from slavery in Egypt.

5 6 *Gimel*. For example, the children learned, God had helped their ancestors, in Moses' day, overcome the Amalekites in a great battle. Thereupon using the Semitic hyperbole that Jesus also employed when, for example, he said, "If your right eye offend you, pluck it out" (Matt. 5:29), they learned that this is what God does to all the enemies of his grand plan both in this world and for all eternity.

7-8 *He* (*Daleth* is missing). So the teacher emphasizes the reality of God's justice. In the picture that he paints he describes God as seated "in eternity" (rather than *for ever*), not in repose, but in active rule, executing justice, impartially to all men, that is, *with equity. He established his throne for judgment, mish-pat*, we read, this last word meaning the revelation of a whole and very different way of living from the heathen, one that is both just and responsible. And this *mishpat* he offers to Israel! *And he judges the world with righteousness, tsedeq*, meaning, in its masculine form, as we have already seen, his saving creative love. What an extraordinary vision of God's loving, creative purpose this teacher here offers to his pupils. He remembered that Abraham had declared to God before the destruction of Sodom: "Shall not the Judge of all the earth do right?" (Gen. 18:25). This passage may have inspired Henry Scott Holland to write his powerful hymn, "Judge Eternal, throned in splendour".

9–10 *Waw*. This divine Judge leans over backwards, we might say, to be both judge and advocate at the same time for the oppressed peoples of the earth. What a wonderful message those school children were learning, one which they were meant to pass on to the world as they grew up, even as we are meant to do today. We are meant to say to the masses of impoverished humanity in the Third World what we ourselves are glad to say to God in prayer: *For thou, O Lord, hast not forsaken those who seek thee.* How far this message is from that of certain Christian sects who suppose that the "poor heathen" are all perishing and will surely go to hell! We see clearly here, then, that to the psalmist faith is to be understood, not as belief in the existence of God, but as trust in the Lord as a living Person who has taken up the case of the poor of the world in the divine courtroom as their Advocate, when he ought, by rights, to be only their Judge!

SING PRAISES TO THE LORD

Psalm 9:11–20

11   Sing praises to the Lord, who dwells in Zion!
      Tell among the peoples his deeds!
12   For he who avenges blood is mindful of them;
      he does not forget the cry of the afflicted.

13   Be gracious to me, O Lord!
      Behold what I suffer from those who hate me,
      O thou who liftest me up from the gates of death,
14   that I may recount all thy praises,
      that in the gates of the daughter of Zion
      I may rejoice in thy deliverance.

15   The nations have sunk in the pit which they made;
      in the net which they hid has their own foot been caught.

16 The Lord has made himself known, he has executed judgment;
   the wicked are snared in the work of their own hands.

   Higgaion. Selah

17 The wicked shall depart to Sheol,
   all the nations that forget God.

18 For the needy shall not always be forgotten,
   and the hope of the poor shall not perish for ever.

19 Arise, O Lord! Let not man prevail;
   let the nations be judged before thee!
20 Put them in fear, O Lord!
   Let the nations know that they are but men!   *Selah*

11-12 *Zain.* Accordingly we should encourage each other to sing in gratitude to this God in that he is ever concerned for the masses of humanity. But such a faith is no form of Pantheism, the idea that God is to be found in Krishna and Siva, and in any or all of the ideologies of mankind. *The Lord dwells in Zion!* This is to say that he has revealed himself to one people only, and it is now their turn to pass on what they have learned of him to all the peoples of the earth. Nowhere in the Bible do we find the notion that God has used a vast megaphone, so to speak, to enable his voice to be heard by all nations and all peoples at once. Nowhere do we find the idea of "the noble savage". Israel is his chosen people. To them alone has he spoken and upon them alone has he laid the task of being his voice to the rest of mankind; for they are to tell all nations of the inexplicable things God has actually *done* in Israel's history, as we noted in verses 1-2. Similarly, in the NT, God did not reveal himself to the Greeks and Romans of Paul's day. But he *had* now done so *within Israel, in* Jesus, *in* Zion, the city of Jerusalem. Thereafter God commanded the disciples of Jesus to be his witnesses to the ends of the earth.

We may receive a wrong impression of God through this psalmist's description of him here, because the English Bible uses only nouns in relation to him. But in Hebrew the description is made in verbs, that is to say, in words of action. Our words Saviour, Redeemer, and so on, do not accurately picture for us what the *living* God is actually doing for his world at all times.

13–14 *Heth.* The Lord's command to Israel to *tell among the peoples his deeds* does not exclude the fact that they are to tell each other about his love. So the school class learns that each of them should take note of God's loving care for them, such as when they may be desperately ill, or have wandered like lost sheep far from the fold. Then they are to say, "Thank you" to him in public for his rescuing care. *The gates* of a city were where people congregated for public meetings and where they could bring a lawsuit against a neighbour and lay it before the equivalent of our JP of today. So that was where they were to tell about God's love and justice, at the point where people looked for justice to be done to them! *The daughter of Zion* is an attractive way of speaking of the inhabitants of Jerusalem. They were all one communal "she" whom God loved as his daughter, even as God loved the king as his "son" (Ps. 2:7). Notice how the speaker had already been down to *the gates of death.* Now he finds that *the gates of Zion* have opened for him into the life of the living God.

15–16 *Teth.* The time came for the Director of Education of a whole British Dominion to retire. He had imposed a completely secular form of education upon a whole generation of children, basing his philosophy upon the works of Plato and Aristotle. Only at the end of his days did he come to change his mind. When asked, "If you had your time over again, is there any difference in the emphasis you would make in your educational policy?" "Yes," he replied. "I would take into account the reality of original sin." These verses certainly do just that. The children in this school in Jerusalem were certainly shown the effects of original sin on the lives of the nations. As the great historian, A.J. Toynbee, has formulated with clarity, where the moral core of a nation decays, evil's power to destroy itself is made manifest, and when this happens, the nation that embraces the evil then lives it out, "enfleshes it", in its own political and social life. In Israel's history, on the other hand, unlike that of the many nations whose decline into Sheol Toynbee describes so accurately, God has revealed himself as the Judge of all the earth.

What a climactic declaration of faith this is. No wonder the orchestra has to strike up with a loud chord at this point, just as the film-makers do when the hero has successfully laid low his enemy on the screen. That is *Selah*. But what is *Higgaion*? We wish we knew. But it was evidently another musical direction. Perhaps, as some suppose, it means, "Play here some quiet, meditative music."

17–18 *Yod* and *Kaph*. If we consider that Sheol is where God is not, then to forget God is to start living in Sheol, here and now. To *forget* here, however, is really to *ignore* God—and that is actually a much more reprehensible thing to do. Then the word *for* (verse 18), which is *ki* in the Hebrew, would be better understood as *that*, when it is used after an unspoken oath or promise. So we read: "(On the other hand, I declare) that the poor shall never be forgotten." Then again, when the verb is used in the passive in this way, then its subject is God. Finally, therefore, the words *for ever* may well mean *in eternity*!

19–20. This couplet does not use the next letter in the alphabet. Consequently, as is the case in a number of psalms, it seems to have been added as a kind of chorus to be sung by all the congregation present; for in it we hear summed up the message of the whole psalm so far. By almost being a quotation from Num. 10:35, this verse puts the message of the psalm in line with what God had been doing ever since the days of the Wilderness Wanderings. For, in his wisdom, God has used fear to bring men to their senses, if nothing else has availed to turn their thoughts about their mortality into thoughts about the eternal God.

A TIME OF TROUBLE

Psalm 10:1–8a

1 Why dost thou stand afar off, O Lord?
  Why dost thou hide thyself in times of trouble?

2   In arrogance the wicked hotly pursue the poor;
      let them be caught in the schemes which they have devised.

3   For the wicked boasts of the desires of his heart,
      and the man greedy for gain curses and renounces the Lord.

4   In the pride of his countenance the wicked does not seek him;
      all his thoughts are, "There is no God."

5   His ways prosper at all times;
      thy judgments are on high, out of his sight;
      as for all his foes, he puffs at them.

6   He thinks in his heart, "I shall not be moved;
      throughout all generations I shall not meet adversity."

7   His mouth is filled with cursing and deceit and oppression;
      under his tongue are mischief and iniquity.

8a   He sits in ambush in the villages;
      in hiding places he murders the innocent.

It may well be that the children were studying in a period of social anarchy. The prophet Hosea, speaking in Samaria, for example, lived through the reign of five kings, hardly one of whom died in his bed. In fact, much of Israel's history could force people to ask, "Where are you, Lord, in all this crisis?" That kind of history repeats itself so often. When Bonhoeffer was in his Nazi prison, awaiting his death as Hitler's special prisoner and object of hate, he wrote that he perceived no evidence of God's presence in what was happening. Yet by faith he overcame that looming horror. This whole psalm does so also, and in the same way.

1–2 *Lamed*. The wicked *hotly pursuing the poor* could at times be taken literally, as when, last century, the Scottish Highland and Irish crofters had their roofs burned over their heads and their families shipped off to the Colonies in conditions worse than those obtaining in cattle-boats.

3–4 (*Mem* is missing). So we have pride, persecution and arrogance rampant in the world, basically because men reject the fact of God and of his concern for the poor. To be rapacious and covetous is actually to curse and renounce God the Lord, without needing to say so explicitly. With these passions in a man's heart there is no room left for God to visit there. This man has become too supercilious to condescend to thoughts of God. So, in all his plans he leaves God out. "Supercilious" here is literally "In the height of his nose"—what a devastating picture of some people whom we ourselves know! A university lecturer in philosophy declared recently in a public lecture: "Professional philosophers now know many moral and ethical principles as absolute fact. For example, we know that God does not exist, that there is no life after death . . . and that the meaning and purpose of life is to have as much fun as possible." That is an example of "academic superciliousness".

5–6 *Nun*. The wicked *seems* to get away with his evil plans, especially if we suppose that God's moral law is an anachronism, a vague and unrealistic set of rules. This man or woman here may be a financial success like the rich farmer in Jesus' parable at Luke 12:15–21, or he may be that successful type vigorously portrayed in many modern novels—the man who is "successful" in seducing many women. In his view the mills of God grind too slowly to bother about whether they turn or not.

7–8a *Pe*. Paul quotes this verse at Rom. 3:14. Even in his period the business world was what we today call a "jungle", with dog eat dog. Unfortunately there are still countries where it is virtually impossible for the peasant to obtain justice, because he cannot afford to pay the necessary bribes.

THOU DOST SEE

Psalm 10:8b–18

8b His eyes stealthily watch for the hapless,
9   he lurks in secret like a lion in his covert;
     he lurks that he may seize the poor,
        he seizes the poor when he draws him into his net.

10 The hapless is crushed, sinks down,
        and falls by his might.
11 He thinks in his heart, "God has forgotten,
        he has hidden his face, he will never see it."

12 Arise, O Lord; O God, lift up thy hand;
     forget not the afflicted.
13 Why does the wicked renounce God,
     and say in his heart, "Thou wilt not call to account"?

14 Thou dost see; yea, thou dost note trouble and vexation,
     that thou mayest take it into thy hands;
   the hapless commits himself to thee;
     thou hast been the helper of the fatherless.

15 Break thou the arm of the wicked and evildoer;
     seek out his wickedness till thou find none.
16 The Lord is king for ever and ever;
     the nations shall perish from his land.

17 O Lord, thou wilt hear the desire of the meek;
     thou wilt strengthen their heart, thou wilt incline thy ear
18 to do justice to the fatherless and the oppressed,
     so that man who is of the earth may strike terror no more.

8b–11 *Ayin*. These illustrations are drawn from the world of nature, such as the hunting and fishing scenes we can see today on the walls of ancient Egyptian monuments. The last sentence is quite heart-rending if it has been uttered by a poor peasant, when the latter loses all confidence in God, who "doesn't see to all eternity", as the Hebrew puts it, after all.

12–13 *Qoph*. In deep pity for such a peasant, therefore, the psalmist raises the old Wilderness cry again, the battle-cry of the Lord of hosts in his war against the powers of evil. For God alone can put right the mess his people are in.

14 *Resh*. In answer to verse 11, he declares not just that God *does* see what is happening all the time; he actually turns his declaration into a challenge to God: "Thou *dost* see, and thou *dost* note!" What is more, after seeing these troubles and vexations, *Thou dost take them into thy hands*! In this wonderful way then he declares that the Lord himself deliberately shares our vexation of spirit. The hapless peasant in question consequently learns to call God his Father.

15–16 *Shin*. However, the psalmist can't quite put a full stop here. His very humanness causes him to call upon the Lord to use force to stop the evil man in full course, rather like Peter wanting to call down fire from heaven on those who were against Jesus. He knows that God is King for all eternity, and therefore possesses the right to exercise judgment upon evil nations.

17–18 *Tau.* Not only *can* God help his people (verse 12), he *wants* to do so. Once this psalm had become available for public worship and was preserved in the choirmaster's collection (see the heading of Psalm 9), this last couplet may have been added and sung as a response by the congregation. "O Lord, thou *dost* hear . . . " always, at all times, and so these verses become a kind of profession of faith. So the following lines now "profess" that what was said at verses 10–11 is not in fact the last word. The divine Judge actually does two parallel things at once, the congregation now sings. (a) The Lord cares in justice for the *weak* and the oppressed peasant. (b) The Lord won't let mere *weak* men and women ever again be driven ruthlessly off their land (as the Hebrew may be rendered). Of course, since men have been and still are forced by their conquerors to be displaced persons by the million, this profession of faith really means: "Never are we to suppose that such ruthless behaviour goes unnoticed by the divine Judge."

STAY WHERE YOU ARE

Psalm 11:1–7

To the choirmaster. Of David.

1 In the Lord I take refuge; how can you say to me,
  "Flee like a bird to the mountains;
2 for lo, the wicked bend the bow,
    they have fitted their arrow to the string,
    to shoot in the dark at the upright in heart;
3 if the foundations are destroyed,
    what can the righteous do"?

4 The Lord is in his holy temple,
    the Lord's throne is in heaven;
    his eyes behold, his eyelids test, the children of men.

5 The Lord tests the righteous and the wicked,
       and his soul hates him that loves violence.
6 On the wicked he will rain coals of fire and brimstone;
       a scorching wind shall be the portion of their cup.
7 For the Lord is righteous, he loves righteous deeds;
       the upright shall behold his face.

We should try to write our own inverted commas into this psalm to discover precisely who is speaking.

The psalmist declares first: *In the Lord I have taken refuge*, the word *Lord* coming first in the Hebrew to show where the emphasis lies; for there are many wrong-headed ideologies or religions I might have fled to to find refuge, he means. So he makes clear what is the motto of his life.

Now a friend questions his motto, advising him rather to *flee like a bird to the mountains.* (a) A bird is a living creature, it is able to fly where it wishes. But a bird does not have a conscience like you and me. I must use my freedom with a deep sense of responsibility. I must not fly away from the problems of human life, or, to change the metaphor, bury my head in the sand like an ostrich. (b) *Flee* here is in the plural. A couple took their baby with them to live the simple life on a small island off the Queensland coast. They were traced by a TV cameraman. "We are seeking an alternative life-style", they informed the interviewer, "away from the world of greed, lust for power, and the fear of nuclear war." "What will you do if your baby should fall ill?" "Oh, we would sail over to the mainland and put her into hospital." "That seems a sensible thing to do," replied the cameraman. "But if you don't pay any taxes, are not others paying for the hospital care that goes with the civilization from which you have opted out?"

Such a flight from life has always been a temptation for the believer. He or she sighs for the peace of a monastery or a nunnery, or longs to retire early and opt out of the rat race. In fact, these very words here were uttered by poor Mary Queen of Scots as she laid her head on the block. But then, poor soul, she had no option! A famous American millionaire, taking the words of this psalm literally, bought a small cottage as a retreat, and kept doves to help him relax and forget. But of course he found no peace in his cottage, for he had carried his tensions and worries with him in his heart to the cottage. In fact, this word *dark* (for there are a number of different words for darkness in the OT), does not speak of ordinary night-time, but of the darkness of the soul's despair and of the gloom of Sheol that can lead even to insanity or suicide.

So the heart-rending cry is made by this friend: "Evil is all about us. So *if the foundations are destroyed, what can the believer do?*" These were the foundations of the earth which God had set in place in the beginning when he created the heavens and the earth (see Ps. 46:1–3), when he lowered the pillars on which the earth rests right down to the roots of Sheol. This friend had evidently forgotten that there is a close connection between faith and courage. Cowardice reveals a lack of faith that God is on his throne.

The psalmist now in his turn actually makes a great reply: "Don't flee from the spot or from the experience in which God has put you. It is just *there* that you are meant to give your witness by your obedience to his will for you. If an earthquake occurs and you think the *foundations are destroyed* remember that both the good and the wicked are being tested by God together. Never forget that the Lord is in full charge of your life."

So he assures his friend: (a) that God is alive and at work *in his holy temple*, that is, hearing prayer, forgiving sins, welcoming home sinners, waiting for people to *flee*, or to *take refuge* (verse 1) in *him*, and not away off in the mountains; (b) that God is ruling his world from on high, noticing and testing every little detail of human life. He does so, moreover, without favouritism; he tests both those whom he has embraced within his covenant, and the wicked of the earth, equally. By putting these two ideas together, we find that this friend is using *theistic* language and not *deistic*. *Deism* comes from the Latin for "God", *deus*. It is a theological term that means accepting the idea that God is the God of creation and of nature, but no more.

Such was the prevailing theology in England in the eighteenth century. Against such a view we have the rebellion of churchmen such as John Wesley: He preached the God of *theism*, from the Greek for "God", *theos*. From a psalm such as this Wesley knew that God was not only the original Creator, he also maintained a personal relationship with his children.

Then follow two strange words. (a) The Lord's *soul*. This is the word *nephesh*, which means in the OT the whole of a man, body, soul and spirit. Yet the psalmist dares to use it of God, believing that man who is a *nephesh*, is created in the image of God. In this way he reminds us that God too is *Person*. Then (b) God *hates*. Only those who are unable to recognize the horror of human degradation, rebellion and utter egotism start back in surprise at finding this word used thus. But the psalmist knew that God must hate the thug, the vice and dope peddler, the anarchist, the kidnapper, and all those other degraded persons who greedily and violently mar the life of ordinary folk even today. It is a very unbiblical thing to declare, beloved as it is of some kinds of evangelists, that "God loves you, but hates your sins."

Verse 6 uses parabolic language, so that every word hits home to people in all cultures. Today we drink a cup to another's good health. In those days they handed a friend a cup to drink as a mark of goodwill. That cup however could contain within it either a blessing or a curse. For a vivid picture of the cup of God's wrath, there is no more moving parable than that found in Jer. 25:15–29. That passage well illustrates the statement made in verse 5 that God hates, not just violence, but the violent man.

Finally we find ourselves singing verse 7 along with the Israelite congregation as a postlude to the psalm. And we do so with joy. For (a) it declares that we shouldn't worry about the universe. God can be relied on to defend the moral order; and then (b) it contains a remarkable promise. In origin *to behold God's face* meant to enter the temple to meet him there in praise and worship. Remember that what the AV translated as *shewbread* (Exod. 25:30; 1 Sam. 21:6) is actually *the bread of the*

Face. But as the years went by the phrase was undoubtedly spiritualized until it spoke of a promise that went beyond even the death of the body. Moreover, we see how this came about when we realize that the suffix *his* on the word *face* is what grammarians call the "pathetic" form, used to induce strong emotion. Consequently we might dare to translate now by the words "God's dear face".

"I, EVEN I ONLY, AM LEFT"

Psalm 12:1–8

To the choirmaster: according to the Sheminith.
A Psalm of David.

1 Help, Lord, for there is no longer any that is godly;
   for the faithful have vanished from among the sons of men.
2 Every one utters lies to his neighbour;
   with flattering lips and a double heart they speak.

3 May the Lord cut off all flattering lips,
   the tongue that makes great boasts,
4 those who say, "With our tongue we will prevail,
   our lips are with us; who is our master?"

5 "Because the poor are despoiled, because the needy groan,
   I will now arise," says the Lord;
   "I will place him in the safety for which he longs."
6 The promises of the Lord are promises that are pure,
   silver refined in a furnace on the ground,
   purified seven times.

7 Do thou, O Lord, protect us,
   guard us ever from this generation.
8 On every side the wicked prowl,
   as vileness is exalted among the sons of men.

This poor poet, with whom at some periods of our life we find it easy to identify, is going through a fit of depression, like Elijah did when he fled to Horeb (1 Kings 19:10). Elijah complains to God that "the people of Israel have forsaken thy covenant", and that there was no "covenanter" left except himself. The word *godly* here, *hasid*, means just this, a member of the covenant people, one who seeks to reflect, return to God the *hesed* he has shown to his people. Thus the *godly* are parallel with the *faithful*. There is no one left, he declares, faithful to God.

The basic mark of human disloyalty to the covenant is not so much the way in which people respond to God as how they behave towards their neighbour. This may come as a surprise to those with conventional ideas about what it means to be "religious". To be disloyal to God means being two-faced to one's neighbour, flattering him but at the same time undermining his integrity. Biblical religion is intensely human. This fact has in history often been a charge against it! "Things have come to a pretty pass," declared an English politician in the early Victorian era, "if religion has invaded our private life." The basis of the word *lies* in Hebrew is "hollowness". T.S. Eliot has described the person without integrity or love as "the hollow man"; he is smooth, unctuous, a sycophant.

It is therefore natural for a person to call upon God, who is, after all, Almighty, to deal with such hollow men. For example, G.K. Chesterton once wrote: "From sly speeches of men, deliver us." This slyness includes fast talking; "We'll talk our way to the top, we'll outtalk the simple; no one can stop us," as a novelist has put it. It is possible to beat people over the head with words as well as with truncheons. In his *Memoirs*, Cardinal Mindszenty of Hungary, imprisoned as he was for years in his battle for human freedom, quotes this verse of our psalm: *Our lips are with us; who is our master?*, and says, "It is basically people at the top, in positions of power, who speak like this."

God's reply in verse 5 is a divine statement basic to the whole biblical revelation. It is at such a moment of oppression, Mindszenty continues, that God says *"Now . . . I will arise."* For God is always on the side of the *poor* and *needy*. What the ordinary peasant wants more than anything else in life is security—enough to eat, a place to lay his head, and no one to drive him off his little piece of land. Today we would add to this list, freedom from fear of the secret police, freedom of speech, and freedom of religion.

God's statement reflects the majesty of his Person: "*I will now arise, and will give him the security for which he longs.*" Note: (a) God waits till people are in the depths, at the nadir of their hopes, before acting. Else they might think that they had lifted themselves up by their own bootstraps. (b) God takes the state of *hollowness* (verse 2) and out of *it* he creates a new situation.

God waits, not only till the human situation is at its worst; he may choose to wait for his *promise* to be fulfilled by letting it be tested *seven times* over. His promises may thus have seemed to be unreliable. But the fulfilment of them comes with the perfection of his promise. This idea is shown by his use of the number seven. For seven is the perfect number. God's creation was not perfectly completed till the coming of the seventh day. God's *promises* (which are words spoken like the words of creation, "and God said . . . ") are wrought like silver in the heat and trials of the furnace of life. Only then can his promises be *pure*, that is free of dross caused by the wickedness of man, or as here, of man's *lies*.

In the year 1799, after the French Revolution, Europe was in near chaos. The Cardinals were compelled to meet, not in France, not in Rome, but in Venice, in order to elect a new pope. At that meeting it was believed that "This will be the last pope". How wrong they were. God never breaks his promise, but he may see the need to refine it in suffering seven times over.

Having listened to this great statement of faith, made in answer to the Elijah-like cry of the psalmist in verse 1, the congregation now identifies itself with the theme of this great psalm. "It is now wholly up to you, Lord", the word *you* this time being placed first for emphasis. God's promise is indeed *pure*. *Seven times* in history has his promise to care for the poor been *refined* in man's wars and violence. But today most countries *do* try to produce social justice for all, and make Social Security a fact of civilization. And there are now countless charitable trusts and funds to help the distressed.

And, of course, human slavery has been banished off the earth. And yet, as the poem ends by saying, God's promise of compassion and love amongst mankind is still being frustrated, so long *as vileness is exalted among the sons of men.*

FROM DESPAIR TO JOY

Psalm 13:1-6

To the choirmaster. A Psalm of David.

1 How long, O Lord? Wilt thou forget me for ever?
   How long wilt thou hide thy face from me?
2 How long must I bear pain in my soul,
   and have sorrow in my heart all the day?
   How long shall my enemy be exalted over me?

3 Consider and answer me, O Lord my God;
   lighten my eyes, lest I sleep the sleep of death;
4 lest my enemy say, "I have prevailed over him";
   lest my foes rejoice because I am shaken.

5 But I have trusted in thy steadfast love;
   my heart shall rejoice in thy salvation.
6 I will sing to the Lord,
   because he has dealt bountifully with me.

The cry "How long?" occurs four times in this psalm. It is of course the eternal human cry. We think of the old pensioner living all alone with no one ever coming to the door. We think of the insecurity of life of the masses in India when the monsoon refuses to arrive. We think of the hungry, wretched homeless in lands where there is endemic civil war. No wonder that the response to the proclamation of the Christian Gospel in such lands can go in two directions: (a) "You say that Jesus came two thousand years ago to bring salvation to the world. Then why hasn't he done so by now?" But the opposite response to the cry of "How long?" can be this: (b) "You say that Jesus came two thousand years ago in answer to that cry. Then why haven't you Christians told us about him long before this?"

I speaks here. As we have seen, this may be the cry of an individual, or it may be the cry of a collective personality. We keep up this idea of the collective *I* when in our day we speak of John Bull, or Uncle Sam, or *La Belle France*.

To *bear pain in my soul*, in my whole being, clearly means more than just pain in the body. It can refer to having doubts, or to those conflicts of devices, plans and schemes that keep on racing through the human brain. Day after day a new theological or philosophical solution to one's feeling of *Angst* (as the Germans call this black depression) beats upon the door of one's mind, only to be discarded as inadequate. Depression can be suffocating, worse than mere physical pain. Martin Luther wrote: "Hope itself despairs, and despair nevertheless hopes." The experience can be a real conflict between the spirit and the flesh.

Sleep is not always that blessed relief that we look forward to each night. This *Angst*, this deep sense of despair, can be the sleep of death; and death, in the Psalms, is no less than separation from God. Martin Luther had no hesitation in saying that *my enemy* was the devil. But of course my enemy can take many forms. *Shaken* is not a strong enough term for the Hebrew word here. This verb describes losing one's roots. It is applied elsewhere to the tottering of the very foundations of the earth. We must not scorn the vigour of the language used, however, for at some point in the life of every one of us this experience of tottering on the brink of hell has been a reality of which we have been afraid to speak to anyone else at all. But now this psalmist has done it for us. And what a relief it is to find that others too have gone through that hell which we have experienced ourselves!

In verse 3, however, our poet says a prayer: "*Consider and answer me, O Lord, my God; lighten my eyes.*" This cry quite simply means: "Bring me back to life again." "Let there be a gleam in my eyes once again." But how does God do this great thing? The fact of God's *hesed*, God's steadfast love, that devoted love of his which can never let his beloved go even when he or she feels lost in the sleep of death—that fact, by God's sheer grace, comes right home to our psalmist with fresh clarity as the greatest of all realities. Let us then get our verbal tenses right. What our poet says is this: But as for me, I *have* trusted in your *hesed*; so my heart *shall* exult in your love that turns me into a loving person to others (the feminine form of this noun that we have met before). I have trusted, and I have found that my trust was not ill-placed. God *cannot* let me go, I now know, for it would not be in his nature to do so. So now that terrible experience of *Angst* has completely gone from me—by your grace, God! Now my heart sings. How good God has been to me! Now I know that all through my period of depression he has never taken away his covenant love, his *hesed*, from me.

THE FOOL HAS SAID

Psalm 14:1–4

To the choirmaster. Of David.

1 The fool says in his heart, "There is no God."
    They are corrupt, they do abominable deeds,
    there is none that does good.

2 The Lord looks down from heaven upon the children of men,
    to see if there are any that act wisely,
    that seek after God.

3 They have all gone astray, they are all alike corrupt;
    there is none that does good,
    no, not one.

4 Have they no knowledge, all the evildoers
    who eat up my people as they eat bread,
    and do not call upon the Lord?

The book of Proverbs has a lot to say about fools. There we find six different words for a fool. We can arrange them, we believe, in an ascending scale of foolishness. (a) A *pethi* is a silly ass. (b) A *kesil* is a stupid person. (c) The *ewil* is an idiot. (d) The *holel* is the complete fool. (e) The *nabhal* is actually impious. (f) The *lets* is the sneerer, the arrogant free-thinker. Our psalmist however feels no need to go beyond the fifth category. To his way of thinking to deny God's love and care is the climax of imbecility.

In the ancient world virtually nobody was an atheist, even if he knew his God or gods only through superstition or through a study of the stars. What is meant here by "There is no God" is a God who is not personally interested in people.

This imbecile says as much *in his heart*, that is to say, he shows what he believes as part of his inner being. Thus he reveals in his conversation that the mainspring of his being is "hollow". Therefore, since God is now irrelevant to him, his ways are naturally morally corrupt. The word *good* here describes no mere abstraction. OT man would say that there is no such thing as good*ness*. By goodness he meant the activity of a *person*, a human being who was *good for* the people round him. And that is what our fool knew nothing about.

The God of the Bible is *transcendent*. A theological term like that does not speak home to our minds till we see the idea of it in a picture. We have it here. It reveals to us God as being utterly other than and different from, and above and beyond his creation. But at the same time this verse pictures for us the truth that God is not some kind of absentee landlord. He is also *immanent*, the opposite theological term. God is concerned about his creature, Man, and is present with us in all that we do and say. The phrase, *the children of men*, emphasizes that all human beings are referred to here, and not just Israel, God's own chosen people. Yet note another important theological point. Our poet tells us that God has to find out what people are doing on earth. This is because God has made men free of his control. People are not God's puppets. They are not predestined to do either good or evil. The choice they have is theirs. Yet, if they are to *act wisely*, they are to remember that God is in control!

But God is disappointed in what he finds when he *looks down*. The sweeping statement made in this verse bears out the basic theological picture given us in Gen. 6:5–6, to be followed by Paul in Rom. 3:10–12. The word *corrupt* can even be rendered "gone putrid". It is only the sceptic or the humanist who would object to this seemingly extreme statement, and on two counts:

(1) He would say that anything that is wrong with man can be put right by further knowledge, by psychological help to get him to think straight, and by educating him to seek "the good", as Plato suggested. This idea has been disproved all down the centuries since Plato's day. Man is in fact caught up in a vicious circle. Jeremiah declares at Jer. 17:9: "The heart is deceitful above all things, and desperately corrupt; who can understand it?" The point is, as Jeremiah says, that human beings cannot understand the plight they themselves are in. They cannot understand that education and psychology are not enough to change their whole nature, their *heart*. It can only be done from outside, by a power that is sufficient to break through the vicious circle; and that power is the grace and forgiveness of God.

(2) This renewal of mankind *can* happen, because God is concerned to make it happen.

It is God who asks the question in verse 4. True knowledge, says God, would stop them trying to live out their lives within that vicious circle, and would induce them to call on the Lord to do for them what they cannot do for themselves. What a telling insight we have here into the ways of ruthless men once they have seized power in the community. *They eat up my people as they eat bread.* Amazingly, however, despite all their folly, they are still *my* people! And yet the modern humanist declares that all that mankind needs to live in peace is education and the furtherance of science! We see then that *knowledge* is not scientific study, it is not something we pursue with the intellect. Knowledge is awareness of the workings of God through his fellowship with us and us with our fellow human beings.

RELEASE FROM THE VICIOUS CIRCLE

Psalm 14:5–7

5 There they shall be in great terror,
　for God is with the generation of the righteous.
6 You would confound the plans of the poor,
　but the Lord is his refuge.

7 O that deliverance for Israel would come out of Zion!
　When the Lord restores the fortunes of his people,
　Jacob shall rejoice, Israel shall be glad.

Suddenly the poet gives a shout. *There!* he says. Where? we wonder. Evidently right in the middle of that vicious circle from which it is impossible to escape—except by grace. It is *there*, in the midst of the life of the ordinary believer who is ruled by evil men that the judgment of God falls. Whilst the RSV says that God is *with* the generation of the righteous (i.e. with the covenant people), the Hebrew says that God is *in* it. That, of course, is what "immanence" means!

Next he speaks straight *at* the corrupt and evil persons who would dominate the lives of simple folk. *You* would frustrate the plans of simple folk, as they discuss the real things of human life, like raising their children, looking after their old people, getting in the harvest on time, keeping the Sabbath as a day of rest and worship, and such like. Hooligans such as these, whether they be the local village hoodlums or the power-hungry who, in a coup, have seized control of a nation and now rule it oppressively, pitilessly and revengefully—*they* shall be in great terror (see Lev. 26:16). For the Lord is the refuge of simple folk.

Once this poem had been added to Israel's "hymn book", worshippers could apply its promise to any of the catastrophic situations they themselves had to live through down the centuries. They found strength from this psalm to be sure that God would surely rehabilitate his people; (this is the best translation of the words *restore the fortunes of his people*). There were civil wars in the days of the kings of Israel, and there were wars with neighbouring Syria. There was the destruction in 722 B.C. of the northern capital, Samaria. There was the shattering experience of the fall of Jerusalem in 587 B.C. when the greater part of the covenant people were taken off into exile in Babylon. But right on up to this day the promise and the hope of this psalm applies, as countless Jews and Christians alike can amply testify.

ANOTHER TEN COMMANDMENTS

Psalm 15:1–3

A Psalm of David.

1 O Lord, who shall sojourn in thy tent?
     Who shall dwell on thy holy hill?

2 He who walks blamelessly, and does what is right,
     and speaks truth from his heart;
3 who does not slander with his tongue,
     and does no evil to his friend,
       nor take up a reproach against his neighbour . . .

How varied the psalms are! This time we are given a new set of ten commandments! They are set down in the form of a liturgy to be sung outside the main entrance to the temple. The people have come up to Jerusalem from the villages on the plain and in the highlands to take part in one of the three great festivals that divided up the year. They are stopped by a group of priests, and taught to repeat or sing the ten following statements. Only then were the pilgrims allowed to enter and worship God.

The people of Israel were always pilgrims. They were always on the move to the Kingdom of God, even when they were settled in their own land. In the Wilderness God was present with his people in the *Tent* which Moses erected for him. Each morning the people pulled up their own tent-pegs and made a day's march nearer to the Promised Land. But the Lord's tent-pegs were pulled up also. He then went with his people that day's march onward, in a cloud by day and by fire at night, as the tradition recorded, until the evening, when both he and the people erected their tents again for the night (Exod. 40:34–38). What a great piece of symbolism this was to help Israel understand the meaning of the word *immanence*! But now that Israel was using a stone building as its sanctuary, built upon God's *holy hill*, Israel was to remember that "here we have no continuing city", as Heb. 13:14 puts it. The worshippers were therefore to regard this solid stone building as still reflecting the symbolism of the Tent, with God still in their midst on their daily journey.

What then were they to learn off by heart before they could enter the temple grounds? This psalm supplies worshippers with ten statements to remind them that in the Wilderness journey they were given the basic Ten Commandments we find at Exod. 20. Other prophets had used similar lists to help people understand their faith. Isaiah offers six precepts; see Isa. 33:15 16. Micah offers three such, at Mic. 6:8. Isa. 56:1 produces two, and Amos concentrates on one (Amos 5:4). Looking at these statements in another way, the Rabbis in the early Christian centuries declared that all the 613 precepts of the *Torah* are to be found in these few lines. So now as they approached the gate of the temple, people asked the "cultic prophets", or, as we might say, the ministers on duty, to teach them the basics of their faith (see Zech. 7:3). Here then is an instance of what they were taught. After the question in verse 1, verse 2 begins the reply.

(1) He who *walks blamelessly*, as in Psalm 1. The root of this second word means "complete", "whole". So it describes a man of integrity, the opposite of "double-minded", and so rather like what Jesus calls "pure in heart" (Matt. 5:8). The same two words are to be found used at Gen. 6:9 to describe Noah. They are followed at once by a description of the corruption of all mankind. Yet there is no suggestion made in Genesis that Noah was not a sinner.

(2) Does what is *right*. This refers to one who, being in a right relationship to God, does what God would do, his *heart* being turned towards God and not towards his self.

(3) Who speaks *truth from the heart*, that is, without dissembling, a person who really means what he says. "Not everyone", says Jesus at Matt. 7:21, "who says to me 'Lord, Lord', shall enter the Kingdom of heaven."

(4) Catty, spiteful *slander* is forbidden. This is because you cannot love your neighbour and tell tales about him at the same time. In a similar situation Jesus warned that you dare not enter the sanctuary to worship unless you first go and ask him to forgive you for telling catty tales about him. Queen Mary II once gave a dinner party at which some of her guests conducted a tittle-tattle about alleged elopements, adulteries, debt-collecting, and so on. She quietly changed the whole course of the conversation by asking them if they had read this verse of our psalm. She then repeated it to them.

(5) Slanderous *talk* can lead on to evil *actions*. Fancy *doing evil* to a friend!

SOME MORE COMMANDMENTS

Psalm 15:4–5

4 in whose eyes a reprobate is despised,
  but who honours those who fear the Lord;
 who swears to his own hurt and does not change;
5 who does not put out his money at interest,
  and does not take a bribe against the innocent.

 He who does these things shall never be moved.

(6) The righteous person despises those who have been rejected (by God, and so are now outside the bonds of the Covenant). That does not mean he sneers at them, or gives them up for lost, for God has not done so. Just as God is concerned about them still, so must the worshipper be. But he must learn to see the distinction between loyalty and disloyalty to God.

(7) The OT has no words for religion or religious, a point we should constantly remember. For the Bible is not about religion but about (a) God, and about (b) life. By the words *Those who*

fear the Lord our psalmist is expressing the idea, not of being religious, but of recognising in awe and wonder the mystery of the living God.

(8) A person may make a promise whose outcome he could not have foreseen; but that does not mean he dare go back on his word. A person, for example, may marry another, declaring in so doing: "I take you ... in sickness and in health ... till death us do part." Then she (or he!) turns out to be rotten, deceitful, and unfaithful. But that is no reason for the other party to be disloyal in turn.

(9) According to the Law of Moses money was a gift from God that was meant to be used only as a means for the exchange of commodities. Money had no value in itself. Thus it was not to be used for making more money. People are more important than money. Thus if a brother or a friend should fall on bad times, one ought to lend him enough money to set him on his feet again. Then, when he was able, he was to repay the sum lent to him (Exod. 22:25; Lev. 25:35–37; Deut. 23:19). But you must not take any interest on such a loan. The point is that you have been privileged to help someone who is poor, especially if he has become so by bad luck, for then you do what God does (Ps. 14:6). Moreover, when you discover that "taking interest" in Hebrew is the word for "biting", you realize what the Law of Moses thought about the whole business! On the other hand, lending money for purposes of foreign trade was quite another matter (Deut. 23.20).

(10) One of the scourges of the East has been, and still is, the taking of bribes; worse still, when an innocent man is thereby condemned. Such an act is a terrible sin against the solidarity of love and compassion.

These ten moral commands are clearly taken merely as samples of many more that could be extracted from the Law of Moses. They are not actually "commands", just as the list in Exod. 20 are not called commands either, but "words". They are the Decalogue, God's "Ten Words". But the above selection is sufficient to show the plain man that true faith does not mean just "keeping the commandments". True faith bears fruit. The fruit comes from a loving, kindly, generous personality, from one who is always the same, utterly reliable, one who can *never be moved*. For such a personality is the kind who, as Jeremiah puts it, has the Law written on his heart, in that he now both (a) "knows the Lord", and finds (b) that his sin is forgiven (Jer. 31:34).

After five years in office, President Franklin Roosevelt quoted this last line at a service of Thanksgiving, and then added: "The old ship of state is still on the same course, because the nation has based its life on moral principles."

THE CONFESSION OF A NEW CONVERT

Psalm 16:1–6

A Miktam of David.

1 Preserve me, O God, for in thee I take refuge.
2   I say to the Lord, "Thou art my Lord;
    I have no good apart from thee."

3 As for the saints in the land, they are the noble,
    in whom is all my delight.

4 Those who choose another god multiply their sorrows;
    their libations of blood I will not pour out
    or take their names upon my lips.

5 The Lord is my chosen portion and my cup;
    thou holdest my lot.
6 The lines have fallen for me in pleasant places;
    yea, I have a goodly heritage.

The word *Miktam* found in the heading of this psalm has long remained a mystery. The Greek for it, as found in the LXX's heading of the psalm, reads "stone inscription". No one could think what that meant until recently. For the word has appeared in the Ugaritic language (a cousin of Hebrew, deciphered only about 1930), and there also it seems to mean "inscription on a stone slab". I am only going to make a very tentative suggestion from this. Off and on for a century now the suggestion has been made that this psalm was composed by a convert from one of the Canaanite peoples. This would include those persons who spoke the Ugaritic language. Does our heading thus suggest that this convert from outside the covenant people has found in Israel's faith in Yahweh, the Lord, what he had long hoped to be true, that God is indeed that Rock which Israel said he was (Ps. 18:2, etc.)?

This foreigner finds the experience to be one of *taking refuge* as does the writer of Ps. 18.2. Till now he has known God as *el*, the Ugaritic name for the supreme Being that appears in our psalm at verse 1, and which is translated "God". His words remind us of those Greeks, foreigners, who said to Philip, "Sir, we wish to see Jesus" (John 12:21). We may actually legitimately read verses 2 and 3 as "I said to Yahweh. You are to be my Lord; my whole good depends on You".

I have found, he continues, that the covenant people have received me warmly, so that I now delight in my new friendships. They have behaved to me as only nobles, aristocrats, would. He refers of course, by the word *saints*, to the people of the covenant now in their own *land*, that God had promised to them before they arrived (Exod. 19:6).

As is shown in the RSV *ftn.* the text of the next verse is not clear. But what our writer seems to be saying is that usually when people change their religion they seldom find themselves completely at home inside the new cult. If he had joined with a Canaanite cult, he would have said, "I will not use the names of their gods." If our friend had chosen the god Moloch of the Canaanites, for example, he would have had to sacrifice one of his babies to that god (Lev. 20:2). If he had gone to live in Carthage, and had adopted its religion, he would have had to participate in human sacrifice. Obviously he shrank in horror from the very idea of both such practices.

But, he goes on to say, I have deliberately and in complete freedom of choice, chosen *Yahweh* as my *portion*, and found him to be all that I could long for. The phrase *chosen portion* comes from the time when the land of Israel was being allotted amongst the twelve tribes of Israel. Each tribe then received his portion. His *cup* is just another way of saying the same thing. Obviously he can't help repeating himself with joy. Then he says it a third time! For one's *lot* is the same thing as one's portion. Furthermore, he adds, when they measured out for me with their dividing lines (see Mic. 2:5), so to speak, that which was to be my share in Israel's heritage, I found I had been granted a splendid dower. Once again, he can't help but say this also a second time. "Indeed it was an inheritance that is beautiful to me."

Theologically speaking, this confession is of deep import. There are those who take for granted that ancient Israel thought of their God as being meant for them only. Foreigners could have what gods they wanted. So this leads such people to declare that Israel had little or no feeling for mission. But this psalm is just one passage amongst many that give the lie to such a view. And it gives the lie too to those who today tell the Church in a loud voice that they should leave the heathen alone. They should not disturb them in their inherited faiths, whatever these might be, for they suit those peoples better than Christianity ever would.

THE JOY OF THE NEW CONVERT

Psalm 16:7–11

7 I bless the Lord who gives me counsel;
   in the night also my heart instructs me.
8 I keep the Lord always before me;
   because he is at my right hand, I shall not be moved.

9 Therefore my heart is glad, and my soul rejoices;
   my body also dwells secure.
10 For thou dost not give me up to Sheol,
   or let thy godly one see the Pit.

11 Thou does show me the path of life;
   in thy presence there is fullness of joy,
   in thy right hand are pleasures for evermore.

Our friend is clearly enthusiastic about his new-found faith. He is grateful to *el* (see verse 1) for guiding his thoughts and for leading him to convert to this God whom he has now found to be *Yahweh*. Yahweh has been leading him even in the night hours and motivating his kidneys to help him think theologically! The English says *heart*, the Hebrew says *kidneys*. Those organs are the most sensitive and possibly the most vital part of the human frame. The ancient world accepted as fact that all our inward parts are involved in our thinking and feeling, and that each part can stand for and work for the others. Some suggest that the kidneys were the seat of the conscience. But what is meant is that God uses the whole of his being, feeling, imagination, reason, logical thought and even his digestive system to instruct him in his new faith: "I have set the Lord right in front of me, unremittingly; (I know that) he is also alongside me, so I shall be quite unmoved."

When our friend "converted" he didn't change his God. That would not be possible, for there is only one God. *El* is the basic root of the Hebrew for "God", which is usually *elohim*. *Allah* in Arabic is, of course, from the same root. *El*, however, occurs quite commonly in the OT. We see it, for example, in the name *Immanu-el* (God with us). *Yahweh*, on the other hand, is the name by which the only God, *el*, revealed himself to Moses. The root of the name Yahweh is the verb *h-y-h*, *to become* (rather than the static idea of *to be*). But we must make three additions to that statement.

(1) There is movement and action in the word *h-y-h*. This is seen clearly, for example, in the first words of Hosea: "The word of the Lord that *came* [Hebrew *h-y-h*] to Hosea."

(2) This movement is from God to man, because God is the living God, and man is only creature. That is why God, by grace, always takes the initiative. God says to Moses at Exod. 3:12, "I will become [*ehyeh*] with you." So we see how at Exod. 3:14 the words I AM (also *ehyeh*) mean much more than what those capital letters in English suggest. The point is that God's name "I am who I am" is not there at all in the Hebrew. It is to be found in the LXX, even more badly translated, as "I am the

existent One". That, of course, is a Greek philosophical idea, far removed from the *living* God of the OT.

(3) The name Yahweh, built from our root, seems to have been formed from the active, transitive form of the verb *h-y-h*. So, putting all these ideas together we believe that the divine Name may mean something like "He who causes to become with", and at Exod. 6:3–4, he is to *become with* Moses, and through Moses, with all Israel. Exod. 3:15 adds that this God of Israel is the God of the ancient Fathers of Israel, he who had long ago made covenant with Abraham, Isaac and Jacob. And it was into this ancient covenant that our foreign friend was now made welcome, to find God ever growing closer to him. Finally, through reverence, the Jewish use of the word LORD, (in capitals in the AV) was taken over by the Christian Church in place of the Hebrew *Yahweh*. The name *Jehovah*, by the way, should never be used. It was the invention of printers in the fifteenth century.

Because the Lord of the Covenant is a God who has revealed himself to be like this, and since our foreigner has found him to be so, no wonder he rejoices, the whole of him, body, soul and spirit. "Even my body rests blissfully in You." And since this God of the Covenant has now said to him in person, "I will never let you go, my *godly one*" (meaning " he who loyally keeps covenant with me"), his promise must extend even beyond death. Sheol was the underworld of the dead, and the Pit was the "sump" down at its very bottom. But God is the living God, both now and always, so our new convert will also live for ever.

Did the later congregation join in too at this point, as in other psalms? If so, they had by now learned from this foreigner to declare with complete conviction that since *life* comes as a gift from the living God, God will certainly not take back his gift if he is to be true to himself. This means that God's covenant people will rejoice in his love for all eternity.

A BLESSED HOPE

Psalm 17:1–15

A Prayer of David

1　Hear a just cause, O Lord; attend to my cry!
　　Give ear to my prayer from lips free of deceit!
2　From thee let my vindication come!
　　Let thy eyes see the right!

3　If thou triest my heart, if thou visitest me by night,
　　if thou testest me, thou wilt find no wickedness in me;
　　my mouth does not transgress.
4　With regard to the works of men, by the word of thy lips
　　I have avoided the ways of the violent.
5　My steps have held fast to thy paths,
　　my feet have not slipped.

6　I call upon thee, for thou wilt answer me, O God,
　　incline thy ear to me, hear my words.
7　Wondrously show thy steadfast love,
　　O saviour of those who seek refuge
　　from their adversaries at thy right hand.

8　Keep me as the apple of the eye;
　　hide me in the shadow of thy wings,
9　from the wicked who despoil me,
　　my deadly enemies who surround me.

10　They close their hearts to pity;
　　with their mouths they speak arrogantly.
11　They track me down; now they surround me;
　　they set their eyes to cast me to the ground.
12　They are like a lion eager to tear,
　　as a young lion lurking in ambush.

13　Arise, O Lord! confront them, overthrow them!
　　Deliver my life from the wicked by thy sword,
14　from men by thy hand, O Lord,
　　from men whose portion in life is of the world.

> May their belly be filled with what thou hast stored up for them;
>   may their children have more than enough;
>   may they leave something over to their babes.

15 As for me, I shall behold thy face in righteousness;
       when I awake, I shall be satisfied with beholding thy form.

Like Job, this psalmist believes himself to be innocent. This does not mean that he claims to be sinless. But like the rich young ruler who came to Jesus for help with his faith (Matt. 19:16–30; Mark 10:17–22; Luke 18: 18–30) our psalmist "has kept all the commandments ever since I was a boy". We note two things from the NT story. (a) Jesus, looking upon him, loved him. And so God looked at our psalmist here, and loved him. (b) Jesus shows him how morals are not enough, and so does God now. What God looked for was *hesed*—total commitment to the God of the Covenant in response to his total commitment to us. Our psalmist has not quite believed that God loves him in this way, so he is not quite ready for total commitment to God.

Yet, in his goodness, God had actually *visited* him when in bed at night (there is no *if* in the Hebrew). God had actually tried him and had given him a special private experience of his loving presence. In response therefore our psalmist declares: *Notwithstanding the ways of men I have kept to the words of Your lips, and so have avoided violent ways.* He has in fact chosen to follow God's path, not man's.

Now he chooses to address God as *el*. This makes us ask the question: Is he our friend the foreigner who gave us the previous psalm? Is the "honeymoon" period of knowing the ways of the Lord now over, and is he having difficulties with his faith—as we all do? Anyway, he declares: "I called upon You; I am sure [*ki*] You will answer me, *el*." The word *wondrously* is used here to mean "God's steadfast love that comes to me in a miraculous way". "I am one of those who have taken refuge in You and have found salvation from those who rise up against Your activities"—for the *right hand*, of course, is what one uses to *do* things.

The lovely expression we meet in verse 8 is a quotation from

Deut. 32:10, one of the earliest pieces of writing in the OT. There it is Israel who is called by those words; so here this "new" Israelite, this new convert, wants God to do the same for him. In Old English the pupil of the eye was called a "mannikin", meaning "little man", because the pupil gave back the reflexion of a grown man as a little man. So too with the Hebrew, for it too means "little man", or even "dear little man". Again, *the shadow of thy wings* appears in the following verse of Deut. 32 with reference to what God did at the Exodus. For, as Exod. 19:4 puts it: "You have seen how I bore you on eagles' wings and brought you to myself." So now our psalmist prays God to include him in the whole people of God whom God has brought up out of the land of Egypt, that is to say, whom God has redeemed.

To live in the shadow of God's wings does not mean that one is removed to safety from all the wickedness of this life. This could not be so, for God himself is not removed from this world. God is here, present, *in* this world of human treachery. Therefore even when kept in God's care, evil men, like wild beasts, still surround the believer and seek to ambush him. The wild, searing eyes of the tiger, "burning bright in the forests of the night", can reach and pierce me through, he says. The believer must not fall into the trap of being an optimist; nor dare he be a pessimist; he must always remain that most difficult thing, a realist.

But since he had already said that God is *he who saves those who seek refuge in him* (verse 7), our new convert now realistically claims his right to receive God's help. For God had already done so to Israel in the Wilderness when the cry went up "Arise, O Lord!" Being a sinner still, however, as we said at verse 1, he has not yet learned what total commitment in love can mean, and how such commitment must include love even of one's enemies. By the way, the word *world* here is that which Paul uses when he means, not this material globe, but the evil worldly life of people.

What a lot the congregation has now learned as it listened to this song, sung by a new convert witnessing to his doubts, but still holding on to his faith. All present, therefore, now join in the following great final statement. What exactly does it mean?

(1) The word *righteousness* has to be translated in various ways, depending upon the context, as we pointed out in the Introduction. Here it probably means *victory*, that is to say, the time when God will *put things right*. When that happens, as each individual in the congregation now sings, *I shall see thy face*, that is, really see what God is like as the Saviour of the world.

(2) *Thy form*. It is foolish to be dogmatic here. At Num. 12:8, to behold the *form* of the Lord means something like being aware of the outline of his presence. We recall that God said to Moses: "You cannot see my face; for man shall not see me and live" (Exod. 33:20). For God is Spirit, and so cannot be seen by the human eye, or grasped by the human intellect. So this line *may* mean: "Each morning when I wake up I am saturated (as if, like a sponge, I could hold no more) with the outline of Your presence." Or, it may mean: "When I awake on the other side of death, I shall be saturated (what a vivid term!) with Your form," that is to say, even as little as a mere creature can grasp will totally suffice for my knowledge of God in eternity.

This last line is carved on the headstone of that great Scottish preacher, Dr. Alexander Whyte, of Edinburgh.

A ROYAL PSALM OF THANKSGIVING

Psalm 18:1-5

To the choirmaster. A Psalm of David the servant of the Lord, who addressed the words of this song to the Lord on the day when the Lord delivered him from the hand of all his enemies, and from the hand of Saul. He said:

1 I love thee, O Lord, my strength.
2   The Lord is my rock, and my fortress, and my deliverer,
        my God, my rock, in whom I take refuge,
        my shield, and the horn of my salvation, my stronghold.
3 I call upon the Lord, who is worthy to be praised,
        and I am saved from my enemies.

4 The cords of death encompassed me,
   the torrents of perdition assailed me;
5 the cords of Sheol entangled me,
   the snares of death confronted me.

The heading declares that David wrote this long psalm once he had finally won all his battles and had become sole ruler in Jerusalem. The whole psalm, with occasional verbal differences, is to be found also at 2 Sam. 22. We ought therefore now to read the story of David once again, and so to discover why he could pen this great expression of faith. Then, of course, once we see how the poem could neatly fit David's situation, we can understand how it was adapted to be used by the whole succession of Israel's kings.

The plain man usually assumes that each passage or verse in the Bible has only one original and, could we say, "correct" meaning. But this is not what we find; otherwise the biblical text would be mere dead matter. It would be like the old religious texts coming from the Babylonians and the Egyptians that we now possess in great numbers. The OT is the living Word of God. This psalm has not remained "stuck" in David's days. After the royal line came to an end in 587 B.C., and Israel had been dragged into exile in Babylonia, still more light emerged from this and from other psalms. Now they were found to be speaking directly to a new generation in quite new and different social circumstances.

In the century before Christ, the Dead Sea Scrolls discovered new depths in the psalms that not even David knew. Matt. 11:14; Mark 2:23–28; John 10:34–36; Acts 2:25–28, again, all regard OT passages as taking on new meaning on the lips of Christ, or on others' lips as interpretations of Christ. Paul can develop an OT passage to mean something not obvious in the original (see Gal. 3:6–9; 4:21–31). Yet at the same time this psalm is rooted in what is basic and unchanging in the biblical revelation, that is, in the love of God. So we should be aware that the psalms are not only ancient literature, they are also an element in our modern Bible.

The first verse is not found in 2 Sam. 22. We hear of a Greek intellectual who, with all his background of mythology and philosophy, when he first heard these words, declared: "Fancy actually saying that you *love* your god!" But David loved his God only because his God had first loved David.

For the Lord had given him in this often dangerous world and amongst unpredictable human beings—security. Each picture the poet uses here is a parable in itself:

(1) *The Lord is my strength*. He enables me to live a life of love to others in my turn.

(2) *He is my Rock*. How this image grew as time went on! The idea behind it became visible as people travelled and visited that strange city built on and inside a rock, Petra (or Sela), in nearby Edom. We remember too the significance of the name Peter, the rock on which Christ built his Church, and so on.

(3) A *fortress* was a place where one regained one's breath and initiative to sally forth once again as a soldier should.

(4) His *deliverer* saved him from his many enemies and gave him *shalom*, peace.

(5) *My God*: so this was no mere human saviour David speaks of.

(6) Now we have a second word for *rock*, this kind being one in which David could take refuge as in a fissure, for it was "cleft for me".

(7) This kind of *shield* was five feet high, and could protect the whole body up to the eyes.

(8) The Jerusalem *altar* had four horns, one at each corner. If one was in trouble and fled to the sanctuary and grasped one of the horns, then one was safe (1 Kings 1:50).

(9) A *stronghold* was like a Levantine fortress built on the top of a precipice.

David, we see, has now learned to possess complete confidence in God's care. (a) I call, he says, just that, and (b) God answers me—I am saved!

All of us at times face the horror of death; perhaps our poet is now speaking of the kind of nightmare that anyone in David's period of history could suffer, the horror of being dragged off by ropes down to the underworld; for death, called by the name *Moth*, was a kind of god; and so this was a personalized experience of horror. That is one picture here, the first nightmare. The other describes the deep current that flows along the very bottom of the sea and which runs into the ocean of chaos right down below the pit of Sheol. Such a vision of horror is not far removed from a science-fiction nightmare we might suffer in our day. *Perdition* was the name given to these currents, or *Belial* in the Hebrew. That was the name of the god of deliberate and wanton destruction, whose spirit you met in those disagreeable characters whom the OT calls "sons of Belial". They were the local, violent, evil-minded gangster types who were ever willing to assault or murder either for kicks or for cash, such as Queen Jezebel hired to do her dastardly will on poor Naboth (1 Kings 21). These hired thugs exhibited the spirit of that chaos or *tohu*, as the Hebrew names it in Gen. 1:2, out of which God's creative plan arose. So two American scholars in a joint work have produced the delightful name of "*hell*ions" to describe them! Yet note how God can use even such horrible creatures to his glory. It is *out of tohu* that God creates light, the universe and man in Gen. 1, not out of nothing. The idea of *creatio ex nihilo* is not biblical. How else could we understand the significance of the Resurrection of Christ if it had not been *out of* the Cross?

THE LORD OF NATURE

Psalm 18:6–24

6 In my distress I called upon the Lord;
   to my God I cried for help.
From his temple he heard my voice,
   and my cry to him reached his ears.

7 Then the earth reeled and rocked;
   the foundations also of the mountains trembled
   and quaked, because he was angry.

8 Smoke went up from his nostrils,
   and devouring fire from his mouth;
   glowing coals flamed forth from him.

9 He bowed the heavens, and came down;
   thick darkness was under his feet.

10 He rode on a cherub, and flew;
    he came swiftly upon the wings of the wind.

11 He made darkness his covering around him,
    his canopy thick clouds dark with water.

12 Out of the brightness before him
    there broke through his clouds
    hailstones and coals of fire.

13 The Lord also thundered in the heavens,
    and the Most High uttered his voice,
    hailstones and coals of fire.

14 And he sent out his arrows, and scattered them;
    he flashed forth lightnings, and routed them.

15 Then the channels of the sea were seen,
    and the foundations of the world were laid bare,
    at thy rebuke, O Lord,
    at the blast of the breath of thy nostrils.

16 He reached from on high, he took me,
    he drew me out of many waters.

17 He delivered me from my strong enemy,
    and from those who hated me;
    for they were too mighty for me.

18 They came upon me in the day of my calamity;
    but the Lord was my stay.

19 He brought me forth into a broad place;
    he delivered me, because he delighted in me.

20 The Lord rewarded me according to my righteousness;
    according to the cleanness of my hands he recompensed me.

21 For I have kept the ways of the Lord,
    and have not wickedly departed from my God.

22 For all his ordinances were before me,
    and his statutes I did not put away from me.

23 I was blameless before him,
    and I kept myself from guilt.

24 Therefore the Lord has recompensed me according to my right-
      eousness,
      according to the cleanness of my hands in his sight.

By David's day the peoples of the Near East supposed that the
forces of nature were the playthings of the gods and goddesses
of their various religions. What we have here is a striking poem
which comes from a period actually before David's day, but
which he must have loved and quoted. But before he repeats it
here, in verse 6 he makes a great statement of faith. He cries to
God, he says, but like Elijah on Mount Horeb, he does not hear
God's voice in the roar of the earthquake or the crackle of the
fire (1 Kings 19:11–12). His cry does indeed reach right to God's
ears, however; but God answers him from his temple, and not
from the earthquake, and in his own still small voice.

This mighty poem following should be read straight through
in one piece. One should not analyse it verse by verse, or ask
what the various pictures mean. It is poetry of the highest order.
We note that it could be regarded as an answer to the cry made
in the previous psalm (Ps. 17:13)—*Arise, O Lord, confront
them!* Its description of a majestic thunderstorm seems to have
been recited first in the Canaanite language, so that what we
have here is its Hebrew translation. But Israel's singers took it
over from its pagan origins, inserted the name of God in verse
13, and turned it from a nature poem into a song of deliverance
from the powers of evil.

God's act of deliverance is described in terms of the same
"mythological" picture-world of the poem. For *God drew me
out of many waters*, and set me on good *broad terra firma*. But
why should he do so? There comes the astonishing answer
unknown to the Canaanite worshippers of Baal: "Because he
delighted in me." Even in the event of world catastrophe, it
seems, God "cares for me".

How wrong those biblical expositors are who say that in the
process of the long biblical story God shows his concern and
love for the individual, rather than for the nation, only when we
reach the NT!

There is one remark we should make however before leaving the poem, and that is to note that the *cherub* (verse 10) in the OT was not an angel, far less the baby angel of the medieval painters. The cherub (like the seraph) was a horrible half-man, half-beast, perhaps best envisaged when we look at a picture of the Sphinx in Egypt. The cherub was the creation of the mind of man. It was a representation of human religious ideas, of what the divine ought to be like if man could have his way. We see many such representations in our time in modern India, all heads, all arms, all feet, like curling serpents. But at Isa. 6:1–3 we find that the *seraphs* are actually bowing down before and praising God! In our poem the *cherub* is a vehicle that God *uses* to reveal his glory, even though a cherub is an evil concept. This then tells us today that God can use even the strange ideas of the world's religions, and use them to his glory! For our biblical faith transcends all human religions. Christianity, we should always remember, is not just one of the religions of the world. The Christian *Faith* (not the Christian "religion") has to do with the living God, his creative love, his compassion, and so with that fulness of life of which both Testaments speak. And fulness of life is not "religion" (Amos 5:4; John 5–6)! Nor was Christianity "born at Bethlehem", so that "the Church is only two thousand years old"—unlike Hinduism and some other religions. Our psalms here are all about the *Faith* that God gave us in Abraham, and so "Christianity is as old as the days when men began to call upon the name of the Lord" (Gen. 4:26). Then again, we note that this poem uses the picture-language of a *theophany*, that is, the appearance of the divine Being to the human mind, such as we find at the giving of the Law to Moses on Mount Sinai (Exod. 19:16–24). Thus we might go so far as to say—"The Lord came down at Sinai—for *me*"!

We have now had pictured for us the truth expressed in Gen. 1:1–3, that God creates light, that is to say, his majestic purpose of love, not out of nothing, but out of the chaos, put in the form (for our human imagination to grasp) of a storm above and of an earthquake below. In this way we learn that God acts with man upon the earth in a manner similar to the way in which he acts with nature. God takes man as he is with all his chaotic soul, and through grace he renews him, just as he renews the face of the earth (Gen. 9). Thereupon God gives him a creative job to do. Noah had to work the soil after it had been renewed when the floods subsided. And so, in the same way, just as God made Covenant with Noah, so he makes it with us to keep his people *blameless* and useful by grace alone.

GOD'S COVENANT LOVE

Psalm 18:25–30

25 With the loyal thou dost show thyself loyal;
    with the blameless man thou dost show thyself blameless;
26 with the pure thou dost show thyself pure;
    and with the crooked thou dost show thyself perverse.
27 For thou dost deliver a humble people,
    but the haughty eyes thou dost bring down.
28 Yea, thou dost light my lamp;
    the Lord my God lightens my darkness.
29 Yea, by thee I can crush a troop;
    and by my God I can leap over a wall.
30 This God—his way is perfect;
    the promise of the Lord proves true;
    he is a shield for all those who take refuge in him.

We have noted before that the AV translated the Hebrew *hesed* by a great number of English words. These the RSV manages to reduce to a handful. And we have also noted how the word, no matter how we translate it, describes the nature of that relationship between God and his beloved people now that they have been "glued" together by the Covenant. Here, however, the RSV shows very clearly the basic meaning of *hesed*. For it means *loyalty*. God has given himself to us in love. That has been his primary act of *hesed*. But now he keeps on supporting us, his beloved, from day to day within the Covenant. That then is the continuing expression of his *hesed*; in other words, God is always totally loyal to us whom he has chosen. So our response to God can only be one of *hesed* also, that is, of absolute loyalty on our part. But with the devious, as the poem says, with those who have (literally) *twisted* the unspeakably wonderful *hesed* of God, God must act accordingly.

Now follow some illuminating phrases that illustrate all this. "[I believe that] *thou dost deliver poor people*"—because of Your loyalty to them; but the *haughty eyes* of those who dare not look God in the face in gratitude, God must deal with.

Once again, then, we see the *creative* work of God, the God who never ceases to create. Here he is called *this God*, that is to say, the *el* who is the God of all the religions of men. This great God actually creates for me the means of showing folk the path of life, by doing for me what I cannot do for myself. I have no matches, so to speak, no means of my own to be a light to the world; so he lights my lamp for me (see Matt. 5:14–16). Such a phrase as this brings the idea of "light" right out of the area of abstract ideas and fits it neatly into my own small life. The consequence is that I feel I can do anything he asks me to do; I can take on all comers. I *know* this to be so, because God's promise is *true*, this word actually meaning "tried in the fire and come out pure gold". His promise has "stood the test of time". The early Church sang those truths afresh as they are expressed in the light of Christ in the words of the *Magnificat*, Luke 1:46–55.

THE VOICE OF DAVID

Psalm 18:31–50

31 For who is God, but the Lord?
And who is a rock, except our God?—
32 the God who girded me with strength,
and made my way safe.
33 He made my feet like hinds' feet,
and set me secure on the heights.
34 He trains my hands for war,
so that my arms can bend a bow of bronze.

35   Thou hast given me the shield of thy salvation,
     and thy right hand supported me,
     and thy help made me great.
36   Thou didst give a wide place for my steps under me,
     and my feet did not slip.
37   I pursued my enemies and overtook them;
     and did not turn back till they were consumed.
38   I thrust them through, so that they were not able to rise;
     they fell under my feet.
39   For thou didst gird me with strength for the battle;
     thou didst make my assailants sink under me.
40   Thou didst make my enemies turn their backs to me,
     and those who hated me I destroyed.
41   They cried for help, but there was none to save,
     they cried to the Lord, but he did not answer them.
42   I beat them fine as dust before the wind;
     I cast them out like the mire of the streets.

43   Thou didst deliver me from strife with the peoples;
     thou didst make me the head of the nations;
     people whom I had not known served me.
44   As soon as they heard of me they obeyed me;
     foreigners came cringing to me.
45   Foreigners lost heart,
     and came trembling out of their fastnesses.

46   The Lord lives; and blessed be my rock,
     and exalted be the God of my salvation,
47   the God who gave me vengeance
     and subdued peoples under me;
48   who delivered me from my enemies;
     yea, thou didst exalt me above my adversaries;
     thou didst deliver me from men of violence.

49   For this I will extol thee, O Lord, among the nations,
     and sing praises to thy name.
50   Great triumphs he gives to his king,
     and shows steadfast love to his anointed,
     to David and his descendants for ever.

David now puts together all the various thoughts that have passed through his mind to this point. First, the God who has done all this for him is the Rock, the picture-name with which

the psalm began (verse 2). Consequently he has enabled *me* to
do anything he asks me to do, even to take on all comers (verse
29). As Rock, he has of course been there from the beginning.
Our psalmist shows this conviction by using at verse 31 still
another word for God, *eloah.* This form of *el* occurs in ancient
poems like Deut. 32, but is also present in later literature when
the "ancientness" of God is being stressed. Brought up out of
the chaos of the watery deep, David now finds his feet on *terra
firma*, the sure, *true, proven* nature of God's love (verses 19, 36).
And so, in grand eastern hyperbole, and in the rousing language
of poetry, he declares how the power of God (verse 1) has
enabled him to overcome all his enemies; we might say that he
feels like kicking up his heels in light-heartedness at the wonder
of this power of God.

Note the attractive line we can recover from the Hebrew if we
follow the RSV *ftn.* at verse 35: "Your gentleness has made me
great." Consequently we are led to quote Shakespeare's Portia
in *The Merchant of Venice*, connecting the words of verse 35
with those at verse 28:

How far that little candle throws his beams!
So shines a good deed in a naughty world.

All the majesty and mystery of God's redemptive power as it
works in human life is now focused on the person of David.
Consequently, and now for the third time, we hear the words
The Lord is my Rock. This time they clearly issue from the lips
of David; for *Head of the Nations* is one of the titles given to the
messianic king who sits upon the throne of David.

Finally we have the chorus spoken by the worshipping
congregation. Because it is not David himself (or any of his
successors) who now speaks this passage, the whole congregation acknowledges aloud that it is God himself who does all
these mighty works, not man, not David, not any of the kings
descended from David, one of whom was probably now being
addressed on some great festive occasion. At the moment of his
anniversary, if it was such, his right to rule God's people was
being *re*-newed by God's authority, and not by any human

"divine right of kings"; but most of all because of God's unshakeable *hesed*, his *steadfast love*, to the whole line of David. (See Luke 1:54, where the word *mercy* is still another translation of this vital, living word, that *steadfast, sure love for David* that Isa. 55:3 assumes to be as firm as the Rock itself. And see how Paul quotes this passage to good purpose at Rom. 15:9.)

The outcome of such linking between the OT and the NT is this, that if God has promised in this absolute way to work through the sinner David *to extol him amongst the nations*, then how much more will he do so through the perfect Son of David for whom the NT claims those very promises that God has made in this psalm—*for ever!*

THE WORD OF CREATION

Psalm 19:1–6

To the choirmaster. A Psalm of David.

1 The heavens are telling the glory of God;
    and the firmament proclaims his handiwork.
2 Day to day pours forth speech,
    and night to night declares knowledge.
3 There is no speech, nor are there words;
    their voice is not heard;
4 yet their voice goes out through all the earth,
    and their words to the end of the world.

  In them he has set a tent for the sun,
5 which comes forth like a bridegroom leaving his chamber,
    and like a strong man runs its course with joy.
6 Its rising is from the end of the heavens,
    and its circuit to the end of them;
    and there is nothing hid from its heat.

Poem I

The poem begins, as does Psalm 8, with the poet gazing at the heavens and wondering at the mystery of creation. Yet man does not see God by looking at the sky; what he sees is the *glory* of God. "No man can see God and live." *Glory*, for OT man, was the outward "clothing" of God. It did not hide or cover his "being", rather it *revealed* his actions. As the living God, he is always *doing*, creating, recreating, producing order out of the original chaos (Gen. 1:2), bringing light at each dawn out of the darkness of night, ever creating new species of animals, birds, insects, and so on. In fact the word *rakia* that we find at Gen. 1:6, and which is there translated by *firmament*, is found only twice again, here and at Dan. 12:3. Its use makes us wonder if the psalmist was writing a commentary on Gen. 1.

But to say that we *see* the glory of God in this poem is a reading into it by a modern, scientifically-minded person. The poem talks of *hearing* the glory of God. It declares that behind the whole majesty of nature there is *sound*, the sound of the Word of God. The whole creation, even without the use of *words*, sounds forth the divine Word; when put into Greek, this is the word *Logos* that we meet at John 1:1.

The RSV *ftn.* to verse 4 reminds us of the old translation we used to know in the AV, "Their line is gone out . . . " But the Hebrew word seems to employ a pun which we can perhaps convey by saying that "cord" can also be spelt as "chord". So we might even put it this way: "Their tune has gone out . . . "

But *Logos* can mean more than *word*. It can also mean *reason, meaning*. And so this poem is proclaiming that the heavenly bodies are not mere matter, to be understood merely as scientific phenomena. They shout to all who have ears to hear that behind them and their movements lies the *meaning* of the universe.

Joseph Addison's well-known hymn, "The spacious firmament on high" expresses this well:

What though no real voice nor sound
    Amidst their radiant orbs be found?
In reason's ear they all rejoice,
    And utter forth a glorious voice,
For ever singing, as they shine,
    "The hand that made us is divine."

The word *knowledge* in verse 2 may be translated, ponderously, by "observable scientific data". It is in poetic parallelism with the word *speech* in the previous line. Thus the poet is saying that natural phenomena are means through which the *meaning* of the universe is expressed. And the *ftn.* to verse 4, in saying that "their line goes out", is declaring that each heavenly body must follow the prescribed route laid down by the Creator.

Then he pin-points the sun. In the Egypt of his day the Sun was the supreme god, and each Pharaoh was his incarnation on earth. But here the sun is no god. As G.K. Chesterton puts it, each morning God tells it: "Come on, get up", and it does! Yet even in "Christendom" there are people who cannot believe this, and as part of their Yoga exercises, they turn and face the sun as the source of all life. But here, as our poet says, for the sun *God* sets a tent.

From the Akkadian period in Mesopotamia (2350-2150 B.C) we possess cylinder seals showing the sun, all dressed up and gloriously apparelled as a young hero, entering the earthly regions with a powerful leap from a gate between two mountains. Here our poet has liberated himself from such myths, and simply uses their imagery to display poetically the greatness of God.

THE WORD OF REDEMPTION

Psalm 19.7-14

7 The law of the Lord is perfect,
       reviving the soul;
    the testimony of the Lord is sure,
       making wise the simple;
8 the precepts of the Lord are right,
       rejoicing the heart;
    the commandment of the Lord is pure,
       enlightening the eyes;
9 the fear of the Lord is clean,
       enduring for ever;
    the ordinances of the Lord are true,
       and righteous altogether.

10   More to be desired are they than gold,
         even much fine gold;
     sweeter also than honey
         and drippings of the honeycomb.

11   Moreover by them is thy servant warned;
         in keeping them there is great reward.
12   But who can discern his errors?
         Clear thou me from hidden faults.
13   Keep back thy servant also from presumptuous sins;
         let them not have dominion over me!
     Then I shall be blameless,
         and innocent of great transgression.

14   Let the words of my mouth and the meditation of my heart
         be acceptable in thy sight,
         O Lord, my rock and my redeemer.

Poem II

Poem I deals with what we today call *General Revelation*.
God has revealed himself through the wonders of creation as he
speaks the *Word* to all men everywhere. But Israel, as the
Covenant People of God, is privileged to possess a *Special
Word* that has been delivered to her alone. It is the *Torah*, the
Law of Moses, as much of it as was available and complete by
the poet's day. So now the poet adds a whole new psalm to the
one he has inherited, to sing the praise of God's *Special
Revelation*. The first poem is in praise of the Word of Creation.
The second is in praise of the Word of Redemption.

The two poems that comprise Psalm 19 are perfectly paralleled. The Word that comes to Israel through the Law means
nothing, its voice is not even heard, until faith opens it up to our
human understanding. The sun has a path to travel daily; the
Law, however, is my path, says the poet, one that has been given
me by God. As Kant the philosopher put it: "The sky above us
and the moral law within us witness to the same God." See how
Paul, quoting this psalm, puts the two together at Rom.
10:17–18.

(1) The Law is *perfect*—of course, because it is the Word of
God.

(2) It *revives the soul*, the *nephesh*, the whole of one's person, or better, "gives life" to it. The Word that we meet in Christ also declares, "I came that people might have life and have it more abundantly."

(3) *Testimony* means "meeting-place"; and so it refers to divine guidance or instruction within the Covenant. In his grace the all-wise God speaks at the level of the ordinary person.

(4) The *precepts* or proclamations of the Lord, those things he has charged us to do, are of course, right. Thus they are the kind of things that we rejoice to obey. Even the "Thou shalt nots" we are glad that God *said* as his Word, for we all need a bridle like a horse.

(5) The one basic commandment, which we find at Deut. 6:5 is *pure*, that is, unalloyed by containing impurities in the gold: "Thou shalt love the Lord thy God . . ." Jesus confirmed this for us at Mark 12:29–30. *Enlightening the eyes* is another way of saying *reviving the soul*. Just give the lost wanderer even a little food and drink and the light will come back into his eyes. Such cannot be said about any of man's ethical systems in a secular society. None of them is *pure*, because none of them depends upon the fear of God. This is not understood by those educationalists who wish to put "ethics" into the school curriculum in place of "religious studies".

(6) As we have noted before, the OT has no word for "religion". Our poet's definition of true religion is this, then: it is living before God in a proper sense of *awe*, *reverence* and *obedience*—and now he claims that that attitude belongs actually in eternity. Such honest *fear* is *clean*; that is to say, it is completely uncontaminated by our dirty human minds.

(7) The *ordinances*, of which there are many in the *Torah*, and these include the Ten Commandments, are the most desirable things in life—not the pursuit of wisdom, not heaping up riches, not owning the expensive gewgaws that money can buy. They do three things for him or her who is God's servant. (a) They *warn* us of the dangers of the way, or rather, as the word means, they *lighten it up* for us. (b) A servant expects payment. Just *doing* God's revealed will, however, is all the payment we need. As God had said so long ago to Abraham: "*I*

am your exceeding great reward." (c) Being God's servant is your and my *personal response* to both types of revelation described in this double psalm, i.e. response to God's Order in Creation, and to his Order in Revelation.

THE BARRIER TO FAITH

Psalm 19:7–14 *(cont'd)*

The plain man, who has thought deeply about the mysteries of God's universe, that is to say, about the whole issue raised in Poem I, can say to himself—Yes, but what about earthquakes, and diseases, and death itself? How do these proclaim God's handiwork? Is his creation then not yet complete? And where do I fit into it all?

It is when we come, by grace, to ruminate on what Poem II deals with that we make the one discovery necessary to help us understand the Word of God. Till now our worshipper has not noticed that, as a sinner, he has erected a barrier between himself and the Word, so that he does not even possess the ears necessary to hear. It is the Word of Redemption, therefore, which alone can help him to faith. He himself cannot *discern his own errors*, because his *faults* are *hidden* even from his own eyes. As Robert Burns the poet puts it:

O wad some Pow'r the giftie gie us
To see oursels as others see us!

—not to speak of how God sees us!

The two classifications of sin mentioned here come from the Law of Moses. (a) *Hidden faults* are those "sins of inadvertence" that could be dealt with by the sacrificial system outlined in Leviticus. (b) But *presumptuous sins*, what are called in Hebrew *sins with a high hand*, could not be. You can see the aggressor with his knife in the air ready to strike! And you can see the lustful voluptuary pursuing his prey in order to rape her or to "uncover the nakedness" (as Leviticus puts it) of his own little daughter! Murder and adultery were the two particular sins that excluded a person from obtaining forgiveness through sacrifice—the very two sins that David committed, as Nathan his court chaplain had to point out to him. But here both kinds of sin are covered by the mercy and grace of God!

Since it is our sin that prevents us from hearing both the music of the spheres and the *honey*-sweet words of God's commandments, it is only God himself who can help us out of our impasse. He does so by taking us as we are, and forgiving our sin. Only *then*, says the psalmist, *shall I be blameless* and, by implication, able to hear the Word of life.

A great preacher came to the end of his days. When asked, supposing he could have his time over again, would he preach any differently from what he had done, he replied: "I would keep coming back much more often to the forgiveness of sins."

Chorus. The words at verse 14 are often made part of our liturgy today, for they are the response of each individual *me* and *my heart* to the profound revelation made in this double psalm. For surely, all speculation about the nature and revelation of God's love ends here! C.S. Lewis, the great critic of English poetry and style, once wrote: "This is the greatest poem in the Psalter and one of the greatest lyrics in the world."

THE LORD BE WITH YOU

Psalm 20:1–9

To the choirmaster. A Psalm of David.

1 The Lord answer you in the day of trouble!
　　The name of the God of Jacob protect you!
2 May he send you help from the sanctuary,
　　and give you support from Zion!
3 May he remember all your offerings,
　　and regard with favour your burnt sacrifices!　　*Selah*

4 May he grant you your heart's desire,
　　and fulfil all your plans!
5 May we shout for joy over your victory,
　　and in the name of our God set up our banners!
　May the Lord fulfil all your petitions!

6 Now I know that the Lord will help his anointed;
   he will answer him from his holy heaven
   with mighty victories by his right hand.
7 Some boast of chariots, and some of horses;
   but we boast of the name of the Lord our God.
8 They will collapse and fall;
   but we shall rise and stand upright.

9 Give victory to the king, O Lord;
   answer us when we call.

Originally this psalm may have been a prayer written *for* David, to be used on the occasion of his going off to war. Then, in later years, and in face of the congregation standing in the temple courtyard looking eagerly toward whatever king was seated on the throne, the high priest (though it was only late on that that particular title came into use), acting as the mouthpiece of all Israel, would proclaim this prayer. He spoke it, of course, to God, but addressed it to the king. Note that verses 1–5 are a prayer, not a song. But this psalm has fitted many another situation. It has been used in modern times as a farewell to missionaries setting forth to "fight the battle of the Lord"; it has even been used as a blessing said over simple soldier lads, members of the local congregation, as they set off to defend their loved ones. Its theme is: "May God not keep silent when you need him most."

The Prayer. The *day* of trouble means more than any twenty-four-hour period. Of course *day* in the OT may mean just that. But in Israel's worship the word refers to that moment in human experience when the eternal world breaks in upon our human experience of time. We can all look back upon such *days*, such experiences, most of which are too sacred to discuss, or even to describe to other people. But there can also come a "moment" when the powers of evil seem to have been let loose in a person's heart. If such a thing does happen to us, then there is only one defence against it, and that is the power which comes from the *name* of the God of Jacob.

Since there was a *Selah* at the end of verse 3, that is, a pause following upon a blast of loud music, it may be that at this point in the proceedings the priest offered up a *burnt offering* on behalf of the young man seated before him on the throne. Then there would follow the recitation of the prayer we find at verse 4. Human beings can make stupid plans, but, says our poet, God can overrule even these for good.

The God of Jacob is Israel's Redeemer God. All down the centuries he has rescued Israel from each and all of her foes. So he can be relied on now at this juncture to do the same as he has always done. The *name* in olden days was an exact picture of the nature of its owner. So the *name* of Yahweh, as we have seen before, means something important now: "I will be with you" (Exod. 3:12,14). See also comments at Ps. 16:7.

The king's defence and care will come, not from the sky, but from the Word of Redemption uttered in the sanctuary. We saw how this is so in the previous psalm, which speaks both of the God of Nature and the God of Redemption. Not only so, but *we*, the congregation, now want to support the king, so that he does not feel he is left to go to war in his own strength. *We* want to set up our banners in the *name* of our God, the God of redemptive love. And so we see a kind of early Israelite "Salvation Army" (!) giving prayerful support to the one who has gone forth to battle on behalf of the congregation. It is surely a good thing to take pleasure in another's joy.

Probably there was a pause made at the end of verse 5. It could be that this young man or woman—or king   met next with the "minister", the cultic prophet, whom we have met before. In this way his hope and faith were renewed. Consequently he now returns to the sanctuary and proclaims in a loud voice: "*Now* (after my prayerful meeting with the minister) I *know* that the Lord will help his anointed." Kings were anointed, priests were anointed, individuals chosen for special duties were anointed. This anointed king has now regained his certainty of faith. *I know*, he says, that God will not let me down. *Some boast of chariots*—of tanks and nuclear weapons, we might add. But the *name* of *Yahweh* our God is stronger by far. This, let us note, is the only kind of boasting allowed to a believer, says Paul (Eph. 2:8–9). This is because it is just at that moment when things seem to be at their very worst that *in the name of the Lord our God we shall rise and stand upright.* What a great statement of faith! God's *right* hand was the one that acted for him. That is why, using this theological picture, the NT can speak of Christ being seated at the right hand of God; for Christ is now the executor of God's saving love and redemptive judgment.

The congregation has listened with joy to their young king's statement of faith. So at verse 9, to end the proceedings, they join in a shouted prayer to God for both him and for themselves. The original Hebrew can be seen in the RSV *ftn*. It runs, *O Lord, let the king answer us when we call.* But if we take the two lines as we have them, what we find emerging is the inspiration of the first verse of the British National Anthem.

THE KING'S KING

Psalm 21:1–13

To the choirmaster. A Psalm of David.

1 In thy strength the king rejoices, O Lord;
     and in thy help how greatly he exults!
2 Thou hast given him his heart's desire,
     and hast not withheld the request of his lips.   *Selah*
3 For thou dost meet him with goodly blessings;
     thou dost set a crown of fine gold upon his head.
4 He asked life of thee; thou gavest it to him,
     length of days for ever and ever.
5 His glory is great through thy help;
     splendour and majesty thou dost bestow upon him.
6 Yea, thou dost make him most blessed for ever;
     thou dost make him glad with the joy of thy presence.
7 For the king trusts in the Lord;
     and through the steadfast love of the Most High he shall not be moved.

8 Your hand will find out all your enemies;
     your right hand will find out those who hate you.
9 You will make them as a blazing oven when you appear.
   The Lord will swallow them up in his wrath;
     and fire will consume them.

10 You will destroy their offspring from the earth,
      and their children from among the sons of men.
11 If they plan evil against you,
      if they devise mischief, they will not succeed.
12 For you will put them to flight;
      you will aim at their faces with your bows.

13 Be exalted, O Lord, in thy strength!
      We will sing and praise thy power.

Throughout the last half-century much scholarly research has been carried out on the Psalms, especially in the light of the large body of information we have gained through archaeological discovery ("digs") and through the science of palaeography (the deciphering and interpretation of ancient writings, whether on stone, parchment or papyrus). This information has helped us to understand better the life, religion and practices of the peoples who were Israel's neighbours. One result is that, while it cannot be proved beyond question, it would appear that some of our psalms were composed to be sung at a royal coronation, some even for the occasion when the king was *re*-crowned on the anniversary of his coronation. We shall apply this theory now to Psalm 21.

Let us note the following issues arising from the psalm:

(1) The king himself is not worshipped, as he was, say, in Egypt.

(2) The king rejoices in the strength of the *Lord*, not in his own strength.

(3) God has been gracious to the king throughout the past year, and has answered his prayers. This is what Solomon discovered (see 1 Kings 3:11ff.).

(4) God had responded to his deepest needs, had fulfilled his innermost longings, and had brought good even out of his sin-stained behaviour in the past.

(5) God had *gone ahead* of him with *goodly blessings*. This is the word *meet* (verse 3). The king, as a human being, is travelling down the road of life in the one direction we must all go, from birth to death. But now God has reached down out of

eternity and has *met* him, coming from the other direction, so to speak. This is an instance of the picture-language that we should still try to use, even in these sophisticated days. Jesus used it when he employed parables. Surely the idea of "prevenient grace" comes home to us far better in this way than if we use theological jargon. Martin Luther, the great Reformer, is said to have declared that when God speaks to humanity he uses baby-talk. He does so, he added, for the simple reason that he is love.

(6) The king does not crown himself. Every year he is reminded that, in the words of Andrew Melville, the Scottish Reformer, to King James, he is just "God's silly vassal". It is the Lord who is King, not he. On the other hand, the king is head of all Israel. He sums up all the people in himself. In this way, then, ordinary people learned that the Lord God is also King of Israel, and even more so! How thrilling then the ceremony must have been for each successive "son of David" to go through. Though knowing himself to be a helpless sinner (and 2 Kings is not shy of describing the sins of the line of David!) yet he is once more being allowed to say—imagine it!—"*I* am that king to whom God speaks in this wonderful way." Whereupon all Israel is invited to recall that they too are called to be a "kingdom of priests and a holy nation" (Exod. 19:6) under this king and so as subjects of the King of kings.

(7) He asked for life, as we all do, and got love as well! He asked for human life and received immortal life (see 2 Sam. 7:15)!

(8) God had now irradiated his life with something of his own glory, just as he had done before to Moses (Exod. 34:29,35). Actually the splendour of the royal buildings and of the temple was a gift from God in all *his* splendour.

(9) But above all, his great *reward* was God's personal *presence* in his life (verse 6). There are those today who suppose that one has to go out and search for faith—even go off to India and sit at the feet of a guru in order to find the salvation of one's soul. Our psalmist would have been puzzled at such unbelief. God, he knew, had chosen and called this king, and had promised to *make him most blessed for ever*. So all that the king

need do was simply accept that miracle in joy: "For the king trusts in the Lord."

(10) Following from this, and from the fact that the king was the king and head of Israel, all Israel was thus being reminded that they too had been chosen, and that God was making them most blessed for ever; for they too "trusted in the Lord". Consequently, *in* God's *hesed* (not *through* it, as the RSV has it) both the king and Israel will remain totally safe for ever. But "God" here is not only "the Lord", the name of the God of the Covenant. He is now called *the Most High*, that name by which Abraham had come to know him of old (Gen. 14:19). This means that since God had remained faithful to Israel throughout the previous thousand years, he could be relied on to remain faithful to his people to all eternity.

Verses 8–12 now record for us what the priestly spokesman said to the king in his address on this solemn occasion. We shall note only two points, however. (a) We should not be alarmed at the poetic licence and exaggerated way of speaking which was customary in the period. More important (b) is that God's will will be done only when the king acts. For only then can God's justice be executed. The king will have become a kind of right hand of God. This, of course, is out of the question in the case of a sinner. And so, once again, we are made to see a "messianic hope" sounding forth on this happy occasion, the hope that some day a true and sinless king will come who will truly be the right hand of God. In fact, verse 10 is not a description of a literal event at all; for it hints of the fall of all the wicked in the "end times".

So the congregation responds (verse 13) with a song of praise– not about the king, let us note, but about the strength and power of the God who is the king's King.

THE LONELY DEER FINDS REST

Psalm 22:1–8

To the choirmaster: according to the Hind of the Dawn.
A Psalm of David.

1 My God, my God, why hast.thou forsaken me?
   Why art thou so far from helping me, from the words of my
      groaning?
2 O my God, I cry by day, but thou dost not answer;
   and by night, but find no rest.

3 Yet thou art holy,
   enthroned on the praises of Israel.
4 In thee our fathers trusted;
   they trusted, and thou didst deliver them.
5 To thee they cried, and were saved;
   in thee they trusted, and were not disappointed.

6 But I am a worm, and no man;
   scorned by men, and despised by the people.
7 All who see me mock at me,
   they make mouths at me, they wag their heads;
8 "He committed his cause to the Lord; let him deliver him,
   let him rescue him, for he delights in him!"

The heading we have suggests singing this psalm to the tune
(unknown to us, of course) called *The Hind of the Dawn.* Why
the dawn? In old Arab poems this particular *hind* describes a
lonely deer, cut off from the rest of its herd. Dawn finds it
standing on a crag, gazing into the distance in the hope of
discovering its friends at last. It is for us to say, then, whether
the idea behind that tune is a good one!

A cry for help, verses 1–2. Does God really forsake us? If we
find ourselves when dawn breaks like a lonely deer, does it
mean that God is not present with us any more? Our poet may
experience "God-forsakenness", as we all do at times, but he
does *not* say in consequence, with the fool (Ps. 14:1) "There is
no God." On the contrary he exclaims "*My* God, *my* God!" It is
true that, in his wisdom and compassion God may not answer

my prayer as I expect him to; but I know him too well as *my* God, the psalmist is saying, the God who has covenanted with me, to doubt his faithfulness and loyalty to me.

Of course we remember that Jesus uttered these words on the Cross (Mark 15:34). That occasion was the supreme moment when the faithfulness of the God of the OT was finally put to the test. Moreover, it was at that moment that Jesus found that God had, in fact, actually answered his prayer. He did not discover this to be so in Gethsemane. But now the answer came in the reality that God was *there*, with Jesus, in all the horror of the Cross, sharing his suffering and tragedy as only a Father can do with a Son. The awareness of this supreme reality therefore reached deeper than Jesus' cry of loneliness, so that, before he died, he quietly committed his spirit into the hands of his Father.

It is the psalm as it was written in OT times, even as it has come down to us intact, that we are to study now, however, and not the life and work of Christ. Yet, even as we do so, we should be aware that in all probability Jesus repeated not just the first line of the psalm but the whole of it in his agony. It is therefore worth keeping in mind, as we read on, that he found God speaking to him in still other sections of this psalm, even though it was penned so many centuries before his day. Jesus was a Jew. As such, he might have been herded into the gas chambers of Auschwitz if he had lived in our century. Such is the hell that men can create for each other which is utterly other than the will of God for human life. And so this generation, all over again, asks the same old question: How could God have been present there in that *man*-made hell of Auschwitz?

True prayer, verses 3–5. Here we see what prayer ought to be, particularly when we are struck down with any kind of depression. It is telling God that he alone is holy, righteous, good, loving, not "me"; that he alone is loyal, not me. It is declaring to God that he never once let down the poet's ancestors as they marched through the centuries from Egypt on till the day of David. And so it is to believe that God must inevitably be present in any of the hells that human beings can create on the earth; and just because he is present in them, he must save, not from *outside* of all the pain and sorrow of life, but from *inside*—for he too is there, present, inside, all the time.

This kind of a God is enthroned, held up high for all the world to see, not by philosophical speculation, not by scientific investigation, but by the grateful praises of the people who—not understanding intellectually what pain and evil are all about—yet shout his praise in love and gratitude. Their ancestors, Abraham, Isaac, Jacob, Moses, Joshua and David had *trusted, and were not disappointed.* Is that not enough for faith *now*?, he declares.

I am a worm, verses 6–8. These three verses plumb the depths of human awareness of the reality of sin and suffering. Isa. 41:8–13 is one of the so-called "servant" poems that describe Israel as God's chosen servant. It points out that God had fulfilled his promise to Abraham by choosing Israel, by calling them from far-away Babylon, that is, *from the ends of the earth, saying to you, "You are my servant, I have chosen you and not cast you off. Fear not, for I am with you"* right there in the heart-rending degradation of life in exile, that is to say, back again now in that Babylon where it all began in Abraham's day. But the poem goes on (verse 14): *"Fear not, you worm Jacob, you men* [or perhaps the word is "louse"] *of Israel . . . your Redeemer is the Holy One of Israel."*

That passage is echoed here. It contrasts vividly (a) the mere "nothingness" of man, and (b) the greatness of the compassion and love of God extended to mankind, not from "out there", but from *inside* all the pain and suffering that the servant had to go through. Incidentally, such a passage enlightens for us the meaning of the baptism of Jesus. He asked John to baptize him, not for the sake of the forgiveness of sins, but that he might reveal sacramentally his total identification with a people that was, in God's sight, a mere worm or louse—but yet, paradoxically, a people whom God had called, through suffering, to be his servant.

"Roll your cause on the Lord", the poet's neighbours had called out sarcastically. "Here is the proof that God is not what he has been puffed up to be. You think he delights in you? But he has done nothing at all to rescue you from your plight!"

YOU TOOK ME FROM THE WOMB

Psalm 22:9–21

9 Yet thou art he who took me from the womb;
  thou didst keep me safe upon my mother's breasts.
10 Upon thee was I cast from my birth,
  and since my mother bore me thou has been my God.
11 Be not far from me,
  for trouble is near
  and there is none to help.

12 Many bulls encompass me,
  strong bulls of Bashan surround me;
13 they open wide their mouths at me,
  like a ravening and roaring lion.

14 I am poured out like water,
  and all my bones are out of joint;
  my heart is like wax,
  it is melted within my breast;
15 my strength is dried up like a potsherd,
  and my tongue cleaves to my jaws;
  thou dost lay me in the dust of death.

16 Yea, dogs are round about me;
  a company of evildoers encircle me;
  they have pierced my hands and feet—
17 I can count all my bones—
  they stare and gloat over me;
18 they divide my garments among them,
  and for my raiment they cast lots.

19 But thou, O Lord, be not far off!
  O thou my help, hasten to my aid!
20 Deliver my soul from the sword,
  my life from the power of the dog!
21 Save me from the mouth of the lion,
  my afflicted soul from the horns of the wild oxen!

The poet now speaks on behalf of all Israel, the servant people of God. He declares that he had actually been chosen before he was conceived in the womb, as young Jeremiah came to discover later on about himself (Jer. 1:5). Paul throws the divine election even further back in time. Since Christ was there before the foundation of the world, he writes at Eph. 1:4–5, God chose us, *in* him, actually before the foundation of the world. Our poet never needed "to get converted" in later life. Even as a child he had quite naturally accepted the fact that God had been looking after him from his mother's knee; and now he lived in confidence and faith in that awareness. So meaningful was God's election of him, despite the fact that he was a worm, that he *knew* that, even when God did not seem to be present with him ("hold aloof" is the Hebrew), that was no cause for anxiety. For God cannot be untrue to the loyalty of his nature.

Now follow three word-pictures.

(1) *Bulls and lions.* An angry bull is a terrible adversary; he can charge with the momentum of a hippopotamus. A Bashan bull (like a Jersey or an Aberdeen Angus) was the choicest and heaviest breed of the day.

(2) *Sickness and death.* It is no mere chance that the words *I am poured out* should be the basis of much theological debate. A similar usage at Isa. 53:12, employing another verb, however, describes how the servant *pours himself out* to death. This last verb would more accurately mean "emptied himself out". Consequently it is the idea that Paul uses, in Greek translation, when he speaks of the action of the cosmic Christ (Phil. 2:7). Here in our psalm, however, God takes up, so to speak, the unwilling and unsought for suffering of Israel, and turns it into the creative suffering of the chosen servant.

(3) *Dogs* were what the Greeks called barbarians—"lesser breeds without the Law", to quote the poet Kipling. Can't you see, for example, the rich inhabitants of Gaza, who had piled up their great wealth from a slave trade that had world-wide ramifications, sneering at the way of life of little "uncultured" Israel? After a raid into the hills of Judah they had taken off the cream of a village's youth to Philistia, girls as well as boys, where the young folk must now stand, chained together, naked, in the Gaza market and be gloated over lasciviously by fat eastern merchants and slave traders. Truth is truth in all ages of

man. This devastating picture was still true for the events surrounding the crucifixion of Jesus (John 19:24). There it is not the Hebrew of our psalm that is quoted, but the Greek translation of the OT made about 250 B.C. That therefore explains why the words in the Fourth Gospel are rather different from the original before us here.

So at verse 19 we return to the original theme, one that torments the human soul in all ages, whether in ancient Judah, or at the Via Dolorosa, or in the hellishness of Auschwitz, or again in the suffering to death by cancer of a dear one today. Where is God in all this? "Deliver my *life* from the power of the dog", is really "my only one", meaning "this one-and-only life of mine" (see the RSV *ftn.*).

There is a devastating sentence in Matthew's Gospel, 26:56: "Then all the disciples forsook him and fled." What Jesus had now to go through he then suffered *alone*. And so the poignancy of his cry as he quotes verse 1 of our psalm is all the more terrible.

THE ANSWER OF THE SAVIOUR GOD

Psalm 22:22-31

22 I will tell of thy name to my brethren;
    in the midst of the congregation I will praise thee:
23 You who fear the Lord, praise him!
    all you sons of Jacob, glorify him,
    and stand in awe of him, all you sons of Israel!

24 For he has not despised or abhorred
    the affliction of the afflicted;
    and he has not hid his face from him,
    but has heard, when he cried to him.

25 From thee comes my praise in the great congregation;
    my vows I will pay before those who fear him.
26 The afflicted shall eat and be satisfied;
    those who seek him shall praise the Lord!
    May your hearts live for ever!

27 All the ends of the earth shall remember
        and turn to the Lord;
    and all the families of the nations
        shall worship before him.
28 For dominion belongs to the Lord,
        and he rules over the nations.

29 Yea, to him shall all the proud of the earth bow down;
        before him shall bow all who go down to the dust,
        and he who cannot keep himself alive.
30 Posterity shall serve him;
        men shall tell of the Lord to the coming generation,
31 and proclaim his deliverance to a people yet unborn,
        that he has wrought it.

What happened between verses 21 and 22 we are not told. But now our poet comes back to announce in supreme faith and confidence the goodness of God. Jesus told even a lunatic that such was his duty under God (Mark 5:19). In fact it is to be the duty of all believers in all ages. They are not meant to hold a theological argument about the *nature* of God. They are meant to praise him for what he has *done. For his very name* is Saviour (Isa. 43:11 and see Matt. 1:21). It is his saving activities that are the revelation of his nature.

The last half-line of verse 21 had read: "From the horns of the wild cattle—*thou hast answered me.*" So something seems to have happened to him in the nick of time. Then we might enclose the next three verses in one set of inverted commas, for they are all one hymn of praise. God has acted; God has saved him; this God is he whose nature it is to save. He saved David, and our poet, and Jeremiah, *in Christ*, as Paul teaches, long *before* A.D. 33, just as he saves today, long *after* that central date in the world's history. Or, to put it in another way, with Paul again, God has saved me "from the foundation of the world". This reality is not found through General Revelation (see Psalm 19), echoed as it is in all the religions of humanity, but only through the Special Revelation the Bible gives us. God's love is personal. God does not despise one so small and unimportant as me, believes our poet, a mere peasant come up to Jerusalem for the great festival.

Another worshipper now takes up the recitation (verses 25–26). He addresses God: "Here I am praising You in the great congregation," that is, at one of the three great annual festivals when everyone who could attend, did so. "But even praise itself is a gift from You; it is Your grace that has given me even the desire to praise You, and You are the source of the vows I am now prepared to pay up before all these worshippers here." Being a simple person himself the speaker now speaks thus for his friends: "Poor folk will now receive plenty to eat. Those who seek God won't have to ask 'Why have You forsaken me?' For he is there waiting to be praised." The last line of his speech may mean: "Never lose heart," that is, knowing and receiving the grace of God. But it may also mean: "The poor shall eat and be satisfied, and find that their hearts belong to eternity." What an expression! And what a fool the modern sceptic is who says that human beings invented the Bible and even invented God!

How like Jesus the God of the OT is (see Isa. 55:1)! For he is always concerned that ordinary folk should have enough to eat. The love of God shown here and throughout this whole psalm is aimed not only at sinners, but also at sufferers, at the hungry, and at those who may find themselves going down into the depths of the meaninglessness of the pit of despair.

Still another voice now (verse 27) invited those present to remember that Yahweh is in fact Lord of all the earth, so that they should tell people everywhere to remember that fact. The king from his throne must then have humbly joined in declaring this to be so! So the invitation goes out into all the highways and byways of human life. Nor should we forget that the nations at the end of the earth were all Gentiles, and not the chosen people of God!

At verse 29 a final voice takes up the praise: "Yes, even the affluent shall bow down before him" (the word is really *fat ones*!). This will be a miracle indeed (just think of that fat slave-owner in Gaza!) as Jesus himself tells us at Mark 10:23–27.

Scholars have had to agree that there are at least two interpretations of the next couplet. (a) Even all those who already sleep in the dust of death (that is, in the underworld, according to the thought of the day) will bow the knee to him, though they have not been able to *give themselves life.* (b) All those who do not believe except in their own powers, who are too proud to bend before God, even these shall be saved. Whichever way we take it, we have here an expression of the universalism believed in by the Second Isaiah, who, living amongst the poor, unhappy, superstitious masses of Gentile humanity, when in exile in Babylon, could exclaim:

> Turn to me and be saved, all the ends of the earth!
>> For I am God, and there is no other.
> By myself I have sworn,
>> from my mouth has gone forth in righteousness
>> a word that shall not return:
> "To me every knee shall bow, every tongue shall swear."
>
> (Isa. 45:22–23)

The Bible is concerned with the ongoing movement of God's purpose throughout history. All people are linked in the stream of life. So each generation must tell their children about what God has done in the past. The command is to *tell.* One tells a *story.* The Bible is the story of what God has done as he pursues his loving purpose of salvation, not only of all people, but of heaven and earth as well.

"Proclaim his *deliverance.*" This is the feminine form of the word *righteousness* we have noted before. This form, we have seen, is used for the effect in our human lives once God has *put us right* with himself, put us in a right relationship with himself, by bringing us back home to himself. When that happens we are delivered from our egotism and bondage to sin, and are not only set free to love our neighbour as ourself, we are also actually given the power by God to do so in practice.

A FEAST OF GRACE

Psalm 23:1–6

A Psalm of David.

1 The Lord is my shepherd, I shall not want;
2   he makes me lie down in green pastures.

He leads me beside still waters;
3   he restores my soul.
He leads me in paths of righteousness
       for his name's sake.

4   Even though I walk through the valley of the shadow of death,
       I fear no evil;
     for thou art with me;
       thy rod and thy staff,
       they comfort me.

5   Thou preparest a table before me
       in the presence of my enemies;
     thou anointest my head with oil,
       my cup overflows.
6   Surely goodness and mercy shall follow me
       all the days of my life;
     and I shall dwell in the house of the Lord for ever.

The previous psalm ended by speaking of the joy of salvation, that is, of discovering what it means to have been put into a right relationship with God, brought back home into fellowship with him in the Covenant. This psalm, which almost surely stems from David himself, describes what it feels like thus to be back at home with God. It is expressed in language that really spoke home to the country folk of his day. David had been a shepherd. Now he was the shepherd of his people. In what way must he now care for them? This problem opened up for him a new awareness of what God, the true Shepherd, is himself like in his relationship with his people.

Psalm 23 is the world's favourite psalm. It is the favourite of Jew, Eastern Orthodox, Western Protestant, and wistful agnostic alike. It comes alive when used at a wedding, even more so when said or sung at a funeral. And it expresses more vividly than any other portion of Scripture the individual's private experience of God's grace.

The "sheep" imagery is probably more universal than any other that could be selected—though of course it has to be explained to an Eskimo or a Pacific Islander. But the human imagination does not need any help in order to "feel" the loveliness and beauty of the allusions to green pastures, still waters, and the like.

The *valley of the shadow of death*, however, is what faces all people of every race and clime. A Greek village woman of olden time once took her baby to a wise man, asking him if he could foretell the child's future. "There is only one thing that I can tell you for sure about your baby," he replied, "and that is, he is going to die." The tremendous lesson of this psalm, then, is that God is love, God is loyal, God will never let us go. It unfolds this loyal-love of God for us in three stages.

(1) While we live our life here on earth, so long as we live it "with" him, and allow him to live it "with" us, then we experience the deep joy, satisfaction and security that the sheep knows in the presence of its good shepherd.

(2) The second stage is this, though. Life is not all a bed of roses. We can be deeply and gratefully aware of God's continuing presence with us in days when all goes well. It is just because of that, however, David declares, that we can be sure of him when all does *not* go well, even when the light fades and we find ourselves in darkness. The phrase he uses is literally "Valley of Deep Darkness". So the idea is that God's comfort and strength are "with" us in all kinds of darkness, in times of depression, serious illness, rejection by one's friends, horror at discovering the disloyalty of one's own heart, and so on, as well as the experience of death itself. David does not argue that this is so. He *tells* us that it *is* so! Hamlet spoke of "the undiscovered country from whose bourn no traveller returns", as he mused upon the coming reality of his own death. But God's loving presence, declares David, will be as real and true then as it is now when all goes well. We are to remember that in biblical thinking, although God *is* light, yet he dwells in the darkness into which we must go in our turn.

How different David is from Hamlet! He tells us that God is the God of hospitality, the Father who sets before the returned prodigal a special fatted calf. Why does David think of himself in this light? Because of the expression, "He restores my soul", which is really "He gives me back my life". God longs to be

hospitable, even to David's enemies, if only they would also
come home and share in the feast. In the NT God's hospitality
in eternity is pictured as our being invited to sit down at the
Supper Table of the Lamb (Rev. 19:9).

But we are to remember that David was king over God's
"royal kingdom", one in which all God's subjects share in his
royal rule. So the *me* in the phrase "*Thou anointest my head
with oil*" refers to each and all of the simple subjects of the
Kingdom of God. Consequently, the sheer excitement we feel at
being anointed to serve God is more than we can absorb, take
in, realize; such is God's unspeakable grace that *my cup overflows*.

(3) So we come to stage 3. Since God's covenant love has been
the very basis of my life at stage 1, that is, when all went well;
and since, when I reached stage 2, I found that God's grace was
still with me in the Valley of the Shadow; then *surely*, that is, "*I
know*" that God's being "good for me" (as the Hebrew means)
and God's *hesed*, his unswerving loyal-love, will pursue me all
the days of my life. As the poet, Francis Thompson, calls him,
God is the Hound of Heaven. Indeed, he will never let me go.
Therefore *I know* that I shall dwell in the house of the Lord for
ever. David knew what it meant to be present continually in the
sanctuary in Jerusalem (the temple had not yet been built), just
as another psalmist longed to be (Ps. 63). Because of this he here
refers to the "heavenly sanctuary", the "place" of the presence
of God in eternity, even as Jesus spoke of God's "many man-
sions".

There is the oft-told story, coming from last century, of the two
ministers who went on holiday together tramping in the Welsh
hills. High on the moors they met a shepherd lad and stopped to
chat with him. They found this boy had never been to school
and that he knew nothing at all of the Christian faith. The two
ministers finally read to him the 23rd Psalm, and to help him
find a personal faith they got him to repeat the words, "The
Lord is *my* shepherd". Next year they were back in the same
hills. This time they called at a cottage to ask for a drink of milk.

The lady noticed them looking at a photograph of a lad on the mantlepiece. "Yes," she said, "that was my son. He died last winter in a snowstorm while tending his sheep. But there was a curious thing about him, his right hand was clutching the fourth finger of his left hand." "Well now," one of the ministers replied, "we met your boy last year. In fact, since he was a shepherd boy, we taught him to repeat the first line of the 23rd Psalm, and we told him whenever he said it to himself, to pause at the fourth word, and think 'This psalm was meant for me'."

THE KING OF GLORY

Psalm 24:1-10

A Psalm of David.

1 The earth is the Lord's and the fullness thereof,
   the world and those who dwell therein;
2 for he has founded it upon the seas,
   and established it upon the rivers.

3 Who shall ascend the hill of the Lord?
   And who shall stand in his holy place?
4 He who has clean hands and a pure heart,
   who does not lift up his soul to what is false,
   and does not swear deceitfully.
5 He will receive blessing from the Lord,
   and vindication from the God of his salvation.
6 Such is the generation of those who seek him,
   who seek the face of the God of Jacob.   *Selah*

7 Lift up your heads, O gates!
   and be lifted up, O ancient doors!
   that the King of glory may come in.
8 Who is the King of glory?
   The Lord, strong and mighty,
   the Lord, mighty in battle!
9 Lift up your heads, O gates!
   and be lifted up, O ancient doors!
   that the King of glory may come in.
10 Who is this King of glory?
   The Lord of hosts,
   he is the King of glory!   *Selah*

This 3,000-year-old psalm has taught people all down the centuries the absolute priority in their lives of the worship of God. It is recited by Jews first thing on the first day of each week. It is used by Christians world-wide on Ascension Day, and verses 7-10 are sung before Holy Communion in many Reformed Churches.

It began, in all probability, as a song to be used when a great procession of priests and people carried the Ark of the Covenant into the sanctuary in an annual celebration. David had been first to do so, even before there was any temple there (2 Sam. 6:12-15). The Ark, traditionally built by Bezalel for Moses in the wilderness of Sinai (Exod. 37:1-9), signified God's presence in the midst of his people. The Philistines had captured it, so it had seemed at the time that the Lord was no longer with them (1 Sam. 4:11; 5:1). Then again, it was the Ark of the *Covenant*, the symbol of God's special relationship in love and loyalty, first, to all Israel, and then later, to David and to his line of kings (Ps. 132:8). Because of this, in deep gratitude to God, it seems that this ceremony was held year after year in such a manner that everyone could take part, from king to commoner, in a renewal of loyalty to God.

Moreover, what now takes place is an act of worship of the Creator of all things, of whom we read in Gen. 1, not just of the local god whom the Jebusites used to worship before David captured the city and made it "the City of David". There that city now sat, solid, on its rock, before all ages, right on top of the chaotic waters that boil and bubble away under the earth (Exod. 20:4). These waters reminded Israel of the chaos mentioned in Gen. 1:2, out of which God had originally created life and order. Who then dare ascend the hill of such a Holy City to worship the kind of God who ruled the world from there?

It may be that one particular priest was delegated to proclaim verses 1-2 to the great crowd assembled outside the walls of the city. Thereupon another priest took up the cry. He asks the question with a loud voice: "Who is worthy to come in and worship in the holy place?" Then still another makes answer on behalf of all present.

We note that the qualifications are not: (a) "Have you kept the Law?", or (b) "Have you performed the required sacrifices?" The qualifications have to do with a person's *will*. The individual must have (a) clean hands, which mark outwardly the cleanness of the heart within, and (b) carefully avoided any overt evil ways. That is sufficient for God to accept and to bless. And so the third speaker categorically declares that all such people will be welcome to join in the procession and to come right into the holy place.

Of course the two qualifications announced are not a description of a believing person. All they point to is that the intending worshipper should *want* to come in, sinner as he undoubtedly remained. But right back a thousand years earlier that is all that this God of Jacob had asked of Jacob, not perfection of life, but just sincerity of purpose. That is sufficient for God to grant a person his blessing. A blessing, people believed, was something almost physical, when something in the way of power passed from one to another, as when Jesus touched the woman with the issue of blood. This power conferred the gift of *tsedaqah* (*not* to be translated as *vindication* as the RSV does). It is this feminine word we have met before and which is usually rendered by *righteousness*. So verse 5 would run: "The God who, in his love, has put him (the one blessed) right (using the masculine word) has now empowered him to put others right (the feminine word) by means of his love" (see the Introduction). How deep and moving those OT words are, and how important it is that we should study them! Without doing so we would find it difficult to discover what St. Paul is talking about in his NT Letters. No wonder a *Selah* sounds forth at this point.

The procession moves forward (verse 7). They reach the gates in the city wall and it may be that now we hear two choirs singing antiphonally.

Choir 1 addresses the gates, telling them to open up to let the King of glory come in. Yet the Great King is represented only by that little six-foot box which was known as the Ark of the Covenant. But that little Ark was sufficient for God's purposes. For the whole gracious plan of the King of glory was represented in what the Box stood for, just as, in later years, that same gracious purpose was made known in full to the whole world in the person of only one man.

Choir 2 replies at verse 8a in one line. They ask: "Who is the King of glory?"

Choir 1 rejoins at verse 8b with a mighty shout: "He is the Almighty, the God who is for ever at war with the powers of evil." This we know to be the emphasis, for the Ten Commandments incised on their stone tablets were quietly resting in that little box, the Ark.

Choir 1 now loudly commands (verse 9) the gates to open and to let the King of glory in.

Choir 2, however, (verse 10a) puts the same question again. The worshipper has to learn that faith in God does not come easily and automatically. He still needs assurance and help. And help comes (verse 10b). Probably the whole concourse of priests and people now joyously shout these last two lines in one voice, "The Lord of hosts" (meaning the armies both of Israel and of the heavenly beings) *"that* God is the King of glory!"

It would be a good experience in our understanding of the grace of God if we were to reportray these ancient words outside the closed doors of our own local church. In doing so, moreover, we would be reminding ourselves that this psalm also points forward to the time when the gates of the heavenly Jerusalem, to use the picture language of the book of Revelation, will be thrown open in eternity and the whole world of men, women and children alike will be invited to enter in. And such a presentation would bring to our consciousness the amazing fact that the King of glory did not enter in from the sky above, but from below in the shoes of that jostling crowd as they excitedly pushed their way into the courts of the temple behind the Ark of the Covenant.

King George VI asked that verses 7 and 8 be sung at the opening of the Glasgow Exhibition in 1938, and Queen Mary requested that the tune *St. George's Edinburgh* be played. This was because the psalm had already been used at the opening of the Great Exhibition in London in 1851.

THE WAY, THE TRUTH AND THE LIFE

Psalm 25:1–10

A Psalm of David.

1 To thee, O Lord, I lift up my soul.
2   O my God, in thee I trust,
      let me not be put to shame;
      let not my enemies exult over me.
3 Yes, let none that wait for thee be put to shame;
      let them be ashamed who are wantonly treacherous.

4   Make me to know thy ways, O Lord;
      teach me thy paths.
5 Lead me in thy truth, and teach me,
      for thou art the God of my salvation;
      for thee I wait all the day long.

6   Be mindful of thy mercy, O Lord, and of thy steadfast love,
      for they have been from of old.
7 Remember not the sins of my youth, or my transgressions;
      according to thy steadfast love remember me,
      for thy goodness' sake, O Lord!

8   Good and upright is the Lord;
      therefore he instructs sinners in the way.
9 He leads the humble in what is right,
      and teaches the humble his way.
10 All the paths of the Lord are steadfast love and faithfulness,
      for those who keep his covenant and his testimonies.

This is another acrostic or alphabetic psalm, like Psalms 9 and 10 together. In this case, each single verse begins with a letter of the Hebrew alphabet. We have not shown the names of these letters this time; it was sufficient to do so at Psalms 9–10. But we realize how, when we were children, we found it was easier to learn a poem off by heart if it rhymed. One line, however, is deficient. We shall note it when we come to it, and see what we should do about it. Then verse 22, the last line, seems to be an

addition to the original poem, as it follows after the last letter of
the alphabet.

I trust is how we begin. The *soul* is, of course, as we have seen,
the whole personality, body, soul and spirit. This is what God
expects of us, total trust. But the rest of the paragraph reminds
us of the heart-rending conclusion to the great Christian hymn,
the *Te Deum*: "Let me never be confounded." The idea is so
terrible that our poet turns rather to pray for others besides
himself: (a) Let nobody's prayer go unanswered, he implores
God, and (b) let those who are *wantonly treacherous* (what a
very strong expression!) come to their senses and admit their
wickedness in shame. We believe that today we are living in an
age of unusual violence. We hear constantly of dope-running,
embezzling, mugging, hi-jacking, kidnapping, arson, the blowing up of buildings, and so on. What should our Christian
response be to such? Our psalmist does here what Jesus too has
told us to do—pray for our enemies.

Teach me what I already know he says at verse 4. Perhaps we
might say: "Make what I learned in Sunday School come alive
for me now." Note that *to know* does not mean "to know
about". In the same way that a man *knows* his wife (not knows
that she is his wife) so we can *know* the ways of the Lord. In
these verses then we discover that we are actually dealing with
the three realities Jesus speaks of and applies to himself—the
Way, the *Truth* and the *Life*. This has been noted by many
commentators. OT man searched and longed for these three
aspects of God's self-revelation. Surely God is more important
than anything else there is, he believed. The poet is thus saying,
"No matter what happens else, make me to *know*. . . ."

So at verse 6 he asks God to remember two things! The first is
positive. (a) Remember your covenant love which has been
there right from *of old*. Isa. 51:16 likewise makes a tremendous
statement:

Even as I was stretching out the heavens
  and laying the foundations of the earth,
I was saying to Zion, "You are my people."

The negative comes next. (b) Don't remember the sins of my youth. God knows how virtually all young people want to "try everything once". How else could they discover what they ought *not* to do, they argue. This is the meaning, of course, of the forbidden fruit in the Garden of Eden and of the subtle temptation in the question, "Why not?" So he prays that the past might be all swallowed up in the *hesed* of God, which, he adds, is *good for* me. As we have noticed before, God's goodness is no mere abstract quality. God's goodness means his *being good for* me. (See how the word is used at Ezra 8:22.)

Therefore, just because God is like that, and not, as we might suggest today, a self-satisfied fat Buddha in the sky, his teaching is far from what we meet with in the East in the shape of the three monkeys: "Hear no evil, see no evil, say no evil." The Lord is *positively* good for us, and so we are meant to be positively good to our neighbour, not just abstain from evil. *Therefore*, says the psalmist, God takes time, trouble and energy (to use human terms) to instruct sinners in the Way, and to lead the humble to know *his* Way (his *mishpat*, seen in the *Torah*). And if we ask "Whose way?", then we discover that *his* can now refer either to God's way or to the way of the humble man—for they are now one. God's Way covers all the *paths of the Lord*, one for each different humble person. But all are held together within the bonds of the Covenant where God's *hesed* and faithfulness are to be found. Such people do actually find that they, in their turn, *can* actually keep their side of the bargain (their *hesed*) and perform God's will as they have learned it in his *testimonies*, that is, what God has revealed by way of his commandments and judgments.

THE FRIENDSHIP OF GOD

Psalm 25:11-22

11 For thy name's sake, O Lord,
    pardon my guilt, for it is great.
12 Who is the man that fears the Lord?
    Him will he instruct in the way that he should choose.

13 He himself shall abide in prosperity,
    and his children shall possess the land.
14 The friendship of the Lord is for those who fear him,
    and he makes known to them his covenant.
15 My eyes are ever toward the Lord,
    for he will pluck my feet out of the net.
16 Turn thou to me, and be gracious to me;
    for I am lonely and afflicted.
17 Relieve the troubles of my heart,
    and bring me out of my distresses.
18 Consider my affliction and my trouble,
    and forgive all my sins.

19 Consider how many are my foes,
    and with what violent hatred they hate me.
20 Oh guard my life, and deliver me;
    let me not be put to shame, for I take refuge in thee.
21 May integrity and uprightness preserve me,
    for I wait for thee.

22 Redeem Israel, O God,
    out of all his troubles.

No suggestion is made in this psalm that the speaker feels himself to be pure by nature. Rather he would regard himself as a forgiven sinner. Moreover, he now declares with joy that it is to forgiven sinners that God offers his *friendship*. This word means God's intimate, almost secret companionship. Then follows a statement that is basic to all biblical religion: *He makes known to them his covenant*. This phrase echoes what is asked of the believer at verse 10, where we saw that it is up to him to keep his side of the covenant that God has made with his people Israel. Actually today too many believers pay scant attention to this basic act of God. In so doing they turn to an individualistic and private faith in face of the problems of life. But the psalmist in OT times and St. Paul in NT times agree, each representing the mind of the God of the Covenant that (a) the *ancient* Covenant as Paul calls that known to the psalmist, and (b) the *renewed* Covenant as he calls that which Christ has given us on the basis of that known to the psalmist, are one. If this were not so, then we should not use the Psalms in Christian worship. God deals with us as individuals, yes, but only as individuals who are surrounded and encompassed and upheld by the *hesed* he sheds upon all those who dwell within the *friendship* of the Covenant, which is his original gift, not to individuals, but to all Israel, the people of God.

The Lord plucks my feet out of the net which hunters lay on the *way* that wild animals use (by covering with a net the hole they have dug on the path that the animals customarily follow to their drinking-place). Once I am living in covenant both with him and with my friends amongst the People of God, if I try to kick myself free by myself, I get all tangled up. The *friendship* of God is not a commonly used word about God, but it offers, by its unusualness, a fresh perspective upon the meaning of the word *hesed*.

We should note the true sense of verse 13. It would be more accurate to read: "His whole being [*nephesh*] shall abide in what is good for him," that is, in the goodness of God aimed at him; "thus his descendants will find that the whole world belongs to them." In fact, Jesus quoted this verse as we have rendered it when he said at Matt. 5:5: "Blessed are the meek, for they shall inherit the earth." This is what God's goodness does for his covenant folk.

It is good to discover that the words *My eyes are ever fixed toward the Lord* become, in later years, the name of some folk who are listed in the genealogies that make up the People of God. We meet the name at Ezra 10:22 and 27 as *Eli-o-enai*, and at 1 Chron. 26:3 as *Eli-e-ho-enai*. It would take much to live up to such a name, I am sure we would agree.

I need you, Lord is something we all find ourselves saying at times. Unless God *turns* (his face) to us in grace we remain unable to keep our eyes ever toward the Lord, and so we feel as *lonely* as a lost sheep. As any psychologist can tell us, moreover, all kinds of trouble, mental, social, marital, whatever, can set in as a result of egotism and self-centredness. It is sin that corrupts health, marriage, social justice, workable economics, even the life of the Church. For, of course, it is sin that raised the barrier between God and ourselves and which is able to withstand the pressure of his grace upon us. The symbol of *the flaming sword which turned every way*, guarding the way back into the Garden (Gen. 3:24), explains how it must be God alone who can bring us home to himself. And God does indeed take the initiative when he *forgives us all our sins*.

Verse 19 begins with *consider*, even as does verse 18. Those two verses should, we believe, be transposed, and so make better sense. Scholars have suggested a word not found in the text that begins with the appropriate letter that is missing. If they are correct in their choice of word, then we could read: "Confront my enemies, for they are many." And so, in the face of all his foes, our poet *waits* for God to take the initiative and act to save him.

The chorus finally at verse 22 takes this appeal made by one individual and applies it to the whole people of God assembled to worship on this festival day.

I WILL REMAIN LOYAL

Psalm 26:1-12

A Psalm of David.

1 Vindicate me, O Lord,
    for I have walked in my integrity,
    and I have trusted in the Lord without wavering.
2 Prove me, O Lord, and try me;
    test my heart and my mind.
3 For thy steadfast love is before my eyes,
    and I walk in faithfulness to thee.

4 I do not sit with false men,
    nor do I consort with dissemblers;
5 I hate the company of evildoers,
    and I will not sit with the wicked.

6 I wash my hands in innocence,
    and go about thy altar, O Lord,
7 singing aloud a song of thanksgiving,
    and telling all thy wondrous deeds.

8 O Lord, I love the habitation of thy house,
    and the place where thy glory dwells.
9 Sweep me not away with sinners,
    nor my life with bloodthirsty men,
10 men in whose hands are evil devices,
    and whose right hands are full of bribes.

11 But as for me, I walk in my integrity;
    redeem me, and be gracious to me.
12 My foot stands on level ground;
    in the great congregation I will bless the Lord.

The key to this psalm is to be found at verses 6–7. Before reaching that point we must notice a danger we all face of expecting to find our own point of view in the Psalms. Only too easily we read into them the way people think in this day and age. It is essential for us to be humble before the text of Scripture, and let it speak to us, rather than for us to try to speak to it.

We should ask the psalmist here the question: "What do you mean when you say, 'I have walked in my integrity'?", but being careful not to have in mind our modern bias or denominational emphasis. So we put the second question: "Are you pointing to your own self-righteousness?" To which he replies at verse 6: "I go about thy altar, O Lord." We shall see what he means.

He goes about the altar of *the Lord*, not about a set of religious ideas, and *telling all thy wondrous deeds*. These last two words are only one in Hebrew. It means those gracious acts of God that we meet with in our human life but which are quite beyond our human understanding. Consequently it can be rendered at times by the word miracle. However, modern man would inevitably read the wrong meaning into such a translation, schooled as he is by the secular, scientific education of our time.

One of God's profound miracles, an action that is wholly beyond my intellect to grasp, says the psalmist, is that he has taken a sinner like me, has justified me (has put me in a right relationship with himself—as we have seen that the word means), has made me an integrated personality (see verse 1), and so a person who now lives in trust and faith, knowing a new fullness of life. This kind of new life I now possess is definitely not of my own doing; it has happened to me as the result of knowing God's *hesed* (*steadfast love*) and *faithfulness* (see verse 3 *ftn.* RSV). No one is justified by his own faithfulness to God. He is justified by God's *faithfulness* to him (the word we noted at Ps. 25:5, translated there as *truth* or "reliability"). It is only because this is so that one *dare* use the laver that was placed before the sanctuary for this purpose (verse 6, and see Exod. 30:17–21), though in this case the act of washing was probably metaphorical. Thus there were two actions, (a) this one, purification by water, and (b) the other mentioned, purification by sacrifice. These two actions took place *when I go about thy altar, O Lord.*

Because of God's faithfulness, in refusing to let the psalmist fall out of his grasp, he can confidently declare, next, that he has received God's strength. He no longer feels irresistibly compelled to "sit down" in the company of *dissemblers* or hypocrites. This verb should be noted. When Ezekiel the priest finally met up with those exiles who had been taken off to Babylon, and who had had to try to adjust themselves to the strange surroundings of a very new world, it was natural that their thinking should have changed too. Ezekiel found that he and they were strangers to each other. So instead of trying straight away to preach to them, he tells us what he did: "I sat where they sat" (Ezek. 3:15, AV). Our psalmist finds he must take the contrary position. He has refused to sit down and learn to think as the wicked think.

One word used to describe the covenant people of God in the OT is the word *qahal*, translated as assembly, convocation, or company. This was turned into the word *ecclesia* when the LXX appeared around 250 B.C. That, of course, is the word "church" used in the NT. What we meet with here, however, is an *ecclesia* of evil-doers, as if this company were organized in opposition to the *ecclesia* of the Lord. One can belong only in one or the other of those "churches". There is obviously no middle way.

Our psalmist now goes on to say how much he *loves* to be in the *ecclesia* of the Lord, for God's glory dwells in its midst. He desperately wants not to be *swept away* (surely a word of great contempt) should he be fool enough to join up with the enemy force, meaning the wrong *ecclesia*. *Bloodthirsty men* are those who use violence to attain their ends. So long as he remains in the Lord's *qahal* or *ecclesia*, God may indeed try him and prove him (verse 2); but *God himself* will uphold him in those tests, just because he is always faithful and loyal to his loved ones.

God's glory is not describable as a meteorological phenomenon. The glory the psalmist speaks of is the experience of God's gracious presence even as his people live and worship together in love and fellowship. At that moment then God's glory is *seen*. His judgment too is *seen*, on the other hand, when members of the other *ecclesia fill their right hand with bribes*, surely the curse of many so-called civilized lands today.

From the word *dwells*, intertestamental Judaism produced the noun *Shechinah*. By this word they sought to give a name to the localized Presence of God in the midst of his *ecclesia*. Then, of course, the idea was used in the NT as one description of the meaning of Christ: "The Word became flesh and *dwelt* among us . . . " (John 1:14).

Finally, the congregation joins in chorus, each individual *I* proclaiming, "This is what God has done for me too. I find I can walk" (see Psalm 1) "as an integrated personality. But, Lord, do keep on ransoming me" (rather than *redeem*) "and pitying me. From where I now *stand* I can see far into the distance, I can now see so much of the meaning of life. That is why, at the great festivals when all Israel is present together, *I will bless the Lord*."

It is commonly thought today that the Church is there "to teach people to be good". Yet, since one can be "good", live a moral life, without the help of the Church, the Church is irrelevant in modern society. What this psalm is telling us loudly is that "the Church" does not teach people "to be good". It leads them to that source and power which enables them to live in love and *loyalty* to both God and man.

NO NEED FOR FEAR

Psalm 27:1–6

A Psalm of David.

1 The Lord is my light and my salvation;
     whom shall I fear?
   The Lord is the stronghold of my life;
     of whom shall I be afraid?

2 When evildoers assail me,
     uttering slanders against me,
   my adversaries and foes,
     they shall stumble and fall.

3 Though a host encamp against me,
     my heart shall not fear;
   though war arise against me,
     yet I will be confident.

4 One thing have I asked of the Lord,
     that will I seek after;
   that I may dwell in the house of the Lord
     all the days of my life,
   to behold the beauty of the Lord,
     and to inquire in his temple.

5 For he will hide me in his shelter
     in the day of trouble;
   he will conceal me under the cover of his tent,
     he will set me high upon a rock.

6 And now my head shall be lifted up
     above my enemies round about me;
   and I will offer in his tent
     sacrifices with shouts of joy;
   I will sing and make melody to the Lord.

David could well have been the original author of this psalm.
Many of the references in it fit squarely into his life-experience.
If this is so, then it was written (or at least recited in the first

place) between 1,000 B.C., when he came to the throne, and 960
B.C. when he died. But later on this great and moving psalm
found a place in the "hymn book of the Second Temple", as the
Psalter came to be called. The "Second Temple" is the building
that went up between 520 and 516 B.C. and which was dedicated
the following year.

Our modern hymn books go through processes of revision,
each new edition making slight changes in the words even of
"old favourites". So it is with the Psalter. If it were not so, the
Bible would not be the *living* book it is, one that speaks first to
the days of David, then to those of Ezra, then to those of
Jesus—and then to us. In fact we don't possess, and no one ever
has, the original "autograph" of any part of the OT.

If God be for us . . . The two nouns *light* and *salvation* are
written as a hendiadys, a form common to poetry. That means
the poet has chosen two words to say the same thing from two
points of view. God's *light* creates my *salvation*, and my
salvation has come about because God is *light*. Since it is God
the Creator who is such, then there is nothing in all creation to
be afraid of. When the University of Oxford, to be followed by
the Oxford Press, took over the first words of this psalm in
Latin as its motto, *Dominus Illuminatio Mea*, it spoiled the
depths of the psalmist's insight. For without the word *salvation*
we lose so much of the meaning of the word *light*. So much then
for the harm we can do by quoting texts out of context.

Stronghold is really "the source of strength in my life", God's
strength! In verse 2, the RSV *ftn.*, being the original reading
(refuge), is surely more telling than any paraphrase of it. We
have just reminded ourselves that we are reading poetry, not
plain prose!

To David the host would have been a human army. To Ezra it
might have referred to political pressure, as we can discover in
that book that bears his name. Today, without sounding far-
fetched, our enemies might even be a host of destructive viruses.
We have only recently been discovering how viruses can
reproduce themselves by the million like living beings and how
they depend upon their own biological ingenuity to recreate

themselves in ever new destructive forms. So *though a host should encamp against me* can mean a completely new thing to a patient in a modern hospital! We are to remember that in the Bible evil is one, and can assume all kinds of manifestations (that wily old devil!), political, military, psychological, social, religious, so that there is in fact only one army of evil. Yet David *knows* God here. He does not cry to God for help. Knowing God is all he needs.

So there is a war on. The believer at all times is committed, in total *knowledge* of God's "reliability", to wage the "wars of the Lord". These are spoken of in the old poems that precede even the days of David (see Exod. 15:1-18, and verse 21). That is why, in the developing meaning of the psalms, we today can sing with a like commitment of heart and mind the great hymn "Onward, Christian soldiers, marching as to war".

This is a reality that the Psalter helps to set before us. It is that "the Army of the Lord" was not first recruited at Pentecost, as one occasionally hears said today. There is profound truth in the theological assertion that "Jesus did not found a church; he found one". Anything else would be a deep disrespect to the faith of the Jewish people. Nor dare we limit the promise God made to Abraham at Gen. 12:2-3 to the Jewish people alone. For one thing, Abraham was not a Jew, but an ancestor both of the Jews and of many Gentiles; and for another, to deny either the Christian or the modern Jew a place in the promise would be to make nonsense of the Psalms.

The statement in verse 4 is a way of saying: "There is only *one* God. So what follows has *one* basic thing to say to me in my life." Picture-theology is employed to declare what this *one thing* is. It is to remember the First Commandment. "Thou shalt have no other gods before Me." There are other gods—lots of them—health, wealth, games, one's own ego. But the worship of God at all times and in all places and in all activities is Number One. To *dwell* in the house of the Lord is literally to *sit* in it. There were four postures for worship in biblical times. (a) You could sit for meditative prayer, as the Jew does today, and as Jesus sat to teach (Matt. 5:1-2). You did not kneel in the modern fashion in those days. (b) To "kneel" in OT times was to go down on one's knees and then place one's brow on the ground, just as a Muslim does today. But that posture was abandoned when the Church spread to northern Europe, since its buildings possessed only wet, muddy floors, and no seats. (c) The third position, described as bowing down in the Bible, was to go flat on the ground on one's face. One had to do just that in the presence of the Pharaoh of Egypt. This position has survived only in the case of the ordination of a Roman Catholic priest. (d) But very often people just stood to pray.

So the picture here is of a man or a woman worshipping God while sitting in the temple, seeking over a long period (when he could be quite relaxed) to understand the ways of God. Of course he could not sit there if he lived in a village. Consequently these words are surely only a picture of an *attitude of life*. Yet we read next: "And *now* . . . " So because of his meditation he knows what it means to walk with God secure in his faith no matter what troubles assail. "For my head is now *higher than my enemies*!" He can see much further into the meaning of God's love and promises than they can. So he goes about his daily life with a song in his heart.

A DIALOGUE WITH GOD

Psalm 27:7-14

7 Hear, O Lord, when I cry aloud,
      be gracious to me and answer me!
8 Thou hast said, "Seek ye my face."
      My heart says to thee,
   "Thy face, Lord, do I seek."
9   Hide not thy face from me.

   Turn not thy servant away in anger,
      thou who hast been my help.
   Cast me not off, forsake me not,
      O God of my salvation!
10 For my father and my mother have forsaken me,
      but the Lord will take me up.

11 Teach me thy way, O Lord;
        and lead me on a level path
        because of my enemies.
12 Give me not up to the will of my adversaries;
        for false witnesses have risen against me,
        and they breathe out violence.

13 I believe that I shall see the goodness of the Lord
        in the land of the living!
14 Wait for the Lord;
        be strong, and let your heart take courage;
        yea, wait for the Lord!

Now we overhear part of the psalmist's conversation with God, that he held sitting in the temple (or in his village!).

(1) He says: *Lord, hear me when I cry aloud.*

(2) God has already replied, even before the psalmist spoke: *Seek my face—all of you.* The verb is plural, and so is addressed, not just to David, now, but to the whole congregation.

(3) My heart replies, he declares: *I have indeed been seeking thy face,* so don't hide it from me now. Sure of this, then, he can continue to speak, knowing that God is indeed *there*, listening, caring, waiting for his words.

Trouble. What experience has this poor man gone through? We do not need to know. For we all have our own private and individual hells to live through   and no one else knows what we must suffer. But he *does* say, *Thou hast been my help*, in times before this. "It is true that [*ki* in Hebrew] my parents have let me down. They do not understand me; there is really such a thing as the generation gap. But you are both my father and my mother and I am your son/daughter. You will surely gather me up in your arms."

Two-way traffic. In verse 11 he returns to the joy of that fellowship he spoke of in verse 4, but to reach it he declares that both God *and* man must act. But God must act first! "Teach *me*," says the psalmist; I don't know what to do myself and what to do about those false witnesses, those violent opponents of mine whom I spoke of before (verses 2–3). Yet, as we have seen, those enemies may be within us, and one of them may be just lack of faith. Professor Jung of Zürich once wrote: "Among my patients in the second half of life, that is, over thirty-five, there has not been one whose problem in the last resort was not that of finding a religious outlook on life."

If God will do those two things for me (as he does!), he goes on at verse 13, *then*... Now follows at this crucial moment a strange word in the text. See how the various versions try to deal with it, the AV, the NEB, the TEV and others. There is much merit in translating as "If I had not believed that I shall see..." ("then I might have abandoned all faith"), or something like that. We find just such a construction at Exod. 32:32. But as it is, the psalmist does confidently declare his belief that he *will* yet see God *being good to* him, the meaning of the word we have noted before. He makes this affirmation on the simple grounds that God is faithful, reliable, trustworthy.

But what does *in the land of the living* mean? (a) It could be translated as "in the land of life"—whatever that is. (b) The living may refer to us human beings so long as we live upon this earth. (c) It may refer to those who are alive with God now in eternity, in that God is the God of the living; and that he is the living God. The best thing to say, I believe, in the light of our argument at the beginning of this psalm, is that a biblical text, being the living Word of God, may begin in 1,000 B.C. by conveying a meaning on a level that the people of that era could accept. But in the period since those days God has revealed himself ever more and more fully to his covenant people—in fact, as the NT would say, God has by its day revealed himself wholly, completely, and once-for-all (*eph hapax*) in Jesus Christ.

So, no matter at what level we take the statement of belief we find at verse 13, waiting for the Lord is clearly worth while! Joachim Neander wrote:

Hast thou not seen
  How thy heart's wishes have been
Granted in what he ordaineth?

JUDGE THE WICKED, O LORD

Psalm 28:1-9

A Psalm of David.

1   To thee, O Lord, I call;
        my rock, be not deaf to me,
    lest, if thou be silent to me,
        I become like those who go down to the Pit.
2   Hear the voice of my supplication,
        as I cry to thee for help,
    as I lift up my hands
        toward thy most holy sanctuary.

3   Take me not off with the wicked,
        with those who are workers of evil,
    who speak peace with their neighbours,
        while mischief is in their hearts.
4   Requite them according to their work,
        and according to the evil of their deeds;
    requite them according to the work of their hands;
        render them their due reward.
5   Because they do not regard the works of the Lord,
        or the work of his hands,
    he will break them down and build them up no more.

6   Blessed be the Lord!
        for he has heard the voice of my supplications.
7   The Lord is my strength and my shield;
        in him my heart trusts;
    so I am helped, and my heart exults,
        and with my song I give thanks to him.
8   The Lord is the strength of his people,
        he is the saving refuge of his anointed.
9   O save thy people, and bless thy heritage;
        be thou their shepherd, and carry them for ever.

The 150 psalms in our Psalter have been compiled in various
ways. Sometimes we can see the reason for the order in which

they occur. Usually we cannot. But here this psalm comes where it does, because it carries echoes of all the previous five psalms. Anyway, like the Psalter as a whole, it deals, not with mankind, but with God. And so it begins: *To thee, O Lord.*

The Psalter, expressing as it does the theology of the OT as a whole, makes plain that living in the presence of God is no less than LIFE. But living without God or more particularly in rebellion against him is simply DEATH. This is so even when we may still be living on this earth. Jesus made that distinction vividly clear when he said: "Let the dead bury their dead" (Luke 9:60). Our poet "knows" the presence of God (Ps. 25:4); it is as if he could put out his hand and touch God, there, before him, solid as a rock. But the danger is always present of losing touch with God, and then LIFE, if that happens, can so easily turn into DEATH. For *to go down to the Pit* does not necessarily refer to what awaits us after death. In Prov. 7:27 we are told of a full-blooded young man who does not realize that living in the world of lust is equal to going *down* to the chambers of death.

To go the road of this young man is only too easy. *Facilis descensus Averni*, said the old Roman poet—the descent to Hades is easy. In fact, the double-minded people described here—superficially charming to their neighbours, but essentially corrupt inside—can so easily lead us astray with their speciousness (verse 3). If You, God, says the psalmist, don't keep on talking to me and if you don't answer me when I approach You, then I only too easily become just like one of those who are on the downward slope.

Rebuke those trouble-makers, Lord; they destroy people's faith and pervert their minds. That is in fact their chief aim in life! So *render them their due reward* (verse 4), do to them what they wanted to do to me and those like me. For to lead people astray is *evil*. Your actions in saving people from the Pit, that is, *the works of the Lord* (verse 5), are of course the very opposite of theirs.

In our day perhaps no category of persons more adequately fits the description of creative evil-doing than the hard-drug trafficker, making his millions off human degradation. With such a picture in mind, then, we must ask the meaning of the second half of verse 5—*he will break them down and build them up no more.*

Breaking down and then reconstructing is God's method of dealing with the human situation. This was emphasized long ago in that pre-Davidic poem, Deut. 32, where at verse 39 we read: *I kill and I make alive; I wound and I heal.* Jeremiah found that God was calling him *to pluck up and to break down, to destroy and to overthrow, to build and to plant* (Jer. 1:10). Building and planting, it seems, can come only after destruction and overthrowing. This truth about God has of course been given to us in the basic "parable" of the Flood and the Ark of Noah.

What is the theology of all this? Does it mean that certain people must meet final death at the hand of God because they are quite incorrigible? Must they inevitably *go down to the Pit*? Or does it mean that out of sheer grace God will take even those members of the human family, whom he *must*, of course, punish, by *plucking them up and breaking them down*, but then go on to re-create them—all because of his essential forgiving and re-creative love? Would such an action by God not be on a par with what we behold in the Cross and Resurrection of Christ? I believe that biblical theologians would say that both of these eventualities are true, yet that they are held together as one only by that grace of God which goes far beyond what the sinful mind of even a theologian can penetrate. As we are all aware, no more does the NT speak unequivocally as to whether hell is for ever or whether the suffering of those who must necessarily experience it is educative and redemptive. Is the drug trafficker, for example, really beyond all hope and beyond the reach even of the grace of Almighty God?

But at the moment it seems that our psalmist, being a sinner, urges God to stop at the *breaking down* point and not to go forward to the *building up* that would ordinarily follow. He believes God has heard him in this prayer, but whether God will act as he wished is another question.

As usual, the congregation takes the psalm to its own heart. It is *the Lord*, they sing, who is *the strength of his people*. That strength has been made known more and more with the passage of time. His will that the hungry should be fed is being taken more seriously today than at any other time in history, and slavery was abolished a century ago by Christian nations and by the Jewish people pressing other nations to listen to the Word of the Bible. *He* (very emphatic in the Hebrew) is also the saving refuge of his "messiah", or *anointed*—the words are one and the same. For every believer is a messiah (see Isa. 61:1), anointed in order to actually *do* the will of God. Yet, anomalously, the sheep will remain helpless, the psalm recognizes, unless the *shepherd* gives them the power that comes from putting his blessing into their lives (see Isa. 40:11).

THE LORD OF NATURE

Psalm 29:1-11

A Psalm of David.

1 Ascribe to the Lord, O heavenly beings,
  ascribe to the Lord glory and strength.
2 Ascribe to the Lord the glory of his name;
  worship the Lord in holy array.

3 The voice of the Lord is upon the waters;
  the God of glory thunders,
  the Lord, upon many waters.
4 The voice of the Lord is powerful,
  the voice of the Lord is full of majesty.

5 The voice of the Lord breaks the cedars,
  the Lord breaks the cedars of Lebanon.
6 He makes Lebanon to skip like a calf,
  and Sirion like a young wild ox.

7 The voice of the Lord flashes forth flames of fire.
8 The voice of the Lord shakes the wilderness,
  the Lord shakes the wilderness of Kadesh.

9   The voice of the Lord makes the oaks to whirl,
       and strips the forest bare;
       and in his temple all cry, "Glory!"

10   The Lord sits enthroned over the flood;
       the Lord sits enthroned as king for ever.
11   May the Lord give strength to his people!
       May the Lord bless his people with peace!

This is a great nature poem. But as in everything else, praise must go, not to nature, but to the Lord of nature. At Psalm 19 we saw how all peoples may indeed praise the Divine Being for revealing himself to mankind in a General Revelation through the marvels of nature. But we also saw that such is not enough. So the author was moved to praise God for the Special Revelation he has given us of himself in the Law of Moses.

It is not surprising that, since this psalm deals with the first category of revelation, other people too should possess poems in praise of the Lord of nature very similar to our Psalm 29. In fact, several of the phrases here are to be found also in Canaanite poems that we now possess, and which have come down to us from the period of Moses and Joshua.

Glory! So it is no surprise to find in verse 1 the phrase *sons of gods* (*ftn.*) or *heavenly beings* (text), because this is how the Canaanites expressed themselves. On the other hand, however, even though the psalms are completely monotheistic, that is, they are written in praise of the one and only God, by taking over this Canaanite mythological language, the Hebrews were able to express pictorially the idea that creation is not just dead matter. In fact, they suggest that by the very way in which the universe has evolved, it itself has been singing the praises of God. We do not need to be specialist scientists to be aware today that what we once thought to be dead matter is as truly alive as tigers and mice. We now know to speak of the particles of life as "living organisms". It would not then be out of place to suggest that even these strange elements are *worshipping the Lord in holy array.*

The storm. The voice of the Lord is of course the roar of the storm, the thunder that reverberates round the hills. Yet in what follows we read that *the voice* sounds forth seven times, corresponding, it would seem, to the seven words of God's creative activity in Gen. 1. But the poem begins with *many waters*, as does Genesis, rather than with the hills. God's creation is one. As we have said in the Introduction, we should not speak (as the ancient Greek philosophers did) of body *and* spirit, heaven *and* earth, science *and* religion. At Gen. 1:2 we see how the Hebrews pictured chaos as having been there in the beginning, but that, by means of his Word, God created order and light. An aspect of that order is what we today call "the balance of nature". Floods and volcanoes, fires and diseases, seem to us to disrupt the natural order.

But soon *the voice of the Lord* brings all elements within nature back into balance again. For floods, volcanoes, diseases and so on are all merely symptoms of the watery chaos that God has never abolished, but which he has permitted to exist. It was pictured by the ancients as "the waters under the earth" (see Exod. 20:4). In those waters, moreover, monsters dwell. These represent their horrible origin in chaos. He (or she! or they!) are known as *Leviathan, Rahab,* the *piercing* or *crooked serpent,* the *dragon* or the *great fish* such as that which Jonah encountered when he sank right down to the bottom of the ocean, to the "waters under the earth" where the seaweed became entangled in his hair (Jon. 2:5–6). How rich is the imagery that the ancients used to describe the powers of evil! But this one thing is certain—the Lord is in control even of these and all other elements of chaos, no matter how human beings may learn to picture them.

We saw in Psalm 28 that God *plucks up* before he *plants*; and we saw that such is true of his actions in connection with the whole natural world. So now in this poem such a strange plan of action becomes visible to our human eye. For we see him uprooting the giant *cedars of Lebanon* and shaking *Sirion* (the Phoenician name for mighty Mount Hermon) with earthquakes, fire and avalanches.

Why should it be that the forest fire or the hurricane wind

which denudes the trees should actually be proclaiming "Glory!", when we might want to cry instead, "Shame on You, God; why do You destroy the world in this way?" It is because God *sits on* the flood that all nature can shout "Glory!" He rules as King over all the processes of nature. Evolution is not mere natural selection and steady growth from point to point. The living God rules *over* nature because nature itself is alive, *skipping like a calf on Mount Lebanon.* Said Jesus, "My kingdom is not of this world." God's kingdom is what God creates *out of* pain, *out of* sorrow, *out of* floods and avalanches, and even—most strangely—*out of* sins forgiven.

So now, at verse 10, we see God sitting enthroned *over* the flood, the *mabbul* (Gen. 6:17; 7:17), that Flood *over* which God *rested* in Noah (the word Noah means "rest"). Clearly in such a world there is no room left for astrology, ghosts, superstition, and "things that go bump in the night". God is plucking up, destroying, and only then re-creating, creating something new every morning, in fact, as the words of Rev. 21:5 declare: "Behold I make *all* things new." The Baal of the poems of the Canaanites was not like that. They could only speak of him as the Supreme Being. But our poem calls him *Lord*, Yahweh, the God of the Covenant, the God who had redeemed Israel out of the "chaos", the hell, of the utter slavery of life in Egypt. And *out of* that he produced *shalom, peace*, fulness of life—nay more, he is the God who has gone the second mile and who has given his covenant people something of his own re-creative strength to re-create the lives of their neighbours. So the seven days of creation are also the seven days of re-creation, or, to express this last word in another way, of redemption.

Scholars have pointed out that this psalm began, as at the birth of Jesus, with the angels singing "Glory to God!"; and that it now ends with the declaration, "Peace on earth". For that is actually the name of Israel's God (as at Judg. 6:24); he is *the Lord of Peace.*

FROM SORROW TO JOY

Psalm 30:1–12

A Psalm of David.
A song at the dedication of the temple.

1 I will extol thee, O Lord, for thou has drawn me up,
    and hast not let my foes rejoice over me.
2 O Lord my God, I cried to thee for help,
    and thou hast healed me.
3 O Lord, thou hast brought up my soul from Sheol,
    restored me to life from among those gone down to the Pit.

4 Sing praises to the Lord, O you his saints,
    and give thanks to his holy name.
5 For his anger is but for a moment,
    and his favour is for a lifetime.
  Weeping may tarry for the night,
    but joy comes with the morning.

6 As for me, I said in my prosperity,
    "I shall never be moved."
7 By thy favour, O Lord,
    thou hadst established me as a strong mountain;
  thou didst hide thy face,
    I was dismayed.

8 To thee, O Lord, I cried;
    and to the Lord I made supplication:
9 "What profit is there in my death,
    if I go down to the Pit?
  Will the dust praise thee?
    Will it tell of thy faithfulness?
10 Hear, O Lord, and be gracious to me!
    O Lord, be thou my helper!"

11 Thou hast turned for me my mourning into dancing;
    thou has loosed my sackcloth
    and girded me with gladness,
12 that my soul may praise thee and not be silent.
    O Lord my God, I will give thanks to thee for ever.

Which dedication of which temple is referred to here we cannot say, whether it is David's choice of a particular rock to site an altar to the Lord (1 Chron. 21:18–26), or Solomon's dedication of his temple (1 Kings 8), or the dedication of the Second Temple in 515 B.C. (Ezra 6:16), or even the re-dedication of that temple by Judas Maccabaeus in 164 B.C. after its desecration by the Seleucid king of Syria and his general Lysias (1 Maccabees 4:36–59). So it could apply even to the dedication of our own local church building at the street corner! But whichever was the event, the act of dedication certainly led—or leads today—from sorrow to joy.

Knowing God from worship has done a great thing for me, says our psalmist, for *thou hast drawn me up*. We human beings like to think in terms of up-and-down. At one moment we are down in the depths, at the next we are up in the clouds. Down marks sorrow; up marks joy. Perhaps that is why all peoples put heaven "up there", and hell "down below", even when they know that the earth rotates. God has pulled me up, then, says our poet, out of misery into joy. In saying so he does not necessarily imply that his misery was like that of Jeremiah when he was literally down below ground in a dungeon. For Jeremiah could also say metaphorically "My enemies have dug a pit to take me" (Jer. 18:22). Nor does he suggest that he has recovered from a severe illness from which God had "raised him up". But he does say that, whatever he was rescued from, God's act was one of *healing*. Clearly there is no line (as Jesus shows us at Mark 2:10–11) between sickness of the body and sickness of the soul or psyche. God is the *great* Physician of all ills. Ambroise Paré, the father of modern French surgery, once said: *"Je le pansais, Dieu le guérit."*—"I dressed his wounds, God healed him."

When, at verse 4, he says *You* are *his saints*, he is using a word built from the noun *hesed* we have encountered so often. The latter means "loyal-love" and much more, the covenant term we have examined. God's *saints* are thus the members of the Covenant People of God, the people who walk in God's loving care and who seek to pass his love on to others as a result.

His holy *name*. What is his name? It is *the Lord*. In English that word covers the name *Yahweh* which God used to reveal himself to Moses (Exod. 6:2–8). "The name", we recall, was intended to be an exact description of its owner. But this time the Hebrew is not *shem* (name) but *zecher*, "the means by which one remembers him, the description through which one calls him to mind". But that is the same thing as his name! (1 Cor. 11:25 follows this usage.) Note, then, how in this passage the essentials of the divine Name are revealed by recalling that:

(1) God had already made promises to Abraham, Isaac and Jacob.

(2) He had made covenant with them.

(3) He had promised them a land.

(4) He had redeemed Israel from slavery in Egypt.

(5) He is the God who *keeps on remembering* his covenant.

(6) Who takes Israel as his people.

(7) Who promises to be Israel's God.

(8) In such a manner that "They shall *know* who I am".

(9) And now he has revealed himself as my Doctor!

So the name *Lord* means all these things, and more. Thus when we, his *saints*, give thanks in our newly-dedicated local church we give thanks to *his holy name*, we give thanks that he is actually like all that we have tried to list. But there is more to add. There is *a flash in his anger*, we find, and to that we add, *there is life in his acceptance* (of us), to translate the two phrases literally. The effect of this upon us is to give us assurance that our weeping is only for a *night*, but *joy comes with the morning*. It cannot be otherwise, for God is there himself in the morning. Consequently, says the psalmist, *As for me, I said in my quiet* (of heart), the moments of weeping don't count; because the God I worship is the Rock. This God has made covenant with me; and so in consequence, *I shall never be moved*. Moreover, by accepting me (the word we have just used above) he has actually imputed his own rock-like quality to me!

It seems that the Lord tested our psalmist again (verse 7b), just at the moment when the latter had discovered that he himself was now meant to act like a rock to others. Would he be able to remain firm? He complains: In that little *flash of anger* in which *You hid your face, I was dismayed.* I wasn't ready to try out my new self-awareness as a rock to others. (Surely that is what public worship helps me to do—as we saw at verse 1.) I was very forthright in the way I dared speak to God—"Lord, what use am I to You if You let me slip down into the Pit? How can I sing Your praises if I am dead? So listen to me, Lord, and help me!"

Perhaps, by verse 11, he had told the whole story of his doubts and described his theological difficulties to the temple minister. The latter has evidently now helped him to recover his assurance (his rock-likeness) that, despite all appearances, he *is* still rock (verse 7)! So now he gratefully exclaims that God has heard his cry, and has turned his mourning into dancing (literally, the "twist"—this sounds very modern!). A professor of anthropology has said: "The Pacific Islanders are the happiest people on this earth. They love to sing, they love to play, they love to dance. This is because they begin the day with prayer and they end the day with prayer."

Then the poet says a truly biblical thing. With the help of the Greek text (see RSV *ftn.*) we see that he exclaims: "*In order that my glory may hymn You, and I may never be silent.*" A man has of course no glory of his own. "To God alone be glory," we say. But just as God imputed his own rock-like nature to a mere human being (verse 7) so, by grace, he imputes his own glory to mankind too. You can see it in a person's change of character. As Psalm 8 says, "*O Lord my God, I will praise You for all eternity*, for it will be Your own eternal glory which will be speaking through my lips." At last, then, the psalmist has learned the truth. When he cries "Lord, help me!" (as at verse 10), the Lord has in fact all the time been present *in* his very cry to the Lord!

THE LORD PRESERVES THE FAITHFUL

Psalm 31:1–13

To the choirmaster. A Psalm of David.

1 In thee, O Lord, do I seek refuge;
      let me never be put to shame;
      in thy righteousness deliver me!
2 Incline thy ear to me,
      rescue me speedily!
   Be thou a rock of refuge for me,
      a strong fortress to save me!

3 Yea, thou art my rock and my fortress;
      for thy name's sake lead me and guide me,
4 take me out of the net which is hidden for me,
      for thou art my refuge.
5 Into thy hand I commit my spirit;
      thou hast redeemed me, O Lord, faithful God.

6 Thou hatest those who pay regard to vain idols;
      but I trust in the Lord.
7 I will rejoice and be glad for thy steadfast love,
      because thou hast seen my affliction,
      thou hast taken heed of my adversities,
8 and hast not delivered me into the hand of the enemy;
      thou hast set my feet in a broad place.

9 Be gracious to me, O Lord, for I am in distress;
      my eye is wasted from grief,
      my soul and my body also.
10 For my life is spent with sorrow,
      and my years with sighing;
   my strength fails because of my misery,
      and my bones waste away.

11 I am the scorn of all my adversaries,
      a horror to my neighbours,
   an object of dread to my acquaintances;
      those who see me in the street flee from me.

12 I have passed out of mind like one who is dead;
        I have become like a broken vessel.
13 Yea, I hear the whispering of many—
        terror on every side!—
    as they scheme together against me,
        as they plot to take my life.

Once again the word *Lord* comes first; because God is of course all in all. The word *I* only comes after that. Here is a person who believes, who really trusts, but who finds what we all find, that it is not God's plan for us that we should never be presented with doubts and problems. Unless we meet these head on, and *overcome* them, then our faith will never be as strong as God plans it to be.

In thy righteousness deliver me! Note that here we have the feminine form of the word. So righteousness here means that change of life that God creates in me, making me into a loving, creative personality (see the Introduction). Otherwise, as Jesus put it, I would be one of those who cry "Lord, Lord" when I don't really reveal the meaning of the word "lord", because I don't show myself to be the servant of that Lord by my life of love.

Our psalmist uses the same picture-language that we have met before and which goes right back in time to the thinking of David—rock, fortress, refuge, and so on. But now his feet are actually entangled in the net we saw was used to capture wild beasts. Yet, because of his faith, he can still say three things:

(1) "I am wholly at ease, knowing that thou art in control. So into thy hand I commit my spirit." God's *hand* or arm was what he used when he acted in human life. Here he acts to keep me safe.

(2) *Thou hast* (already—in the past tense) *redeemed me.* God's action is finished, it is complete.

(3) Thou art the *faithful, true, trustworthy* God. So why on earth should I be worried? Was this the kind of temptation in Jesus' mind when he quoted these words on the Cross (Luke 23:46)? But many other persons are also reported to have used

this phrase before their execution, for example, both the Anglican and the Roman Catholic martyrs in the days of Queen Mary and Queen Elizabeth, as well as prominent Covenanters in the "Killing Times" in Scotland (1683-1688); and in the Bible, Stephen also uttered these words before he died (Acts 7:59).

At verse 6 the Hebrew has *I hate* . . . (see RSV *ftn.*); but the Versions, that is, the very early translations made into Greek, Syriac and Latin all seem to have had a Hebrew text before them which read *Thou hatest* . . .; and indeed we possess one Hebrew manuscript that also read it so. That is why the RSV uses it.

It is only the modern reader who thinks he knows what the Bible is all about, before he has read it, who would be upset to find that God hates. For it is possible to hate and to love the same person at the same time. In our case the people mentioned went in pursuit of sheer empty gods. In other words, they were snobs, they showed their class-consciousness, they worked hard and ruthlessly to get wealth. But I have come back after tasting all such vanities, says the psalmist, and put my trust in the Lord; for his *hesed* is still there! And now I know what it feels like to find real security. It is not biblical then to say, as some evangelists do, "God loves you but hates your sins." The biblical writers, not being disciples of the Greek philosophers as was Thomas Aquinas the Catholic theologian, know only too well that there are no such things as sins. Sins do not exist as "things" apart from people. Sins are what people *do*; they are actions. That is why God's judgment must necessarily rest, not upon sins, but upon sinners.

The words *my soul and my body* in verse 9 can be rendered by "my throat and my belly". We know how both those parts of the body can be affected by mental distress. In the one case we cannot swallow, and in the other we can experience an "upset stomach" with resultant diarrhoea. Nowhere in the Bible do we meet with that reluctance to mention bodily functions that characterizes many people today (see Matt. 15:17). In the next verse we should read *My strength fails because of my guilt*. The poet is feeling miserable, simply because he has a bad conscience. It is God who has given him this bad conscience by making him aware that he has sinned.

To be out of fellowship with one's friends and neighbours, through one's own perverse fault, is a horrible experience. It is described here in vivid terms, using old eastern social customs to portray its onslaught. But from the Hebrew tenses we see that this bitter experience had gone on for long time; it had built up till this man or woman had become almost paranoid and mentally disturbed. How good that even *that* scourge should be described objectively in God's Word as something that God can heal.

I TRUST IN THEE, O LORD

Psalm 31:14-24

14 But I trust in thee, O Lord,
     I say, "Thou art my God."
15 My times are in thy hand;
     deliver me from the hand of my enemies and persecutors!
16 Let thy face shine on thy servant;
     save me in thy steadfast love!
17 Let me not be put to shame, O Lord,
     for I call on thee;
    let the wicked be put to shame,
     let them go dumbfounded to Sheol.
18 Let the lying lips be dumb,
     which speak insolently against the righteous
     in pride and contempt.

19 O how abundant is thy goodness,
     which thou hast laid up for those who fear thee,
     and wrought for those who take refuge in thee,
     in the sight of the sons of men!
20 In the covert of thy presence thou hidest them
     from the plots of men;
    thou holdest them safe under thy shelter
     from the strife of tongues.

21   Blessed be the Lord,
        for he has wondrously shown his steadfast love to me
        when I was beset as in a besieged city.
22   I had said in my alarm,
        "I am driven far from thy sight."
      But thou didst hear my supplications,
        when I cried to thee for help.

23   Love the Lord, all you his saints!
        The Lord preserves the faithful,
        but abundantly requites him who acts haughtily.
24   Be strong, and let your heart take courage,
        all you who wait for the Lord!

However, our psalmist now makes the only proper response to
his state of misery. *But I have put my trust in thee, O Lord: I
have declared* (and we can hear him almost shouting the words
defiantly), *"Thou art my God"*. Then follows an oft-quoted
phrase: *My times are in thy hand*. The reference is not to clock-
time, but to those special moments in life when something
memorable happens, marriage, birth of a baby, falling ill,
recovering, a sudden awareness of beauty, of hearing "the lost
chord", moments of deep meaning that never return but which
one can never forget. These all come from God; they are
moments of eternity breaking into time. And the profoundest
of these are those moments when one becomes vividly aware
that God's face is shining on his servant. Awareness of that
wonder drives out all the sense of horror at what the wicked can
do to one. "They can go to hell for all I care", is literally what
our psalmist says. They can go *dumbfounded*, because traditionally Sheol was "the land of silence".

We have no right to retort that such a statement is sub-
Christian, and that, since it represents the kind of thinking we
meet with often enough in the OT as a whole, then the OT is a
sub-Christian document. There are those who take even the
next step and who would consequently disregard the OT
altogether, and declare that the Christian Church should use
the NT alone as its Bible. Yet what "sub-Christian" statements
we meet with also in the NT! James and John were amongst the

worst offenders in this regard. We read that when faced with opposition, as was our psalmist here, they said: "Lord, do you want us to bid fire come down from heaven and consume them?" But Jesus turned and rebuked them (Luke 9:54-55). And even *after* the Crucifixion Peter does just that kind of thing to two people who deceived him (Acts 5:1-11). Actually this psalm is much quoted in the NT. The fact is that all the characters and all the speakers in the Bible—psalmists, prophets, disciples alike—are sinners. To set ourselves up today as being "better" people than David and Jeremiah and Peter therefore would be the height of hypocrisy. It is this very fact that enables us to recognize that the Bible, both OT and NT, is not about the religious thought of human beings, but is in fact a revelation of the love of God to all men; for all whom we meet with in the Bible are sinners, and all keep on learning (just as we must do) about the love of God which passes all human understanding.

One aspect of God's grace is the way in which the God of all grace lets our psalmist (and us!) experience the joy of his presence (verses 19-22), even when he (and we) still remain narrow-minded and vengeful. God is good, indeed, but his goodness is *good for* us; he has *worked at it, made it*, for us; and he has kept some of it, as in a store-cupboard, to bring out and pour upon us from time to time. This goodness of his to us is poured out upon us with a missionary purpose in view, for in all that he does, God wants all mankind to see what they are missing if they *do not take refuge in him*. If they would only do so, then they would be in *the covert of thy presence*, he says, or "in the secret of his face" (see verse 16). What daring and powerful imagery all this is!

Despite that, our poet had had his moments of despair (even as we do). *I had said in my alarm, "I am driven far from thy sight," But* . . . I was quite wrong. This is a very strong *but* in Hebrew. It seems that God has been listening for his poor human cry all the time! So he can now declare that (verse 21) God *has wondrously shown his steadfast love to me*. It was at the moment when there was *no way out*, as if from a besieged city, that God had performed a miracle (it is the word *wondrously* again). Thus the loneliness our friend had suffered, out in the cold, so to speak, even to the point of mental derangement, had become the gateway to the fellowship of the great company of comforted sufferers.

The chorus now has its turn (verses 23–24). Our psalmist has completed his great statement of faith. The hymn "O love that wilt not let me go" was written by a blind and lonely old man. But others thought it was too good to be hidden away, and it crept into the world's hymn books. So here the congregation has taken up this Psalm 31 and all sing it together: *"Love the Lord, all you members of his covenant."* The Lord guards those who have found security in him, for he is security itself. Accordingly, we must show the world how God's people become "secure", "faithful", "unshakeable" themselves, receiving the power to be like him who is himself immovable. Then again, "Vengeance is mine, I will repay, says the Lord" (Rom. 12:19), as Paul declares. This is what the congregation is next reminding itself of in song. So instead of repeating what verses 17–18 had declared, they are to remember that, in their turn, they are called to engage in "the wars of the Lord" that lie ahead. To meet that issue, they should remember God's address to Joshua (Josh. 1:5–6): "As I was with Moses, so I will be with you . . . Be strong and of good courage." And, we might add, "Leave the rest to God!"

RENEWAL EVEN FROM GUILT

Psalm 32:1–11

A Psalm of David. A Maskil.

1 Blessed is he whose transgression is forgiven,
  whose sin is covered.
2 Blessed is the man to whom the Lord imputes no iniquity,
  and in whose spirit there is no deceit.
3 When I declared not my sin, my body wasted away
  through my groaning all day long.

4 For day and night thy hand was heavy upon me;
my strength was dried up as by the heat of summer. *Selah*

5 I acknowledged my sin to thee,
and I did not hide my iniquity;
I said, "I will confess my transgressions to the Lord";
then thou didst forgive the guilt of my sin. *Selah*

6 Therefore let every one who is godly
offer prayer to thee;
at a time of distress, in the rush of great waters,
they shall not reach him.

7 Thou art a hiding place for me,
thou preservest me from trouble;
thou dost encompass me with deliverance. *Selah*

8 I will instruct you and teach you
the way you should go;
I will counsel you with my eye upon you.

9 Be not like a horse or a mule, without understanding,
which must be curbed with bit and bridle,
else it will not keep with you.

10 Many are the pangs of the wicked;
but steadfast love surrounds him who trusts in the Lord.

11 Be glad in the Lord, and rejoice, O righteous,
and shout for joy, all you upright in heart!

A *Maskil*. We are not sure what this word means. Its root has to do with teaching. Perhaps the old Hebrew editors, when placing this psalm in their "hymn book", saw how the *godly* (verse 6) have something most important to learn about the relationship between confession and forgiveness.

Blessedness. To experience forgiveness is sheer blessedness, that is, to have one's rebellious acts against God's *hesed* "taken away", and one's ordinary stupid sins "covered over". The two verbs are rhymed in this verse. Both of them give us a picture of what God does. In Zech. 5:5-11 we see Wickedness being pushed into a barrel and the lid slapped down upon her (not upon her sins!). Then two more women, with wings like storks, pick up the barrel and fly off with it to the land of *Shinar*, the land of the tower of Babel (Gen. 11:2). That is the one picture.

The other is that of "covering over", and it comes from the way in which certain sacrifices did just that. The sacrificer had first laid his hands on the head of the beast that went up to God in smoke, in order to identify himself with it. *He* went up in smoke, then, not just his sins. But God lays his hands over the sinner and his deeds saying, "I can't even see them now." Surely that is grace!

We have four words here used to describe our human sin: (a) *Rebellion*—against God's covenant love, or "transgression" in the RSV, unfortunately. (b) The word *sin* in the RSV; it means really "missing out on the true goal of life". (c) *Iniquity* or crookedness of character. (d) *Deceit*, or laziness, or perversion of the spirit. Surely that suffices!

Stubbornness. But this poet, at verse 3,—was it David himself?—expected to receive what the Christian martyr Bonhoeffer described as "cheap grace". There is the famous story of the philosopher Heinrich Heine, in the eighteenth century, who was visited by a friend when he was dying. "Do you believe that God has forgiven your sins?" the friend asked him. To which Heine made the famous reply: *"Dieu me pardonnera; c'est son métier!"*—"God will forgive me; that's his job!" But David has discovered here that God had *not* forgiven him, and that he is still guilty in God's sight. Moreover, since body and soul are all one, even his *body* is showing the effect of his state of unforgivenness. And this physical exhaustion he was undergoing was God's doing! Consequently he was, quite literally, now "worried sick", as we say today. Does *Selah* here suggest that we pause and try to understand what this painful condition means?

Confession. Finally, at verse 5, David has a conversation with himself. That is sometimes a valuable thing to do. He decides at last to confess to God the reason for this festering self-loathing he is undergoing, and not to hide (the word used of God's action in verse 1, viz. where it is rendered "covered") anything at all from God's eyes; and then, in making his confession, he repeats all the words for sin he has used at verses 1–2! *Then*, he says, with emphasis, *thou didst forgive the guilt* (or remove the *penalty*) of my sin!

Then comes another *Selah*. What are we meant to contemplate in the pause that follows? It is surely this, that forgiveness and the removal of guilt are two different things. To take an extreme case— I may murder a man and then turn to God and ask his forgiveness even for such a terrible deed. But the dreadful reality is that I cannot undo what I have done. David himself knew all about this horror. He had given orders that one of his faithful army officers was to be sent to a point of danger where it was inevitable that he would be killed, as he was (2 Sam. 11:14–15)! I cannot face the dead man's wife and excuse myself to her by saying that God has forgiven me. Forgiveness for the sinful act is clearly not enough. Involved in it also is reparation. God offers to remove from my heart the *guilt* of my deed, the sense of horror, of self-loathing, of alienation from the murdered man's wife—in fact to wipe clean the whole horrible situation, and to let me begin again, a new man. But first, I must confess it!

Since (verse 6) that is what the removal of guilt, the penalty of iniquity, implies, David calls upon every one of the covenant people (the *godly*) to pray to God when all hell breaks loose within their hearts, when the chaotic flood that flows under the earth and which represents the powers of evil seeks to drown them. It is the prayer that Jesus has taught us in four simple words: "Deliver us from evil." God does just this by (a) being our hiding-place from trouble, and (b) by placing his saving arms around us, so to speak, whether the evil comes at us from beyond us or from below us.

Now comes the word used in the psalm's heading *Let me instruct and teach you the way*. Who is the speaker here? Is it the psalmist still, now that God has rescued him and heard his guilt-laden confession? *The way* in that case does not mean "following the moral law", even the Law of Moses. It is turning back to the Father, like the Prodigal Son did, and saying, "Father, I have sinned . . ." *Not* to come home and tell him all one has done is completely stupid. An animal cannot feel the blessedness of relief at freedom from guilt; a man or woman can. Fancy living your life with a stone in your heart when there is a *way* to have it removed, a way by which one's whole life can be renewed.

The two ways. And how they contrast! There are the pangs of the wicked, says the psalmist, and there is accepting the *hesed* of God.

The temple musicians now take up the theme of the poet and turn the whole preceding ten verses into a congregational hymn. "Be glad *in the Lord*" they sing, not *in* one's experience of renewal, not *in* the new sense of relief that is so amazing, but *in the Lord.* Keep your priorities right, is what they are saying.

THE WORD OF THE LORD

Psalm 33:1-22

1   Rejoice in the Lord, O you righteous!
       Praise befits the upright.
2   Praise the Lord with the lyre,
       make melody to him with the harp of ten strings!
3   Sing to him a new song,
       play skilfully on the strings, with loud shouts.

4   For the word of the Lord is upright;
       and all his work is done in faithfulness.
5   He loves righteousness and justice;
       the earth is full of the steadfast love of the Lord.

6   By the word of the Lord the heavens were made,
       and all their host by the breath of his mouth.
7   He gathered the waters of the sea as in a bottle;
       he put the deeps in storehouses.

8   Let all the earth fear the Lord,
       let all the inhabitants of the world stand in awe of him!
9   For he spoke, and it came to be;
       he commanded, and it stood forth.

10 The Lord brings the counsel of the nations to naught;
       he frustrates the plans of the peoples.
11 The counsel of the Lord stands for ever,
       the thoughts of his heart to all generations.

12 Blessed is the nation whose God is the Lord,
    the people whom he has chosen as his heritage!

13 The Lord looks down from heaven,
    he sees all the sons of men;
14 from where he sits enthroned he looks forth
    on all the inhabitants of the earth,
15 he who fashions the hearts of them all,
    and observes all their deeds.

16 A king is not saved by his great army;
    a warrior is not delivered by his great strength.
17 The war horse is a vain hope for victory,
    and by its great might it cannot save.

18 Behold, the eye of the Lord is on those who fear him,
    on those who hope in his steadfast love,
19 that he may deliver their soul from death,
    and keep them alive in famine.

20 Our soul waits for the Lord;
    he is our help and shield.
21 Yea, our heart is glad in him,
    because we trust in his holy name.
22 Let thy steadfast love, O Lord, be upon us,
    even as we hope in thee.

This psalm has no heading. But we note that, along with Psalm 38 and Psalm 103, it has twenty-two verses. That is the number of letters in the Hebrew alphabet. You need the alphabet, the poet seems to suggest, to help you "spell out" the Word of the Lord.

We begin with a bidding to worship, one that is possibly intended to follow upon the last line of Psalm 32. The worship described here would require the help of quite a sophisticated orchestra and choirs, such as we read of in the late literature of the OT (e.g. Dan. 3:5). There must also always be a new song, for God is always doing surprising new things.

The Word of the Lord, say verses 4–5, is Love. This is the word *hesed*, his loyal-love which creates goodness of heart in men and women in its turn. God's Word works quietly, continuously, unnoticed, like a flow of thought and a movement of power in human lives. It can seldom be captured in moments or dates; it is like the growth of a child. Probably it is best seen in family life. Yet (a) it is new every morning; (b) it is absolutely reliable, for of course it is *hesed*; and (c) it is to be found everywhere in the whole earth.

The Word is creative. Prov. 3:19 says: "The Lord by Wisdom founded the earth." The Word of our psalm describes this Wisdom of God as if it came out of God's mouth as a spoken word, to enter then the world of space and time. We are to remember that the Hebrew word *dabhar* means both the word as it is spoken, and the word as it turns into event, or fact. We see this stated clearly at, for example, Josh. 23:14, where in the Hebrew "things" is literally "words". The mystery of God's creative actions can be expressed only in parable and metaphor, of course, because it is quite beyond the capacity of our human minds to understand God's mind in any other way. And so this poet says that God *gathered the waters of the sea as in a bottle*. Another poet says that God spoke his creative Word over the space of seven days (Gen. 1). All we can do is to stand in awe and wonder at the greatness of God and pay no attention to the small and niggling minds of those today who take it for granted that mankind must limit God's work to what scientific categories can comprehend.

In Gen. 1:3 all God had to do was to say: "Let light be!" and light *was*. So too God had only to say the words, "Let there be lights . . . " (Gen. 1:14), and the sun, moon, and stars *happened*. And as the climax of it all God just said: "Let us make man in our image" (Gen. 1:26). Here at verse 9 we have, *He spoke* (a very emphatic *He*, meaning the "living" God). *He spoke and it came to be*; *he commanded, and it happened*. What this means is that in his Wisdom God created, first, the world of *nature*, even as the geologist seeks to trace today, and second, *history*. It is the Bible alone, however, not the scientist, that is able to reveal the latter to us.

In the history of mankind, the Bible reveals to us how we can understand the meaning of our own human story, although from afar, in that we are following, a long way behind, the finger of God in our human lives. Professor Jacob Bronowski, taking the plan of God in human history as an indication of what God has always being doing in both areas, says: "Creation is a hand reaching straight into experience and arranging it with new meaning."

If God can create, he can also un create. The *"counsel" of the nations*, the word used in the very next line, is the same word as for God's creative wisdom. The counsel of the Lord is greater than the counsel of men, for it stands for ever. As for man's — "The best laid schemes of mice and men gang aft agley", as Robert Burns, the poet, wisely declared. Therefore how blessed are those who have the Lord as their God; they know that, being his children, they have actually inherited this mighty plan of his. Such an idea is beyond our human grasp, however, even though we may *know* it to be so. That is why it can be the gift of grace alone.

The word *sees* in verse 13 might mean casual looking. But in verse 15 where it occurs again, it is explained by *observes*. The King on the throne, who had *fashioned the hearts of them all*, understands them at a glance. We remember what "understanding" means here, for when Jesus *saw* the rich young ruler, we are told that he *loved* him.

Then follow two verses (16–17) which the majority of mankind have simply refused to believe. They show how helpless a human king really is. But over against him the King of heaven, who is in full control of events, is well contrasted. Look, says our poet, see for yourself. The Lord's eye rests upon those with whom he has covenanted in love. Because such is his *counsel*, his wisdom, he does not remove them from death, for death must come to all; nor does he transfer his loved ones out of a famine-stricken area. What he does do is to *keep them alive in days of famine*, and he does so by his Word.

Once again, then, all join together to sing about God's amazing grace, because, as the chorus says, *we hope in thee.*

A RECIPE FOR SERENITY

Psalm 34:1–7

A Psalm of David, when he feigned madness before Abimelech, so that he drove him out, and he went away.

1 I will bless the Lord at all times;
　　his praise shall continually be in my mouth.
2 My soul makes its boast in the Lord;
　　let the afflicted hear and be glad.
3 O magnify the Lord with me,
　　and let us exalt his name together!

4 I sought the Lord, and he answered me,
　　and delivered me from all my fears.
5 Look to him, and be radiant;
　　so your faces shall never be ashamed.
6 This poor man cried, and the Lord heard him,
　　and saved him out of all his troubles.
7 The angel of the Lord encamps
　　around those who fear him, and delivers them.

This is one of the *teaching* psalms. These were composed by the "Wisdom" school of writers. We read about them at Psalm 1. Others like it are Psalms 37, 49, 78, 105, 106, 111, 112, 127. Probably it belonged to a collection of poems that grew up over the centuries. You can "feel" the classroom in places in it, such as, for example, at verse 11. There young people would learn this poem off by heart, just as many of us did ourselves when we were children in Sunday School. Today the psalm can be suitably presented in a classroom by employing dialogue form. The following division of the text has been suggested: verses 1–3 one child speaks; verses 4–7 another answers him; verses 8–10 a third speaks; verses 11–14 the teacher interrupts; at verses 15–18, and at verses 19–22 two other speakers contribute to the dialogue.

To help the young people of olden days learn it easily in their own tongue, the poem was composed alphabetically. The first verse begins with Aleph, the second with Beth, and so on.

Compare Psalm 25. There are 22 letters in the Hebrew alphabet, but one is not used. Verse 22 here therefore is probably the chorus added on for all to sing. This turned a teaching poem into a psalm of praise.

As far as we know the psalm headings in the Psalter were added in the period of the Second Temple. Someone has evidently made the suggestion that this psalm would fit the period when David was serving as a mercenary soldier in the Philistine city of Gath. But this heading employs a word which was rare in David's day yet which was in general use in the late period of the OT. But then, as we in our turn read the psalm, we find that it also fits a still later period—ours! Throughout the Middle Ages, in the days before the Reformation, Psalm 34 was used as a Proper Psalm for Holy Communion, as well as during Passion Week. Martin Luther kept it in those places in the liturgy in his reformed service.

The Lord is good. That is how we begin. All human beings are born selfish and self-centred. It is only too easy to boast of your own achievements. Come and join me instead in *boasting in the Lord*, says our writer. This means *exalting his name*, not singly, but *together*.

A personal witness by another speaker follows at verse 4. This one declares that he had *sought the Lord*. God had given him, not just help, but himself! The joy of faith and awareness of God's presence will make *your faces radiant*. So far from self-centred boasting is our poet that he now calls himself just *this poor man*. Yet he is not a mere lone believer. He belongs in the fellowship of the People of God, around whom *the angel of the Lord encamped* when they were on their Wilderness journey from Egypt to the Promised Land (see Exod. 23:20). This angel does so still.

TEACHING THE FAITH

Psalm 34:8–22

8 O taste and see that the Lord is good!
   Happy is the man who takes refuge in him!

9 O fear the Lord, you his saints,
    for those who fear him have no want!
10 The young lions suffer want and hunger;
    but those who seek the Lord lack no good thing.

11 Come, O sons, listen to me,
    I will teach you the fear of the Lord.
12 What man is there who desires life,
    and covets many days, that he may enjoy good?
13 Keep your tongue from evil,
    and your lips from speaking deceit.
14 Depart from evil, and do good;
    seek peace, and pursue it.

15 The eyes of the Lord are toward the righteous,
    and his ears toward their cry.
16 The face of the Lord is against evildoers,
    to cut off the remembrance of them from the earth.
17 When the righteous cry for help, the Lord hears,
    and delivers them out of all their troubles.
18 The Lord is near to the brokenhearted,
    and saves the crushed in spirit.

19 Many are the afflictions of the righteous;
    but the Lord delivers him out of them all.
20 He keeps all his bones;
    not one of them is broken.
21 Evil shall slay the wicked;
    and those who hate the righteous will be condemned.
22 The Lord redeems the life of his servants;
    none of those who take refuge in him will be condemned.

A second personal testimony, verses 8-10. This speaker tells of what he has experienced, how God is so humble in his love for him that he will let him put out his tongue and actually *taste* God before committing himself to God's care. Then he invites his friends to see how the young lions can go hungry (or "young bucks" we might say today, turning the picture into a present day one). For these will find that there is nothing to taste. But those *saints* (members of the People of God) who do *seek the Lord*, will never go hungry again.

It is interesting that an unusual word for *man* is used at verse 8. The word describes the heroic type, the big strong individual, the "successful" man, we might say. So it is not the weak or effeminate man who is invited here, the kind of person who might be expected to be more "religious"; it is the lusty young warrior. This big strong character, then, is not above taking refuge in God. It is interesting to recall that Saint Columba of Iona was of this type. He began his life as a warrior. He was strong, capable of great treks over hill and dale, of ruling hundreds who served under him, able to face up to kings and commoners alike. God actually took him home to find refuge in himself on Columba's last evening on earth, for he died just as he was penning this very verse of our psalm.

Teaching the Faith. Prov. 8:32, and many verses in that book, use the very words of verse 11. Yes, it is possible to *teach* the Faith to young minds. You begin, it seems, not by talking about "religion", but about the situation where the young people find themselves at the moment, with all their zest for life. But the full life means keeping the Ten Commandments, and so deliberately seeking to do good to others. (We have already seen that this is the meaning of the Hebrew noun *good*.) It means running after and catching up with peace and harmony in human relationships, for these always seem to be sliding over the horizon and disappearing beyond reach. This passage is quoted in full at 1 Peter 3:10-12.

Members of both the opposing sides during the Spanish Civil War noticed the significance of the words we meet at verse 11, carved as they were over the door of a theological seminary that lay right between the two armies. That building, however, remained no less than a zone of peace.

The Lord is here. You don't need to feel alone (verse 15) in doing all these things. The Lord is with you in them, even as you set about your task in obedience to his call. This is true particularly of those who have felt themselves *crushed* by the wickedness of the world, or those who have almost lost hope. This fact then is good news indeed, an assurance that is offered to all the poor and stricken masses of humanity.

The Lord delivers from within, the poet says at verse 19. Not from "up in the sky", but right from within the *afflictions* which those whom God has *put right* with himself must continue to suffer. Such an act of God is itself his judgement, his decision on how to deal with the situation. His act of rescuing does not happen to the wicked, therefore, but *the Lord redeems the life of his servants*. They have now actually passed beyond the *condemnation*. (See what Paul says about this at Rom. 8:1.) *The Lord keeps all his bones*, or, as Jesus puts it, "Even the hairs of your head are all numbered" (Matt. 10:30). Nor does God even need to *slay the wicked. Evil* itself does it for him. Or, as we would express the idea in today's language, evil is self-destructive.

A CALL TO ARMS

Psalm 35:1–10

A Psalm of David.

1 Contend, O Lord, with those who contend with me;
    fight against those who fight against me!
2 Take hold of shield and buckler,
    and rise for my help!
3 Draw the spear and javelin
    against my pursuers!
  Say to my soul,
    "I am your deliverance!"

4 Let them be put to shame and dishonour
    who seek after my life!
  Let them be turned back and confounded
    who devise evil against me!
5 Let them be like chaff before the wind,
    with the angel of the Lord driving them on!
6 Let their way be dark and slippery,
    with the angel of the Lord pursuing them!

7 For without cause they hid their net for me;
    without cause they dug a pit for my life.
8 Let ruin come upon them unawares!
  And let the net which they hid ensnare them;
    let them fall therein to ruin!

9   Then my soul shall rejoice in the Lord,
        exulting in his deliverance.
10 All my bones shall say,
        "O Lord, who is like thee,
    thou who deliverest the weak
        from him who is too strong for him,
        the weak and needy from him who despoils him?"

Those who live a quiet, peaceful and perhaps uneventful life may find a psalm like this rather strange, and even disturbing. They may be tempted to think that it shows a spirit that is not very "Christ-like". But note two possible answers to such a view:

(1) Do we not bring to our reading of the Scriptures what we think ought to be there if that is our mood? If we were to try to read this psalm through the eyes of Jesus, would we not understand a bit better some of those "Hard Sayings" of his that we prefer to ignore?

(2) The great majority of people in the world do not live a quiet, peaceful and uneventful life; and if we do not realize this to be the case, then we are showing our narrow-mindedness and self-centredness. So this psalm may help us to understand ourselves more realistically. We have only to think of the Barrios of Rio de Janeiro, the slums of Bombay, Calcutta and Lagos, and the misery of the several millions of refugees of the world. Many simple folk are daily squeezed like the meat in a sandwich between the forces of the Right and of the Left in many lands while we sit at home in peace. We are to remember that the Bible is addressed to all people, and to persons in all states of life or physical or spiritual death.

The psalm is in three parts:

Part I. Verses 1–10, *Relentless Persecution*. The cry here could well have come out of a prison-camp, an Auschwitz, a detention centre, a prison-cell, or just be the voice of the helpless poor of many lands. And we are to remember that the God of both Testaments is explicitly the God of the oppressed. The rich and powerful will find it very hard to enter the Kingdom of God. The psalmist asks God to grant him the personal consolation of knowing that God alone is able to say to him, "*I am your deliverance*".

The difficulty, however, is that this unhappy soul takes it for granted that his enemies are God's enemies. He forgets that they too are poor, unfortunate human beings. We know how this view can form in people's minds, for example, in time of war, or even during a political or industrial confrontation. But this individual is really in a ghastly situation. Who then are we to judge him? Rather let us who live in peace and security learn to be compassionately understanding of the overwhelming horror such individuals are experiencing, and leave God to be their Judge.

His choice of words reveals his fear. In verse 3 he says: "*Say to my soul*" (the same word as "*life*" in the next verse—because he believes that his very life is at stake). He is undergoing a soul-shattering experience. Then he implores God to drive his enemies away as if they were *chaff before the wind*. However, God's instrument, he hopes, will be the *Angel of the Lord*; that is truly divine intervention! For this Angel was God's agent in the days of the Wilderness Wanderings of his people. But he was the "Angel" of the *Covenant*, (or "*messenger*" as the word is translated at Mal. 3:1), and so the agent of God as he pursued his loyal-love towards his stricken people (see Exod. 23:20–21). If we had suffered long and horribly at the hands of cruel men, would we not echo with exultation the words our psalmist utters in verses 9–10 once we had found freedom again? Mary, the mother of Jesus, belonged to those whom society called the *weak and needy* (verse 10), and so she begins her great song, at Luke 1:46, with the very words of this psalm, and then continues in the same vein.

MALICE, GOSSIP AND SLANDER

Psalm 35:11–28

11   Malicious witnesses rise up;
         they ask me of things that I know not.

12 They requite me evil for good;
    my soul is forlorn.
13 But I, when they were sick—
    I wore sackcloth,
    I afflicted myself with fasting.
    I prayed with head bowed on my bosom,
14   as though I grieved for my friend or my brother;
    I went about as one who laments his mother,
    bowed down and in mourning.

15 But at my stumbling they gathered in glee,
    they gathered together against me;
    cripples whom I knew not
    slandered me without ceasing;
16 they impiously mocked more and more,
    gnashing at me with their teeth.

17 How long, O Lord, wilt thou look on?
    Rescue me from their ravages,
    my life from the lions!
18 Then I will thank thee in the great congregation;
    in the mighty throng I will praise thee.

19 Let not those rejoice over me
    who are wrongfully my foes,
    and let not those wink the eye
    who hate me without cause.
20 For they do not speak peace,
    but against those who are quiet in the land
    they conceive words of deceit.
21 They open wide their mouths against me;
    they say, "Aha, Aha!
    our eyes have seen it!"

22 Thou hast seen, O Lord; be not silent!
    O Lord, be not far from me!
23 Bestir thyself, and awake for my right,
    for my cause, my God and my Lord!
24 Vindicate me, O Lord, my God, according to thy righteousness;
    and let them not rejoice over me!
25 Let them not say to themselves,
    "Aha, we have our heart's desire!"
    Let them not say, "We have swallowed him up."

26 Let them be put to shame and confusion altogether
     who rejoice at my calamity!
   Let them be clothed with shame and dishonour
     who magnify themselves against me!

27 Let those who desire my vindication
     shout for joy and be glad,
     and say evermore,
   "Great is the Lord,
     who delights in the welfare of his servant!"
28 Then my tongue shall tell of thy righteousness
     and of thy praise all the day long.

Part II. Verses 11–18, *Malicious Legal Proceedings.* The scene changes. But in how many a mock trial today is an innocent person not presented with trumped-up charges, which he knows he will not be given the chance to refute? Or, his accusers may put him through the third degree, even though they know well that he is not guilty of the charges made against him. The psalmist's torturers were people with twisted minds rather than deformed bodies. The psalmist calls them "cripples". It seems he had actually mourned and sympathized with one of his tormentors when the latter wept for a friend who had died, as much as if he had lost his own mother.

Many men and women never grow up to be mature citizens. Children can be excused for mocking a cripple in the school playground. But here it is grown-ups who treat the weak in this way. So these tormentors are what we today would call sadists. They are people who enjoy hurting those who can't defend themselves, and who "take it out" upon such ordinary people because they have a grudge against society as a whole. No wonder this poor man cries to God, in words we find scribbled on many a prison wall, "*How long, O Lord?*" For, of course, it was not given to our psalmist in the early days of Israel's monarchy to discover, in the providence of God, that he was in reality entering into the sufferings of the Servant whom we meet with at Isa. 53, and whose sufferings God himself could turn to his own glory.

Part III. Verses 19–28, *Gossip and slander*. What the psalmist describes here is what goes on in some of those lands that today suffer under a dictatorship, that is to say, political smears, the bugging of private homes, informing against dear ones to the authorities with nasty innuendoes, and so on: "*Aha, Aha, our eyes have seen it!*"

But so has God! he adds. Then why does God not act? This is surely the bitter cry of millions even as we read these words: "Arm of the Lord, awake, awake!" This is the first line of a well-known hymn that is based upon these verses here. "Awake—*for my cause*", cries the psalmist. We would agree that only he who has the simple faith of a child would dare to shout such a cry to the God of heaven and earth. Yet, does he not already receive, at least in part, the answer to his prayer when he discovers that other believers everywhere are praying for him? And for those who even now are rotting in detention: "O God, *Let them not say*, 'We have got him where we want him'; '*We have swallowed him up*'." Rather, let us, the friends of the prisoners of man's inhumanity to man, *who desire my vindication*, my being "put right" by God, *say evermore: "Great is the Lord, who delights in the welfare* [the *shalom*, the peace, fulfilment, completion, wholeness of life] *of his servant*"; or even, and perhaps more exactly, "*whose will is the peace of his servant*".

But how can this cry for help be classified amongst psalms of praise? The answer is that, just to express trust in God in such terrible extremities is in very fact an act of praise.

THE SERVANT OF THE LORD

Psalm 36:1–4

To the choirmaster. A Psalm of David, the servant of the Lord.

1 Transgression speaks to the wicked
      deep in his heart;
    there is no fear of God
      before his eyes.
2 For he flatters himself in his own eyes
      that his iniquity cannot be found out and hated.

3 The words of his mouth are mischief and deceit;
      he has ceased to act wisely and do good.
4 He plots mischief while on his bed;
      he sets himself in a way that is not good;
      he spurns not evil.

Psalm 35 ended with the sufferer calling himself *God's servant*. We had suggested moreover that, all unwittingly, the sufferer was actually sharing in the pain, humiliation and loneliness of the suffering servant of the Lord depicted in Isa. 53. Now, in the heading of this psalm, David is given the name of *the servant of the Lord*. Consequently, if he, the patent sinner, is so called, because he is also and at the same time a "saint", that is to say, a member of the covenant people of God, then we too, who read this psalm, are to see ourselves as servants of God in the same sense.

Picture of a rebel. This picture is presented to us in verses 1–4. The psalm begins with the Hebrew word *ne-um*. It is a strange word. We do not even know whether it is a noun or a verb. It occurs mostly in the writings of the Prophets. We translate it today by "oracle of . . .", or, much watered down in emphasis, by "says the Lord". See, for example, Amos 2: 11, 16. If the Lord is not the speaker (as he almost always is) then the word must clearly ask us to recognize that what is being said is an awe-ful declaration, one that stems of course ultimately from God himself. See, for example, Num. 24:3 and 2 Sam. 23:1. So we are to understand here God's horror at the words and actions of those who have rebelled against his love.

This raises an important issue. Who is it, we must ask, of all the peoples of the earth who are most under the judgment of God? Of course, all people are, for all people are sinners. But the present-day commonly held view that the masses of the "poor heathen of the earth" are all going to hell, and only those who have consciously put their faith in God, or who have been "born again", are "going to heaven", is not what we find in either Testament. About the time when this psalm was first used the prophet Amos expressed the mind of God quite vehemently (using the word *ne-um*). In chapters 1 and 2 Amos had pointed to the sins of the nations around him, and had declared God's wrath upon them (*not* his punishment; that word, found in the RSV, is not there in the Hebrew; only a little "it". The AV is correct at this point). But at chapter 3 verses 1–2 Amos has something else to say, this time, however, about the covenant people. And this time the idea of punishment *does* occur. In other words, it is those who have rebelled against God's initiative in loving them first before they could love him or reject him, who are under the greatest judgment, and not "the poor heathen" whom God has never called or chosen to be his servant people. So we are learning here what the idea of *the servant of the Lord* is all about.

So we see that *transgression* is not a good word to translate the Hebrew *pesha*. It is used of the person who breaks the covenant God has made with Israel, and which includes him as an individual within it. See how the word is used at Isa. 1:2–3. *Deep in his heart* rebellion whispers (as the NEB interprets it) *to the wicked man*, because he is no longer bound up with the God of the Covenant. In fact, the rebel now speaks like the old Greek philosopher who said, "Man is the measure of all things," or, to put the same idea in English public school language, "I am the master of my fate, I am the captain of my soul." Because he has broken with the Covenant, the rebel no longer has a star to guide him by outside of his own soul. That is why he soon begins to obey the whisper that he hears from within. In other words, he has changed his camp, and so his own-created ideas whisper to him from within as a kind of prophetic oracle (the word *ne-um*). On the other hand the rebel is quite unaware that mankind has an enormous ability at self-deception. Actually, if an Israelite put himself outside the Covenant he was no longer *able* to recognize that he was a sinner. Nor was he able to *hate his evil ways*. Without God he can't possibly see the truth of this; and he can't see the truth without God. So he is caught in a vicious circle. He has ceased to ponder the mystery of life and so to attempt to do what is good for God's plan. Oh how objectionable the rebel has now become in his smug assurance that he possesses all the answers!

PICTURE OF A MEMBER OF THE COVENANT

Psalm 36:5-12

5 Thy steadfast love, O Lord, extends to the heavens,
    thy faithfulness to the clouds.
6 Thy righteousness is like the mountains of God,
    thy judgments are like the great deep;
    man and beast thou savest, O Lord.

7 How precious is thy steadfast love, O God!
    The children of men take refuge in the shadow of thy wings.
8 They feast on the abundance of thy house,
    and thou givest them drink from the river of thy delights.
9 For with thee is the fountain of life;
    in thy light do we see light.

10 O continue thy steadfast love to those who know thee,
    and thy salvation to the upright of heart!
11 Let not the foot of arrogance come upon me,
    nor the hand of the wicked drive me away.
12 There the evildoers lie prostrate,
    they are thrust down, unable to rise.

Possessing a totally different view of life from the rebel who has rejected the Covenant, the poet can only exclaim the wonderful things about God that follow in verses 5–6. Notice that, unlike the rebel, the saint has nothing to say about himself. In fact, *Yahweh*, the Lord, is the first word of this new section. In language much like that of the 23rd Psalm he declares that *God* gives *the children of men refuge in the shadow of his wings* (surely a reference to the eagle's wings at God's gracious offer of his Covenant at Exod. 19:4), and that *God* spreads a table before his children, and fills their hearts with exultation and joy. The Hebrew is literally: "They became satiated with the finest delicacies of thy house", that is, God gives to his loved ones the best bits of the sacrificial animal, although the best bits are meant to go up to God (Lev. 3:11). This idea is parallel then to the cup running over of Psalm 23. Yet the picture here is somewhat different. The next line can be translated: "Give us to drink from the rivers of your Gardens of Eden."

This passage is great poetry. It sounds best though when sung with enthusiasm and joy. For it speaks of God's *hesed*, his loyal-love, and of his *emunah*, God's utter reliability. God's saving love (RSV *righteousness*) reaches as if to the mountain-tops, his judgments as if to those waters under the earth mentioned in the Second Commandment.

But *hesed* is a two way term. It can be best illustrated if we hear a man promising at his wedding to be totally loyal to his wife, that is, "till death us do part"; but equally a woman making her promise to him in exactly the same terms. God *creates* in our hearts whatever loyal-love we have towards him. This love then enables us to be loyal to all other members of the covenant people. This, as we have seen, is what we understand from the *feminine* form of the word *righteousness*, as it occurs in verse 6.

God is the source of all grace. It is only *in thy light that we see light*. It is only in God's *righteousness* and loyal-love (RSV steadfast love) that, in our turn, we can be loving to other people. Again, it is God alone who is completely reliable. He does not change. Thus it is that since true life for us is communion with God here and *now*, it follows that, at our death, God cannot be untrue to himself and simply "let us go". We can illustrate this by suggesting that it is not in order for us to ask another person, "Do you believe in life after death?" What we should ask is, "Do you believe in a faithful God?" Dr. Harris E. Kirk has written that "The whole Bible is a story of light". But that light is also life, and the *living* God, is, of course, the *fountain*, or source, of all life and light.

The Chorus. Verses 10–12 tell us the congregation's reaction to all this. To the question, Who is to receive such love, they answer with two statements, sung aloud. (a) Those who *know* God. This verb is another "covenantal" term, as in Amos 3:2. A husband "knows" his wife physically and mentally, in fact, in a total manner. What a description then of the mind of a believer! (b) Those who are erect, vertical, upright in heart—for only such can reveal God's *salvation* to other people! (This is that feminine word again.) Thus, to let one's foot slip and to become ego-centred once again, would be the supreme tragedy for any member of the covenant people of God. For, as we saw at verse 1, a man is helpless to save himself if he has rebelled against the Covenant and departed from it. So we finish with the prayer of verse 10: "Keep on showing us your *hesed*, Lord, for without it we are without hope." Only if God keeps on showering us with his grace can we ever hope to be the servants of the Lord.

THE RIGHTEOUS WILL POSSESS THE LAND

Psalm 37:1–15

A Psalm of David.

1 Fret not yourself because of the wicked,
    be not envious of wrongdoers!
2 For they will soon fade like the grass,
    and wither like the green herb.

3 Trust in the Lord, and do good;
    so you will dwell in the land, and enjoy security.
4 Take delight in the Lord,
    and he will give you the desires of your heart.

5 Commit your way to the Lord;
    trust in him, and he will act.
6 He will bring forth your vindication as the light,
    and your right as the noonday.

7 Be still before the Lord, and wait patiently for him;
    fret not yourself over him who prospers in his way,
    over the man who carries out evil devices!

8 Refrain from anger, and forsake wrath!
    Fret not yourself; it tends only to evil.
9 For the wicked shall be cut off;
    but those who wait for the Lord shall possess the land.

10 Yet a little while, and the wicked will be no more;
    though you look well at his place, he will not be there.

11 But the meek shall possess the land,
       and delight themselves in abundant prosperity.

12 The wicked plots against the righteous,
       and gnashes his teeth at him;
13 but the Lord laughs at the wicked,
       for he sees that his day is coming.

14 The wicked draw the sword and bend their bows,
       to bring down the poor and needy,
       to slay those who walk uprightly;
15 their sword shall enter their own heart,
       and their bows shall be broken.

This is another "teaching" psalm, easy to learn in the original because there it is alphabetic, each two verses (with the odd exception) beginning with a different letter. But the fact that a class-room poem can be included in a "hymn book" of praise to God shows that the Hebrews regarded biblical instruction as a necessary aid to faith. The psalm deals with both the fate of the wicked, and with the fate of the godly, discussing these two groups almost time about. Curiously enough it is addressed, not to God, as are most psalms, but to a class-room of young human beings. Yet it does not form a continuity right through. Rather it is a collection of proverbs, linked only by the letters of the alphabet. Today we find it interesting to discover that this psalm played an important role in the life of the Qumran Community, that Jewish sect which flourished in the century before Christ, and which preserved for us the Dead Sea Scrolls.

  Trust in the Lord. The section verses 1–4 begins with the words *Fret not yourself*, "Don't get hotted up about the *wicked*", or, perhaps, to use our slang phrase, "Don't get het up", for the verb really means to become hot. So also says Prov. 24:19. Clearly these verses belong originally to a school text-book. Equally clearly the youngsters know what it means to have put their trust in God already. So they are now learning that the wicked do not belong in the eternal order of things, and that that is why they cannot last. They are being told that we should just get on with living our lives quietly. Yet to say that the wicked do not last does not mean what some anti-social reformers in England in the Victorian era meant when they brought their charges against the Salvation Army. When it sought to redeem the outcasts of the slums of London these people declared that God had no plan to help those who had made a mess of their lives. But these proverbial sayings do not offer a reasoned doctrinal statement such as Job's friends placed before that poor sufferer. They express in plain, simple language what Israel's faith was all about—(a) Trust in the Lord; (b) Do good; (c) Enjoy the Lord. If you do these things, then (d) God will give you what you want most of all—himself!

Commit your way to him. To be precise what we have is: "Roll your way of life upon the Lord" in utter abandon. That is to say, "Let him look after you completely". Right in the heart of the African jungle, plagued by poisonous insects, gnawed by hunger, harassed by wild beasts and wild men and sickened by the slave trade, and finally dying on his feet, David Livingstone repeated this verse 5 each day, and from it found strength to go on, knowing that God *will act*! Remember, this is God's world, it says, not yours. So, relax!

Hope in him. Anger at the wicked gets you nowhere; in fact the anger you feel *tends only to evil.* As Jesus, who knew the psalms so well, said, "Blessed are the meek, for they shall inherit the earth" (Matt. 5:5). Our teacher now makes this statement twice over!

Verse 10 can mean more than appears on the surface. *Yet a little while* is probably used here "eschatologically", as Jesus uses it at John 14:19; that is to say, the verse may mean that beyond death the wicked will have disappeared. They may appear to be blessed at the present moment, but it won't last that way! Whereas the blessedness of the godly belongs to both this life and to the Beyond. So here we meet virtually with another of Jesus' "secondary" Beatitudes: "Seek first his kingdom and his righteousness, and all these things shall be yours as well" (Matt. 6:33). If the Lord can afford to laugh at the wicked, we read, in that he knows what the future holds for them, then so can we.

J.B. Priestley once wrote: "If I could be granted a virtue I have never possessed, I think I should ask for what the Bible calls 'meekness'. Not Uriah Heep, but quiet humility of the spirit, a not asking and not expecting too much." In his great work *A Study of History*, Arnold Toynbee writes: "This verse [verse 15] *Their sword shall enter their own heart*, can be illustrated from all the human story."

SOME PROVERBS

Psalm 37:16–26

16 Better is a little that the righteous has
    than the abundance of many wicked.
17 For the arms of the wicked shall be broken;
    but the Lord upholds the righteous.

18 The Lord knows the days of the blameless,
    and their heritage will abide for ever;
19 they are not put to shame in evil times,
    in the days of famine they have abundance.
20 But the wicked perish;
    the enemies of the Lord are like the glory of the pastures,
    they vanish—like smoke they vanish away.

21 The wicked borrows, and cannot pay back,
    but the righteous is generous and gives;
22 for those blessed by the Lord shall possess the land,
    but those cursed by him shall be cut off.

23 The steps of a man are from the Lord,
    and he establishes him in whose way he delights;
24 though he fall, he shall not be cast headlong,
    for the Lord is the stay of his hand.

25 I have been young, and now am old;
    yet I have not seen the righteous forsaken
    or his children begging bread.
26 He is ever giving liberally and lending,
    and his children become a blessing.

Our teacher has selected these proverbs to illustrate his theme.

Proverbs are timeless things; English ones like "Pride goes before a fall" have been current in our culture for centuries. So these proverbs chosen here can fit both the days of ancient Israel and our own time.

In verse 18 the phrase *the days of the blameless* explains the opposite of the phrase *the day of the wicked is coming* that we read at verse 13. It tells us that God is concerned even with our small worries. Verse 19 puts in two lines of verse the great biblical theme that a disaster, such as a famine, may in fact be a judgment, but that out of it God can bring no less than a blessing. (See and compare Matt. 6:25–34.) Notice how strong the *but* is which introduces verse 20. The verse then emphasizes the impermanence of the enemies of God, which is described in the language we find at Isa. 40:8: *The grass withers, the flower fades, but the word of our God will stand for ever;* and see Matt. 6:30.

Verse 22 reintroduces the theme that appears throughout this psalm, at verse 9, verse 11 and later at verse 29. It is that which we meet in the so-called Deuteronomic literature in the OT, viz., that there are only two roads set before us. Thus the passage in Deut. 30:15–20 culminates in the declaration: *"I have set before you life and death, blessing and curse; therefore choose life."* There is no third way, declares God. The statements in verses 23–24 find their echo at Prov. 20:24. Psalm 73 also takes up the theme of these two verses, but asks the question why it should be that a man's steps may slip. A person's *steps* are the calling God has chosen for them, whether as a carpenter, a housewife, a teacher, a nurse, an engineer, or whatever. *Though he fall*, for as a sinner this is quite a possible thing to happen, he is to remember that no matter how far he may descend, "underneath are the everlasting arms" (see Phil. 4:12).

At verse 25 we are given an old man's insights. Here is the elderly schoolmaster standing before his class of young people. One could raise theological objections to his statement. But he is not interested in theology. He just gives a personal witness based on a life of trust. He can do so because he is living *in* the

Kingdom where all his neighbours are his brothers and sisters.
Perhaps that is what verse 24 too means. Having been brought
up in a good home he has turned out to be a good citizen, and
has now brought up his children in the same way of faith. The
result is that his children too have now *become a blessing* to
others.

MORE PROVERBS

Psalm 37:27-40

27 Depart from evil, and do good;
    so shall you abide for ever.
28 For the Lord loves justice;
    he will not forsake his saints.

    The righteous shall be preserved for ever,
      but the children of the wicked shall be cut off.
29 The righteous shall possess the land,
    and dwell upon it for ever.

30 The mouth of the righteous utters wisdom,
    and his tongue speaks justice.
31 The law of his God is in his heart;
    his steps do not slip.

32 The wicked watches the righteous,
    and seeks to slay him.
33 The Lord will not abandon him to his power,
    or let him be condemned when he is brought to trial.

34 Wait for the Lord, and keep to his way,
    and he will exalt you to possess the land;
    you will look on the destruction of the wicked.

35 I have seen a wicked man overbearing,
    and towering like a cedar of Lebanon.
36 Again I passed by, and, lo, he was no more;
    though I sought him, he could not be found.

37 Mark the blameless man, and behold the upright,
    for there is posterity for the man of peace.

38   But transgressors shall be altogether destroyed;
        the posterity of the wicked shall be cut off.

39   The salvation of the righteous is from the Lord;
        he is their refuge in the time of trouble.
40   The Lord helps them and delivers them;
        he delivers them from the wicked, and saves them,
        because they take refuge in him.

Verse 27 brings us back to the dividing line that God has set
before his people, and then adds: *For the Lord loves justice.*
God loves ethical behaviour in *his* children, as did the schoolmaster in his pupils. This means that ethics depend upon
religion. You can't teach "Ethics" as a school subject apart from
God. Else men's ideas upon the realm of the ethical become
entirely relative to the mood and social values of the moment. If
we try to do this kind of thing, then we shall have abandoned
our Judaeo-Christian heritage and reverted to the Greek
concept that "Man is the measure of all things", instead of the
revealed will of God. The RSV is misleading when it says at
verse 28, *The children of the wicked shall be cut off*, as if the
children would have to suffer for the sins of their parents. The
word is *seed*, not *children*. So it means that the wicked won't
have children of their own—their women will have become
sterile.

   Verses 30–31 say something very important. *Wisdom* in the
OT does not cover a knowledge of scientific facts, although it
does cover "how to do it", as when one is handling tools. The
wise man is he who knows the mind of God, as God has revealed
himself in *Torah*. This means that an uneducated man can have
wisdom just as much as the educated. In Hebrew this is the
name of the first five books of the OT, and so is inclusive of the
Law of Moses. But *Torah* deals with much more than law. For
it contains an understanding (that is "wisdom") of the Exodus
from Egypt, that is to say, what God was doing at that time.
Thus it is more than knowing the Ten Commandments. In fact,
knowing all this in his heart is the mark of the truly wise man.
Perhaps our teacher knew the words we find at Jer. 31:33.

It is interesting how much of the Sermon on the Mount is to be found in this psalm. At Matt. 5:11 Jesus says: "Blessed are you when men revile you and persecute you . . . rejoice and be glad, for your reward is great in heaven." This is what is spoken of here at verses 32–33. Verses 34–38 express in still further proverbs the issues dealt with earlier in the psalm. But verse 35 is most impressive. We might paraphrase it with: "I have seen the financial empire of a millionaire prince of the dope scene collapse overnight" (see 1 John 2:17). The translation of this verse found in the AV has entered into the popular phraseology of the English language: " . . . the wicked, spreading himself like a green bay tree." But the RSV is more accurate.

The Chorus. As usual with the psalms, we close at verses 39–40 with a chorus to be sung by the congregation. Its words then reiterate the main theme. But we should note that, over against the evil activities of the "dope millionaire", the phrase *the salvation of the righteous*, which makes use of the feminine form of the word, refers to the loving activities of those whom God has first put right with himself. For God is the "source of their strength" (RSV *refuge*) *in time of trouble.* So they, in their turn, now receive the loving protection of the Saviour God.

THE CRY OF A DYING MAN (i)

Psalm 38:1–14

A Psalm of David, for the memorial offering

1 O Lord, rebuke me not in thy anger,
    nor chasten me in thy wrath!

2 For thy arrows have sunk into me,
    and thy hand has come down on me.

3 There is no soundness in my flesh
      because of thy indignation;
  there is no health in my bones
      because of my sin.

4 For my iniquities have gone over my head;
    they weigh like a burden too heavy for me.

5 My wounds grow foul and fester
   because of my foolishness,
6 I am utterly bowed down and prostrate;
   all the day I go about mourning.
7 For my loins are filled with burning,
   and there is no soundness in my flesh.
8 I am utterly spent and crushed;
   I groan because of the tumult of my heart.

9 Lord, all my longing is known to thee,
   my sighing is not hidden from thee.
10 My heart throbs, my strength fails me;
    and the light of my eyes—it also has gone from me.
11 My friends and companions stand aloof from my plague,
    and my kinsmen stand afar off.

12 Those who seek my life lay their snares,
    those who seek my hurt speak of ruin,
    and meditate treachery all the day long.

13 But I am like a deaf man, I do not hear,
    like a dumb man who does not open his mouth.
14 Yea, I am like a man who does not hear,
    and in whose mouth are no rebukes.

In the heading we find the words: *For the memorial offering*, or better, "To bring to remembrance". One of the amazing elements of our biblical faith is that God expects us to remind him of our needs! This psalm moves forward in three sections. Each section contains the cry to God of "Help!" The biblical writers all know that once God *remembers* his promise to be with his children, he will do something about their cry.

This connection between calling to mind and acting is carried on in the life of the Church in the "action" of the Lord's Supper. As Paul records the words of Jesus: "This do, in remembering me" or, "to bring me to remembrance" (1 Cor. 11:24).

The first cry of "Help!", verses 1–8. These are the words of a very sick person. He or she believes (a) that God has caused this physical pain in order to discipline, train, educate, (rather than *chasten*) his human child. And (b) that God has done this because his child has sinned against him. Like the archetypal figure of Cain in Gen. 4, however, he exclaims: "My punishment is greater that I can bear."

Before we expostulate and say: "God doesn't cause us pain; look how Jesus fought against pain and suffering", we should ask ourselves what verses 5–7 really mean. Most expositors find here a reference to the effect of sexual sins, perhaps even of sexual perversion. It was only "yesterday", so to speak, that the sulpha drugs and penicillin were made available to the world. In the literature of days gone by we read of horrible, painful deaths, such as that which is being described here—burning pain in the genitals, festering sores all over the body. The Bible is not mealy-mouthed about human degradation. It is completely realistic about the effects *of my foolishness*; otherwise the significance of the Good News, that God can forgive even the most degraded sinner, would not really be able to be grasped by a fallen world. Here we hear the cry of the unwilling homosexual, the pederast, the lesbian, the drug addict, the cry in fact of all those who have made their own hell in this life, and who are now having to lie in it. Verse 8 reflects the tumultuous self-loathing of many such captives to their own lust. No, indeed, God does not create these festering sores; what he has created is a human body which its owner is free to use or to abuse. On the other hand, in his mercy God may decide to employ the pain of the sores to *chasten me in his wrath* (verse 1), those very sores which *I* am responsible for creating in my own body.

We should note that syphilis is caused by a germ that spreads through the blood to the brain, the spinal cord, and the valves of the heart. It brings about a general paralysis and locomotor ataxia. The disease can be passed on to the unborn child. Gonorrhea, again, through the reproductive organs, can affect even the eyes of the baby as yet unborn.

The second cry of "Help!", verses 9–14. Self-righteous members of the "People of God" may turn from such degraded types in disgust. But what we hear from the lips of one such degraded libertine are the words of a prayer: *Lord, all my longing is known to thee.* Just imagine it! God enters into the tortured mind of even a syphilitic (see Matt. 6:8)! The sufferer feels his pulse failing. He stands face to face with the reality that he is afflicted with a form of *plague*, as it was thought to be in those days. For it is the word we find in Lev. 13–14 to cover the sicknesses dealt with in those chapters. That *the light of my eyes has gone*, could mean that he is on the point of committing suicide. Like a leper, he is cut off from all human company. He is thus all, all alone in the world. Just to be able to tell God about it, to *remind* God of the tortures of the self-damned, is enough to give the sufferer relief.

Was this poor individual really deaf through his own folly (verse 13), so that he could no longer hear human speech, or was it only that he felt like a deaf mute? Some scholars would render *My heart throbs* by "My mind is bewitched". If then that has happened to him by some witch-doctor, could he still be responsible for his own actions? Either way this poor creature had now cut himself off from the warm fellowship of those kindly people whom he had known before as his friends. So now he can offer no plea, for he cannot hide his pock-marks from the gaze of his fellows.

THE CRY OF A DYING MAN (ii)

Psalm 38:15–22

15 But for thee, O Lord, do I wait;
    it is thou, O Lord my God, who wilt answer.
16 For I pray, "Only let them not rejoice over me,
    who boast against me when my foot slips!"

17 For I am ready to fall,
    and my pain is ever with me.
18 I confess my iniquity,
    I am sorry for my sin.
19 Those who are my foes without cause are mighty,
    and many are those who hate me wrongfully.
20 Those who render me evil for good
    are my adversaries because I follow after good.

21 Do not forsake me, O Lord!
   O my God, be not far from me!
22 Make haste to help me,
   O Lord, my salvation!

The third cry of "Help!", verses 15–22. This part of the psalm is on a loftier plane. While human persons may not lift me out of the gutter, the psalmist sees, "*It is thou, O Lord my God who wilt answer*". He has discovered that he must confess that he is helpless. In his prayer he makes certain points:

(1) Just as the alcoholic or the lecher or the drug addict cannot help himself, but must first look to a power outside of himself, so he asks God to stop people crowing over him, since, in his human weakness he confesses he has made a ghastly mess of his life.

(2) He reminds God that he is bearing insufferable pain and that he is "on the point of collapse" (rather than *ready to fall*). However he comes to the point needed.

(3) At long last he makes confession to God of his *iniquity*, and finally declares that he is *sorry for his sin*. Till now he had only been sorry for himself, and had perhaps "blamed society" (as people say today) for the fact that he had *slipped* as he had done into the gutter. He recognizes that he has become a pariah who finds himself under a compulsion he cannot resist.

(4) However, because he is very human, he does say that the forces of temptation had been mighty strong. Yet why had these forces picked on him? Why, O God, had those temptations, those *living* (see RSV *ftn.*) adversaries of the human soul, fastened upon him, and not on someone else? In fact, he says to God, these forces had been behaving to me like Satan just when I had been trying hard to catch up with a decent life.

Finally, each individual in the congregation, having identified himself with this degraded and suffering sinner by singing the above psalm in public worship, now applies the cry of "Help!" to himself and to every person present at the service. All together, then, they beg for God's gift of the new nature of love (the feminine form of the word *salvation*) (see the Intro-

duction). Could we say that the members of the congregation
are now virtually confessing: "There, but for the grace of God,
go I?" This psalm editor was clearly feeling his way towards the
great reality that it is only through suffering love that human
beings accomplish living tasks for God. In fact, the keenest pain
comes forth from the fires of love.

AS I MUSED, THE FIRE BURNED

Psalm 39:1–13

To the choirmaster: to Jeduthun. A Psalm of David.

1 I said, "I will guard my ways,
      that I may not sin with my tongue;
   I will bridle my mouth,
      so long as the wicked are in my presence."
2 I was dumb and silent,
      I held my peace to no avail;
   my distress grew worse,
3   my heart became hot within me.
   As I mused, the fire burned;
      then I spoke with my tongue:

4 "Lord, let me know my end,
      and what is the measure of my days;
      let me know how fleeting my life is!
5 Behold, thou hast made my days a few handbreadths,
      and my lifetime is as nothing in thy sight.
   Surely every man stands as a mere breath!   *Selah*
6   Surely man goes about as a shadow!
   Surely for naught are they in turmoil;
      man heaps up, and knows not who will gather!

7 "And now, Lord, for what do I wait?
      My hope is in thee.
8 Deliver me from all my transgressions.
      Make me not the scorn of the fool!
9 I am dumb, I do not open my mouth;
      for it is thou who hast done it.
10 Remove thy stroke from me;
      I am spent by the blows of thy hand.

11 When thou dost chasten man
     with rebukes for sin,
   thou dost consume like a moth what is dear to him;
     surely every man is a mere breath!   *Selah*

12 "Hear my prayer, O Lord,
     and give ear to my cry;
     hold not thy peace at my tears!
   For I am thy passing guest,
     a sojourner, like all my fathers.
13 Look away from me, that I may know gladness,
     before I depart and be no more!"

David appointed Jeduthun as one of the chief musicians to lead public worship (see 1 Chron. 16:41-42; 25:1-3).

This psalm has been used in various ways: (a) The Synagogue has employed it to interpret Jacob's conversation with Pharaoh, Gen. 47:7-10; (b) The Anglican Prayer Book of 1549 recommended it be read at a funeral; (c) The Catholic Benedictine Order based its rule of silence upon verses 1-2. In all, the psalm raises certain deep questions of faith, questions that go beyond a rational answer.

I said (to, within myself), *I will guard my ways*, that is, my behaviour. My first act, of course, is to watch my *tongue*, my *mouth*, my speech. Yet keeping silent, says our psalmist, has been of *no avail*. I felt my heart boiling inside me, because I simply had to confront the wicked who were *in my presence*. I thought long and hard about it, and only then did I use my *tongue*. Our psalmist evidently shared with Jeremiah the violent experience of having a fire burn within him (Jer. 20:9).

For, even as I mused, I realized that there are far more important attitudes in life than merely getting *hot* (verse 3) about the wicked. For example, what is the meaning of life itself, their life and my life? How long have I got left to live? How short and insignificant my life really is (and therefore also my anger at the wicked) in the sight of the eternal God. In fact, this is so with all human beings. (Fancy shouting "Clash the cymbals!" at this point (i.e. *Selah*). How odd the psalms are!)

As to our wants and desires, well, we pursue money and what money can buy, then we die—and we have no idea who will enjoy the wealth we have heaped up, and for which we worked so hard. Thomas Carlyle condemned any amateur search for truth. He spoke of toying with it and coquetting with it as the sorest sin. Such a man who keeps saying "I think ... " when God has spoken, is living in a vain shadow. He himself *is* falsehood, Carlyle concluded.

So the fire had burned, and now I possessed the one and only answer to the basic questions of life. No human philosophy or science, I now knew, could meet my need. *My hope, Lord is in thee*, in fact, "my only hope", as the Hebrew says. Since God's presence and sustaining love are to be found only within the *covenant fellowship*, then, if I rebel against its bonds, any fool would have the right to laugh at me for such stupidity. (We have seen that "to rebel" (*trangress* in the RSV) is a covenant term.) I have finally realized that I too am a shadow that must depart. Of course I knew that all mankind must do so. But, Lord, I am bound in covenant with You! With You who are eternal! I see now that before this I was dumb, and didn't or couldn't open my mouth, but that it was You who opened it for me. No wonder I was the scorn of the atheist (RSV *fool*—see Ps. 1; Ps. 14:1). Such a man does not realize that You must be "cruel to be kind". Consequently he supposes that my faith makes me no better off than he is. On the other hand I have deserved all the punishment You have meted out to me. But do please remove Your *stroke* from me. (This is the word we find used of the Suffering Servant in Isa. 53:4.) For it is more than I can take. I am exhausted (RSV *spent*) *by the blows of thy hand* (verse 10). Remember, Lord, that my life is very short!

I admit that this divine *chastening* has been well deserved, and that it shows just how much God loves us. He could have ignored us. But no, he believes we are worth chastening for his name's sake. The words *consume like a moth* (or, rather, like the larva of the moth) describe the slow eating away of what is most precious to a man, that is, *what is dear to him*, his beauty of soul, his attractiveness, his desirableness (as at Isa. 53:2).

The final cry expresses the pathetic bewilderment of one who can't understand God's ways with him, his servant and his child, despite the conclusion he (or someone else) had come to above. He cannot fathom what Isaiah calls "God's strange work" (Isa. 28:21). The RSV can mislead us when it says, *Hold not thy peace*; for the verb has nothing to do with *shalom*, peace. What he says is, "Don't be deaf to my tears! (I declare) that I, even I, am but a resident alien with You, that is, I don't believe I am really a citizen of Your kingdom. Along with all my ancestors I am just a squatter, and that too in the very land which You gave us as our possession for ever!" Our psalmist is evidently tempted to suppose that the promises of God made to Israel, recorded at Exod. 19:5, were simply untrue. He had, however, forgotten God's great declaration at Lev. 25:23: *The land is mine; for you are strangers and sojourners with me.* And how often has that curious anomaly not obtruded itself throughout history, especially in the history of the Jewish people.

So our poor man cries: *Look away from me, that I may know gladness.* For when You do look my way You cause me nothing but grief and pain—*before I depart and be no more.* What a tragic end to the psalm!

I WAITED AND WAITED (i)

Psalm 40:1-5

To the choirmaster. A Psalm of David.

1 I waited patiently for the Lord;
  he inclined to me and heard my cry.
2 He drew me up from the desolate pit,
   out of the miry bog,
 and set my feet upon a rock,
   making my steps secure.
3 He put a new song in my mouth,
   a song of praise to our God.
 Many will see and fear,
   and put their trust in the Lord.

4   Blessed is the man who makes
        the Lord his trust,
     who does not turn to the proud,
        to those who go astray after false gods!
5   Thou hast multiplied, O Lord my God,
        thy wondrous deeds and thy thoughts toward us;
        none can compare with thee!
     Were I to proclaim and tell of them,
        they would be more than can be numbered.

The editors of the Psalter may have deliberately placed Psalm
40 to follow Psalm 39. The latter psalm ended in near despair.
This one begins from such a point. *I waited and waited for the
Lord*, says our author, using the Hebrew idiom, which is *not*
that of the RSV, "I waited patiently . . .". In fact, if he was in the
mood of Psalm 39, he waited most impatiently.

There are at least two speakers in this psalm, "me" and the
"minister", the cultic prophet.

I speak, verses 1–3. God does act, then, in his own good time
and wisdom. Just as he did with Jeremiah (see at Ps. 39:3), so *he
drew me up from the desolate pit*. Jeremiah had to undergo just
such physical hauling up when he was pulled out of the mud at
the bottom of a cistern hewn in a rock (Jer. 38:6–13). But on
another occasion Jeremiah declared, *They have dug a pit for
my life* (Jer. 18:20, 22) with clear reference to a spiritual
experience. Here then the psalmist makes use of this kind of
strong pictorial language that goes right back in its usage to
David himself (see, for example, Psalm 18). In this way he
describes what it means to be rescued from the kind of hell that
Psalm 39 speaks of. God's forgiveness wipes the slate clear, so
that the sinner can begin life over again as if the past has never
even happened. No wonder, then, the psalmist can declare, *He
put a new song in my mouth, a song of praise to our God.*
Notice (a) even the song has to be a gift from God, not his own
words; (b) he is *our* God; we all share in the joy of this new
beginning; and (c) the joy he now possesses becomes a witness
to others. It draws them in their turn into *putting their trust in
the Lord.*

There is a passage in Dante's *Paradiso* describing the redeemed in heaven. It tells of how, when they think back to their sins on earth, they can no longer see them as sins but only as opportunities for God to shower his grace upon the sinner.

It appears that this poor sinner (was he in fact the author of Psalm 39?) had come to public worship and there had made this great declaration. Theologically speaking, however, he said more than he knew. The *desolate pit*, or *pit of tumult* (see RSV *ftn.*) was a phrase used to describe the lowest level of Sheol, the abode of the dead. To reach there, God would have had to go down into those depths himself before he could "draw him up" out of the mud. In other words, what we have is a pictorial interpretation of the phrase we find in the Creed: "He descended into Hell." Because of this, St. Francis of Assisi considered this to be his favourite verse in the Bible, and in consequence patterned his own life of love and compassion upon it.

The Minister speaks, verses 4 5. After he had made his great statement in public it seems as if the cultic prophet at the temple, or as we have called him, the "minister", takes up the theme and develops it, giving God all the glory. *Blessed is the man* (the Hebrew word for a person of position in society) *who makes the Lord his trust*, and does not *go astray after false gods,* for example, the wiles of materialism. *Thou hast multiplied thy wondrous deeds* can be understood to mean "Thou art ever adding to thy miracles". Calming a storm is a strange deed, but, after all, it is understandable in terms of natural events. The real miracle the Bible is concerned with is in the area of redemption; for example, that God should go down into the pit to rescue a sinner, and then utterly transform his life to one of joy and compassion. It is a miracle because the sinner did not do this for himself. God had *thought* it out first *toward us*; then the thought had become action—not once, but countless times.

I WAITED AND WAITED (ii)

Psalm 40:6–8

6 Sacrifice and offering thou dost not desire;
   but thou has given me an open ear.
   Burnt offering and sin offering
   thou hast not required.
7 Then I said, "Lo, I come;
   in the roll of the book it is written of me;
8 I delight to do thy will, O my God;
   thy law is within my heart."

I speak. I came here prepared to offer a thanksgiving sacrifice in gratitude to God for what he had done for me. The word *sacrifice* is *zebah*; it is described in Lev. 4 and 7. It included the slaughtering of an animal. *Offering* is *minhah*, a free-will extra gift to God by way of saying "Thank you" (Lev. 7:12–15). But I have now found that God does not want me to offer either of these sacrifices. What he wants of me is to live a life of obedience. And so follows one of the great biblical statements of what it means to be a believer (or, could we say, a Christian?).

We are to realize that God has a plan for the life of each one of us. He has created us with ears to hear, as Jesus put it. This can be understood in two ways: (a) *An open ear* means the ability to know and understand what God is whispering to us, so that from hour to hour we know exactly where our duty lies. (b) As we see from the RSV *ftn.* the phrase can mean *ears hast thou dug for me.* But "dug" is not the best picture-word to use. When a slave had served his time and was set free, under the Law of Moses he was given the option of remaining in service to his master, as a free man, choosing to do so because he loved and trusted his master, and was glad and proud to work for him. In that case his master stood him up against the door-post of the family home and nailed the emancipated slave's ear to the door-post. He thus dug a hole through his ear (for the verb can mean this) with a nail. The hole that remained thereafter always reminded him of the one whom, of his own free will, he had decided to serve in loyalty and obedience (see Exod. 21:5-6; Deut. 15:12-17). Such then is a picture of the willing service of the redeemed sinner, now that he has found forgiveness and freedom. Paul speaks of this at Rom. 12:1.

I now say to God: *Lo, I come*, bringing myself, not any sacrificial gifts, for such is the plan of my life as it is *written* in God's *book*. In that book there is actually a whole chapter written just about me! I am thrilled *to do thy will, O my God*; I know exactly what I am to do, because *thy law* (better, "revelation") exists in my inner being—not just in my heart (RSV) but in all the various organs of my body.

A highly-qualified young man was called upon by a group of church people. They told him they believed he was the right and obvious man to undertake a special task of service. His reply was: "An answer to this will demand a long period of prayer and fasting." How far that answer was from the insight of this psalmist! He declares that he would know *at once*, in his "guts" (as the word *heart* here really means) what the will of God was for him. Incidentally, this young man in question, after weeks of prayer, accepted, but proved to be a failure at the task. What a high degree of egotism there can be in some types of prayer!

This passage has been put into the mouth of Christ in Heb. 10:5-7. But *Hebrews* being in Greek, the quotation is made, not from the Hebrew text we have here, but from the LXX. There it reads: "A body hast thou prepared for me." Where the LXX reading arose from it is difficult to say. But the outcome of the passage is the same. God had given Jesus a body in which to do his will in the flesh, or, in other words, in which to be completely obedient (see John 4:34).

I WAITED AND WAITED (iii)

Psalm 40:9-17

9 I have told the glad news of deliverance
      in the great congregation;
   lo, I have not restrained my lips,
      as thou knowest, O Lord.

10   I have not hid thy saving help within my heart,
     I have spoken of thy faithfulness and thy salvation;
     I have not concealed thy steadfast love and thy faithfulness
         from the great congregation.

11   Do not thou, O Lord, withhold
         thy mercy from me,
     let thy steadfast love and thy faithfulness
         ever preserve me!
12   For evils have encompassed me
         without number;
     my iniquities have overtaken me,
         till I cannot see;
     they are more than the hairs of my head;
         my heart fails me.

13   Be pleased, O Lord, to deliver me!
         O Lord, make haste to help me!
14   Let them be put to shame and confusion altogether
         who seek to snatch away my life;
     let them be turned back and brought to dishonour
         who desire my hurt!
15   Let them be appalled because of their shame
         who say to me,"Aha, Aha!"

16   But may all who seek thee
         rejoice and be glad in thee;
     may those who love thy salvation
         say continually, "Great is the Lord!"
17   As for me, I am poor and needy;
         but the Lord takes thought for me.
     Thou art my help and my deliverer;
         do not tarry, O my God!

I continue. In the face of the large congregation at festival time I
have shouted the one glad word "Deliverance!" I didn't hold
back, *as thou knowest, Lord.* The word *deliverance* is the
masculine word, referring to God's act of rescuing me "out of
slavery". So next the word *saving help,* which is feminine,
follows from it. The change God has made in my life when he
gave me both the desire and the strength to deliver others from

"slavery in Egypt" I have not kept bottled up inside me, meaning, "I have concerned myself for others in love". I have spoken out before the congregation *about thy faithfulness and thy salvation* (which are now aimed at others through me) as well as about *thy loyal covenant love and fidelity* to me as an individual.

As for You, Lord, don't ever withhold your mother-love (not *mercy*) from me (see the Introduction). Keep on caring for me with your covenant love and fidelity. (You know well) that countless evils encircle me, even those I had never noticed before, and that my feelings of guilt keep on catching up with me.

Our psalmist is aware, just as Martin Luther was, that the redeemed sinner still remains a sinner. His famous phrase was *Justus ac peccator.* Consequently he needed God's continuing faithfulness. For of course the more he became aware of God's forgiving love, the more sins he came to recognize within his *heart* that needed to be forgiven.

Be pleased means "Make it part of Your eternal plan written in the roll of Your book [verse 7] to keep on rescuing me". Here, as in other psalms, his enemies may well be the temptations and feelings of guilt that keep on welling up inside him and which *seek to snatch away my life.* Real life is fellowship with God. Anything that deprives me of this fulness of life which is God's gift should be shamed out of existence. Saint Augustine knew the reality of this statement. "Thank God", he once said, "I am not responsible for my dreams."

The Chorus, verses 16–17. So we reach a happy conclusion. The choir contrasts (a) the perverted glee of those who say "Aha, Aha!" with (b) the enthusiastic joy of those who love "making", "creating" God's *shalom*, as Jesus says at Matt. 5:9,12, for it is something that comes alive in the community. For they do so *ad majorem Dei gloriam*, "to the greater glory of God".

As we have noted before, there is no word in the OT for "religion". The Epistle of James 1:27 reminds the early Christians what true "religion" is all about—no sacrifices, as the psalmist had found, no saying of creeds, not even prayer and fasting; it was basically obedience, shown in loving service to others, to the God who had given his loving service to us.

What is this glory of God? It is his concern for *the poor and needy*, for the powerless, for the disenfranchised, for the wretched of the earth (see Prov. 23:10–11). Such people are not "hands" in a factory, or statistics in a United Nations survey. Each one is a *me*, a human soul, a child of God. And *the Lord takes thought for me*, ceaselessly, as the verbal form shows. And, of course, I am bound up in the bundle of *life* in and with the *living* God (1 Sam. 25:29). Moreover, the word for *Lord* here is not the usual *Yahweh*; it is the *Master* for whom a servant must work every day.

In this way, then, we reflect back to the ideas we found at verse 6. But in all this he is *my help and my deliverer*. So, "keep at it, O my God" (rather than, *Do not tarry*), sings the choir, with the almost cheeky familiarity of those who know that their God loves them and does not mind what language they use to him.

BLESSED ARE THE MERCIFUL

Psalm 41:1–13

To the choirmaster. A Psalm of David.

1 Blessed is he who considers the poor!
    The Lord delivers him in the day of trouble;
2 the Lord protects him and keeps him alive;
    he is called blessed in the land;
    thou dost not give him up to the will of his enemies.
3 The Lord sustains him on his sickbed;
    in his illness thou healest all his infirmities.

4 As for me, I said, "O Lord, be gracious to me;
    heal me, for I have sinned against thee!"
5 My enemies say of me in malice:
    "When will he die, and his name perish?"
6 And when one comes to see me, he utters empty words,
    while his heart gathers mischief;
    when he goes out, he tells it abroad.

7 All who hate me whisper together about me;
  they imagine the worst for me.

8 They say, "A deadly thing has fastened upon him;
  he will not rise again from where he lies."

9 Even my bosom friend in whom I trusted,
  who ate of my bread, has lifted his heel against me.

10 But do thou, O Lord, be gracious to me,
   and raise me up, that I may requite them!

11 By this I know that thou art pleased with me,
   in that my enemy has not triumphed over me.

12 But thou hast upheld me because of my integrity,
   and set me in thy presence for ever.

13 Blessed be the Lord, the God of Israel,
   from everlasting to everlasting!
   Amen and Amen.

Book I of the Psalter ends with the end of this psalm. It began with the phrase "Blessed be the man . . ." (Ps. 1:1); now it ends with a psalm that begins in the same way, but whose last line is rather "Blessed be the Lord . . .". Clearly we have learned much about God since we began to read about him forty-one psalms back.

Psalm 1 was a "teaching" psalm. Psalm 32 had used the word *maskil*, which we saw had to do with teaching and learning. Now we find the word *maskil* again, hidden behind the English word *considers*. So we learn here what the blessed life is all about.

There are people who take it for granted that to be "religious" means to enjoy one's personal salvation. So they seek out those groups which, week by week, meet together to clap their hands and feel "happy in the Lord". They believe that to do this makes them "blessed". But this psalmist believes differently. Here is the group of teenagers we have met before, who, as the coming bureaucracy of Israel, are being instructed on their duties. Most unexpectedly then, the very first line that they are given to learn off by heart is: "*Blessed is he who* is keen to learn about the *poor*" (or, equally, the *weak*, RSV *ftn.*). Such an administrator, says the teacher, *the Lord protects*, and the common people *call him blessed*. Even if he falls ill, and has to go off work, *the Lord sustains him*. And then, a lovely touch, (see RSV *ftn.*), *thou changest all his bed*; God sits beside him, so to speak, at his bedside, and, like a competent and kindly nurse, even changes the soiled sheets. Often enough God is called the Great Physician; here he is the Visiting Nurse.

As for me, verse 4. Yet there are always those who do not appreciate the kindly and merciful public servant. They suspect him of ulterior motives. So when this man falls ill, these others actually hope he will soon die. Some of his fellow-employees, with their tongue in their cheek, bring him flowers and grapes (could we say!). "But I know perfectly well that they are pure hypocrites," he says, "for they go away again saying only nasty things about me." That then is why I can only cry, *O Lord, be gracious to me, heal me*, for I have done "the wrong thing for thee" (that is what the verb probably means in this context). "Did I really misunderstand You, Lord," is what he asks here, "when I honestly sought to be Your obedient servant in public life, and tried to serve the poor?"

This is a very important and harrowing question that faces many, many people today, especially if they are salaried by a government that expects its public servants to rule the masses of the poor and weak (verse 1) with an iron glove.

So this man, whose conscience has urged him to obey God rather than Caesar, has to bear the cost of his kindly witness. In a land where the administrator and the police are forced to act harshly, no one dares deviate from the accepted rules. If he dares to do so, he "lets the side down", for by his action he could easily bring trouble on his mates. Here one of this man's "mates", *a bosom friend in whom I trusted*, had informed against him to the authorities. And so there was no one left to turn to but the Lord. Those who are merely "happy in the Lord" can only too easily leave the Cross out of their knowledge of God's goodness.

But poor man, he has become utterly soured and disillusioned by events. Consequently, what he wants God to do for him is to let him get his own back on the informers! If God should do so, he believes, it would show that he was pleased with his way of life and concern for the poor after all. For God has indeed "kept his grip upon me" (RSV *upheld*) and never let me go because, as I believe, he has put in my heart his own concern for the poor and needy.

Just as Jesus shows, in his parable of the Last Judgment (Matt. 25), that it is those who *consider the poor and weak* who enter into eternal life, so does this psalmist now. God forgives him his very human desire for revenge. The poor man had been provoked to that point, indeed. But his wild plea to God could not detract from his total commitment to the service of all God's "little ones". In fact, as the Chorus declares, *Blessed be the Lord*, who, as the God both of forgiveness and of love, can handle all our vicious and stupid thoughts, and use them to his greater glory!

ABANDONED

Psalm 42:1-11

To the choirmaster. A Maskil of the sons of Korah.

1 As a hart longs
   for flowing streams,
 so longs my soul
   for thee, O God.
2 My soul thirsts for God,
   for the living God.
 When shall I come and behold
   the face of God?
3 My tears have been my food
   day and night,
 while men say to me continually,
   "Where is your God?"
4 These things I remember,
   as I pour out my soul:
 how I went with the throng,
   and led them in procession to the house of God,
 with glad shouts and songs of thanksgiving,
   a multitude keeping festival.

5 Why are you cast down, O my soul,
       and why are you disquieted within me?
   Hope in God; for I shall again praise him,
6   my help and my God.

   My soul is cast down within me,
       therefore I remember thee
   from the land of Jordan and of Hermon,
       from Mount Mizar.
7 Deep calls to deep
       at the thunder of thy cataracts;
   all thy waves and thy billows
       have gone over me.
8 By day the Lord commands his steadfast love;
       and at night his song is with me,
       a prayer to the God of my life.

9 I say to God, my rock:
       "Why hast thou forgotten me?
   Why go I mourning
       because of the oppression of the enemy?"
10 As with a deadly wound in my body,
       my adversaries taunt me,
   while they say to me continually,
       "Where is your God?"
11 Why are you cast down, O my soul,
       and why are you disquieted within me?
   Hope in God; for I shall again praise him,
       my help and my God.

Book II of the Psalter begins with the cry of a loyal worshipper who by necessity is far away from the Jerusalem temple; and oh! how this exile would love to be there now to be one of the throng of worshippers!

It is said that there is a hole in the heart of everyone—ancient Israelite, modern Christian, Chinese Buddhist, Californian secularist alike, and that that hole is a God-shaped hole. Only God can fill it, they say, with—himself. The "ecumenical" nature of this psalm thus shows up clearly when we realize that in this book of the Psalter, the name Yahweh, the name of the Covenant God of Israel, seldom occurs. In this collection of psalms nearly always it is *elohim* whom people call upon, the general word for "God" that all men can use. So here we hear the longing of any human soul who knows that life is empty and meaningless without, not just "God", but *the living God*. For there are "gods" galore in the world who are as dead as a piece of wood.

We begin with an illustration from nature, from the vast sandy steppe-land of the area east of Palestine. There we see a lonely female deer roaming aimlessly in circles, desperately searching for a "wadi" or a spring of water. Does the illustration suggest that the psalmist, for this once at least, is a woman? And why not?

When shall I come and behold the face of God? This last phrase "to behold the face of . . ." is a technical term for going up to Jerusalem to attend a festival to worship and to meet with God. It is the OT equivalent of the Arabic word *hajj*, the name given to the pilgrimage to Mecca made by any good Muslim. But where was she when she made her cry? Was she perhaps the wife of a merchant who must make long trips to the East for the sake of trade in such spices as frankincense and myrrh? Was she a captive taken on a slave raid? How often such a horror happened in those days, when a whole village could be attacked, the men killed off, and the women and children sold into slavery. At Amos 1:6 that prophet pronounces the judgment of God upon the city of Gaza—only fifty miles from Jerusalem—which for century after century had made itself rich from a trade in living human beings. Or was the speaker now a political exile residing either on the plateau of the country which we today call the Hashemite Kingdom of Jordan, or was she amongst the mountains of Lebanon (verse 6)?

I remember says she, as we all do. I recall how I used to go (the grammar of the verb implies "regularly") with the crowd of worshippers, even heading the procession, starting from the city gate, then proceeding through the streets, and going right on into the temple courtyard. What a happy time it was; we all shouted and sang songs of thanksgiving. (We in our turn must

now ask ourselves, "What were they saying thanks for?") So
why should I be depressed, she adds. The time will surely come
when I shall make the pilgrimage once again to see the face of
my God, my *help*. This last word is quite extraordinary. The
Hebrew text may be at fault. But it seems to refer, in a very
condensed form, to "a saving act of God each time the worshipper saw his face".

But the fact is, my soul *is* cast down. There is no use in hiding
the reality. But that is exactly why I call You to mind! For You,
God, are my only hope, even here where I am in a far country.

The next verse is not an illustration taken from nature. The
word *deep* is the technical term for the waters of chaos that boil
away under the earth, and which we hear about in the Second
Commandment. Again, the mention of *waves* and *billows* is
certainly not a literal reference to the Mediterranean Sea.
Rather, what our lady psalmist is saying is that she is in danger
of being completely overwhelmed by the powers of evil, such as
we see boiling up in the Gaza slave-market. Yet, *by day*, that is,
each new day, the Lord *commands* (what a vivid form of
speech!) his *hesed*, the name of that covenant love of his that
will never let her go. And, she adds, *in the night his song is with
me*, in the sense of being right in my heart, sounding as a *prayer
to the God of my life*. It is quite possible, of course, that her
enemy might be merely the bad mood she feels herself in, her fit
of depression that overwhelms all of us at times, and not the
slave-owners of Gaza.

There appears, however, to be an awful contradiction here. *I
say to God*, on the one hand, You are *my Rock*, immovable,
unchanging love. But then, on the other hand, *why have You
forgotten me?* The following picture could well be that of a
slave-market, the *enemy* being the Philistines of Gaza. There
she stands, our poor, abandoned, forgotten, despised Israelite
young woman, naked, for sale, with the wounds of a lash in her
flesh, literally, "with murder in my bones", the crowd around
her "slashing me with taunts": "That God of yours who lives in
his temple up there in Jerusalem, why doesn't he save you
now?"

It is at this moment, however, that there wells up in her mouth that cry of faith and confidence (repeated from verse 5) which has been repeated in turn by countless martyrs right till the present day. This wonderful woman can make her quiet response to the jibes of her masters simply because she is utterly sure that the *living* God is there already in her future.

O LEAD ME HOME!

Psalm 43:1-5

1   Vindicate me, O God, and defend my cause
     against an ungodly people;
  from deceitful and unjust men
     deliver me!
2   For thou art the God in whom I take refuge;
     why hast thou cast me off?
  Why go I mourning
     because of the oppression of the enemy?

3   Oh send out thy light and thy truth;
     let them lead me,
  let them bring me to thy holy hill
     and to thy dwelling!
4   Then I will go to the altar of God,
     to God my exceeding joy;
  and I will praise thee with the lyre,
     O God, my God.

5   Why are you cast down, O my soul,
     and why are you disquieted within me?
  Hope in God; for I shall again praise him,
     my help and my God.

Some scholars believe that this short psalm was once continuous with Psalm 42. This may be the case. Psalm 42 could be regarded as being two separate cries for help made by a very lonely person, the first being 42:1-5, the second being 42:6-10, with verse 11 as the Chorus. Perhaps then 43:1-2 forms the third part of this one psalm. If so, then it could be summed up in this further cry: "Then, O God, why don't you fetch me home?"

I may ask an advocate to *defend my cause*. He would then stand beside me and plead on my behalf while the judge listened to the argument put forth from both sides. But in the OT we meet with an extraordinary variation from the way we think a law court should be organized. For in the OT God is *both* the Judge *and* the Advocate at the same time! This is of course one way of saying that he is both Judge and Saviour at once.

Here then (a) God as Advocate has pleaded my cause, but (b) God as Judge has not as yet made any response; he has kept silent. At Job 19:25 Job declares with complete assurance that this *Redeemer*, or "Vindicator" as the RSV *ftn*. translates it, and so even his Advocate, is alive. Consequently, *from my flesh I shall see God, whom I shall see on my side*. The Hebrew text of that passage is in bad repair, but we at least glimpse from it these two aspects of the loving purpose of God. So then, says our psalmist, *Defend my cause*, Lord, against a people who are not members of Your covenant, consequently a people who don't know the Ten Commandments or the meaning of justice. *Why have You rejected me?*, when I am up against unbelievers who are a law unto themselves.

The final answer. Beginning at verse 3 we meet with such a lovely passage that it has been repeated or sung all down the centuries. When mankind was shut out of the Garden they found it impossible to turn round and go back in again (Gen. 3:24). Only God can lead us back home to himself. Moreover God is to be found on *thy holy hill* and *at thy dwellings* (plural in the Hebrew). (As we would say today, he is to be found at any of the local fellowships of believing people.) Then when I get home there I will follow a joyous and exciting experience, the psalmist declares. More even than that is meant however. God does not just give us joy. He *is* our joy itself! He *is* our exultation! No wonder we hear finally the excited and thrilled ejaculation: "O God, my God!"

When Dr. Samuel Johnson made his historic tour of Scotland accompanied by his loyal secretary, the Scot, Boswell, the latter took Johnson one Sunday to hear the local congregation sing this psalm in its metrical version: "And why with vexing thoughts art thou disquieted in me?" To this Dr. Johnson said: "Some men don't have vexing thoughts." To which Boswell replied, "To me they have been very real ever since I sang this psalm in my boyhood days."

Surely we would agree with Boswell. Life is not always a bed of roses. As Bonhoeffer discovered in his Berlin prison, there are times in life when we are evidently meant to live as if God were not. On the other hand, the psalmist finally shakes off his doubts. In ancient Mesopotamia—and we possess information on this from an Akkadian cylinder seal—they had two lesser divinities who conducted the suppliant to the throne of the Great God. Our psalmist adopts this ancient picture, but puts in the place of the two pagan gods two others, whom he calls Light and Truth. He prays God to send these Two who will bring him home to God. But God *is* Light, and God *is* Truth. And so, in still another theological picture, we see God looking after his loved ones both as Advocate and as Judge.

We have described a situation that could well have taken place long ago in a slave-market in Gaza, or in a foreign land far from Jerusalem. But the genius of the psalms is that their message can come right home to us as individuals even today in our daily living. There are so many unhappy circumstances that can make us feel alienated and lost. Some people have to suffer rejection by their family and find themselves living lonely and embittered lives. Some people wonder if the cancer they have been told is in their bones is a punishment from God for their sins. Some people carry about with them year after year a deep sense of guilt, like a great stone in the heart, all because of just one disloyal or horrible act they performed against someone who trusted them implicitly. Some people, brought up in the faith, turn for years of their lives to a desperate search for wealth, for success, for fame, or for a position of power— and than all of a sudden find that they have missed out on what alone gives meaning to life, the loving presence of their heavenly Father. Then perhaps, in their old age, an acquaintance asks them, "*Where is your God?* The God you learned about as a little child?" (42:3). Then you have the effrontery to reply by asking God, "Why hast thou forgotten me?" (Ps. 42:9), when all the time it is you who have forgotten God. And so it is that it can only be the grace of God (for you can't do it yourself) that brings you to the point of saying, like the Prodigal Son, "I will arise, and go to my Father." I shall find him, that I know, when *I go to the altar of God*, and will say at last, "O God, my God" (verse 4).

Hope is *knowing* that God is there and so hope means "waiting for God". But hope arouses us to praise the God we are waiting for when we seem to have lost him from sight. Moreover, just doing so means putting out your hand into the darkness and finding it gripped by Another. The cry of Psalms 42–43 (see how 42:5 is repeated at 43:5) is one that God will certainly answer. For it is a prayer, not to *get* something from God, but one that expresses a longing to be at home with God once again, as a child comes home to his Father.

GOD HAS LET US DOWN

Psalm 44:1–12

To the choirmaster. A Maskil of the sons of Korah.

1 We have heard with our ears, O God,
    our fathers have told us,
  what deeds thou didst perform in their days,
    in the days of old:
2 thou with thy own hand didst drive out the nations,
    but them thou didst plant;
  thou didst afflict the peoples,
    but them thou didst set free;
3 for not by their own sword did they win the land,
    nor did their own arm give them victory;
  but thy right hand, and thy arm,
    and the light of thy countenance;
    for thou didst delight in them.

4 Thou art my King and my God,
    who ordainest victories for Jacob.

5   Through thee we push down our foes;
      through thy name we tread down our assailants.
6   For not in my bow do I trust,
      nor can my sword save me.
7   But thou hast saved us from our foes,
      and hast put to confusion those who hate us.
8   In God we have boasted continually,
      and we will give thanks to thy name for ever.   *Selah*

9   Yet thou hast cast us off and abased us,
      and hast not gone out with our armies.
10 Thou hast made us turn back from the foe;
      and our enemies have gotten spoil.
11 Thou hast made us like sheep for slaughter,
      and hast scattered us among the nations.
12 Thou hast sold thy people for a trifle,
      demanding no high price for them.

This psalm again is something different. It is a community lament. In it it is *we* who speak. A reading of 2 Kings shows us how often the peoples of both Judah and of Samaria went out to battle, and how often they were defeated. This lament could thus fit a number of occasions. We are to picture crowds of people, some of them perhaps villagers who have taken refuge within the walls of the capital city, swarming to the temple precincts to bewail a defeat their army has suffered in the field. Someone has prepared this liturgy for them to use, and of course it could be used on later occasions also. According to the heading it is a *maskil*. We have seen that the word probably means "instructional". From this psalm we can see how much that generation had still to learn about the ways of God. The liturgy is in five parts.

The Past, verses 1–3. The home of an Israelite couple with children was a "Sunday School". Father and mother taught their young ones what they themselves had learned at public worship particularly from the lips of the "cultic prophet" or minister (see Psalm 106). They had learned "how You, God, had called upon Moses to bring our ancestors out of Egypt and guide them into their Promised Land; and how Joshua had won for them a place to live. But that these had only acted for You. It was You who had *given* our ancestors this good land, and in it You had planted them like a vine. It had not been a human arm which had given them the victory, it had been no less than the arm of the Lord. For it had been *thy delight in them*, meaning 'You were glad to be there in Person' [in 'face', or *countenance*] in their midst" (see Deut. 4:37–38).

The Present, verses 4–8. The liturgy now turns to give glory to the God of Jacob, that is, the God who had been Israel's (or Jacob's God—two names for the same man) from earliest days. He is *my King and my God*—the whole congregation declaring with one voice that it was God and not man who had "ordered" those victories of old.

But now the liturgy falls into a dangerous area, a danger that has beset all nations right till today. It is that of declaring that "God is on our side", so that we find ourselves sincerely thanking him for winning our battles for us. We note that verse 7 refers back to the historical statement made in verse 3. There it was God who had *planted* (verse 2) Israel in their new land. Ps. 80:8 calls this plant a Vine; Isaiah, at chapter 5, takes up the imagery, as does Jesus in John 15:1. There Jesus infers that something went wrong with the Vine Israel. This Psalm 44 tells us what did in fact go wrong. When the worshippers shouted, "Thou art my King and my God", they were addressing their human king as he sat in his glory on his throne in front of the sanctuary; for they regarded him as "son of God" (2 Sam. 7:14). So they expected him to be God's instrument to help Israel win their victories.

The Future, verses 9–19. Then why had God stopped helping them at the point he had reached in their history? Why had he allowed their recent defeat in battle to take place? Ezekiel 34 pictures Israel as sheep scattered in defeat (and exile) over the hills. There the reverse had taken place from what God had once done for his people. Of old he had *rescued* his people from slavery and had "concentrated" them in their own hill-country, not *scattered* them among the nations. Now he had actually *sold* them, that is, into slavery, regarding them as having hardly any value. Perhaps the occasion referred to here was in 721 B.C. when Samaria fell to the conquering army of the Assyrians.

WE ARE NOW A LAUGHING-STOCK

Psalm 44:13–26

13 Thou hast made us the taunt of our neighbours,
    the derision and scorn of those about us.
14 Thou hast made us a byword among the nations,
    a laughingstock among the peoples.
15 All day long my disgrace is before me,
    and shame has covered my face,
16 at the words of the taunters and revilers,
    at the sight of the enemy and the avenger.

17 All this has come upon us,
    though we have not forgotten thee,
    or been false to thy covenant.
18 Our heart has not turned back,
    nor have our steps departed from thy way,
19 that thou shouldst have broken us in the place of jackals,
    and covered us with deep darkness.

20 If we had forgotten the name of our God,
    or spread forth our hands to a strange god,
21 would not God discover this?
    For he knows the secrets of the heart.
22 Nay, for thy sake we are slain all the day long,
    and accounted as sheep for the slaughter.

23 Rouse thyself! Why sleepest thou, O Lord?
    Awake! Do not cast us off for ever!
24 Why dost thou hide thy face?
    Why dost thou forget our affliction and oppression?
25 For our soul is bowed down to the dust;
    our body cleaves to the ground.
26 Rise up, come to our help!
    Deliver us for the sake of thy steadfast love!

So God's own people were now *a byword and a laughingstock*

amongst the nations. They had been accustomed to proclaim to their pagan neighbours that their God was (a) Almighty, and (b) that he had made a covenant with their ancestors to be faithful to them for ever. Yet now the strange thing was that, as Israel was sure, she had kept her side of the covenant, but God had broken his side. The result was terrible disillusionment. God had *broken them in the place of jackals.* This is an Israelite picture of hell on earth, of utter desolation. And he had covered them with the deathly *darkness* (AV "shadow of death") of the spirit, the same word that is used of the jaws of hell in Ps. 23:4.

A Picture of Human Impertinence, verses 20–22. We have *not* forgotten God, shouts the psalmist. We have *not* strayed after false gods. We wouldn't dare do any such thing! For *God knows the secrets of the heart.* And then, without understanding the deep import of what is being said, the liturgy quotes a phrase whose mood is that found in the description of the Suffering Servant in Isa. 53 (see also Rom. 8:36). There the Servant People of God are also called a *young plant* which God himself had planted and which was meant to grow up in his presence.

Poor little Israel has so much yet to learn of the ways of God, as we all have:

(1) Israel must learn that, just because God has made a covenant of love with her, they are not the only nation whom God loves. Because they are God's "special people" does not mean that they have taken out an insurance policy with God against any possible defeat in war.

(2) Israel must learn what they had been chosen for. They were not chosen to be saved. They had been chosen to serve. They were chosen to take the Good News of the love of God to all men. As Isa. 49:6 puts it: "I will give you as a light to the nations, that my salvation may reach to the end of the earth."

(3) Israel had to learn that God had made use of war up till now, simply because Israel till then had been a political unit. In this world of force, he who takes the sword can only defend himself with the sword. But Israel had also to learn that, in the process of God's self-revelation of his loving purpose for the

world through the Covenant, she was now meant to take the next step of faith. Because of the Exile, when the body politic of Israel had been smashed, and she had become a "servant people" only, she must recognize that God wished her to be the Family of God, in fact, the "Church", and so be something else than a political power.

(4) This meant that God, in his wisdom, had ordained that Israel was to be his servant in defeat rather than in victory. Israel had to learn that she was meant to be the Suffering Servant of God rather than the victorious warrior people they had been once.

A Cry to God, verses 23-26. Finally:

(5) When Israel cried, *Rise up, come to our help!* (verse 26), they were now to discover that God himself was the Warrior, who was ready to give his own blood that his people might be saved (Isa. 63). But that kind of victory was a whole new world of experience Israel was only now, in God's love, being taught to understand.

. From verse 26 we learn that Israel is not quite so impertinent as to tell God exactly what to do. All she asks is that God should do something—anything, and not just keep silent; rather let him *teach* (*maskil*) his people what he is doing with them. It is we who are in the fortunate position to have hindsight sufficient to realize that God was actually teaching his people his will by letting them suffer defeat! For, with our hindsight, we now know that he who was *the Lamb slain from the foundation of the world* was actually being slain *in* his covenant people when they suffered the defeat of which they were at this moment complaining to God.

GOD SAVE THE KING!

Psalm 45:1-8

To the choirmaster: according to Lilies.
A Maskil of the sons of Korah, a love song.

1 My heart overflows with a goodly theme;
I address my verses to the king;
my tongue is like the pen of a ready scribe.

2 You are the fairest of the sons of men;
      grace is poured upon your lips;
      therefore God has blessed you for ever.
3 Gird your sword upon your thigh, O mighty one,
      in your glory and majesty!

4 In your majesty ride forth victoriously
      for the cause of truth and to defend the right;
      let your right hand teach you dread deeds!
5 Your arrows are sharp
      in the heart of the king's enemies;
      the peoples fall under you.

6 Your divine throne endures for ever and ever.
      Your royal sceptre is a sceptre of equity;
      you love righteousness and hate wickedness.
7 Therefore God, your God, has anointed you
      with the oil of gladness above your fellows;
8   your robes are all fragrant with myrrh and aloes and cassia.
   From ivory palaces stringed instruments make you glad.

This poem is about a royal wedding. We read of at least two
such in the OT, one at 1 Sam. 18:27 and another at 1 Kings
16:31. *According to Lilies* is surely an attractive name for a tune
for just such a happy occasion. This poem is therefore *a love
song*, as every wedding hymn should be.

The OT book, the Song of Songs, expresses perfectly the
holiness of sexual passion when it is ruled and motivated by the
kind of love that our jealous God showers upon Israel within
the covenant. For that covenant is a covenant of marriage. His
jealousy demands that his Bride be faithful to him to the
exclusion of all others. That book is dedicated to Solomon, the
"father" of the king addressed in this psalm. We find that it uses
a number of "covenantal" words. These all interpret the word
hesed which describes God's "steadfast love" for Israel. Thus,
Love is strong as death. Many waters (the waters of chaos that
we have met before) *cannot quench love, neither can floods
drown it* (Song of S. 8:6–7). So this royal marriage is to be
regarded as an acted parable of the passion of the divine
Husband for his Bride, Israel (Hos. 1–2). As we have seen, the

king in Jerusalem, as "son" of God (2 Sam. 7:14–15) is the mouthpiece of God to the people, as well as the mouthpiece of the people to God. But he is not *merely* a king. He is also a husband. This means that his conjugal relationship is part of the means which God uses to reveal the meaning of his own love for Israel. No wonder the people regarded the royal marriage as being vitally important for an interpretation of their faith.

The King, verses 1–8. The orator was probably the chief cultic prophet of the temple, either in Jerusalem, or at the shrine in Samaria. The latter was the capital city of the Northern Kingdom, and it had its own line of kings. The orator begins with the words: "*I* address my verses . . ." He returns to the first person in verse 17, where he ends his poem with "*I* will cause your name . . ," We have before this called this functionary a "minister". Or he may have been a kind of royal chaplain such as Nathan seems to have been to David. Whoever he was, this privileged man will probably have written this poem for the occasion; thereafter the same words could be used at subsequent royal marriages.

He takes over some of the flamboyant language we meet with in the court style of the Great Powers of the day. But he makes significant changes in that royal language when he adapts it to serve the cause of God's chosen monarch. He is tremendously excited at the event taking place. He even begins his declaration by saying, "My heart boils over!"; "I keep thinking—my work is about a king!"; "I will need the tongue of a sophisticated writer!"

He continues: "You are the most handsome of men; (God's) *grace is poured from your lips*; that is because *God* has blessed you [i.e. has put his hands upon your head] till eternity!" Then, even though he continues to use the extravagant language which subjects felt it necessary to employ in the ancient world when they flattered their king, he was really saying something that Paul insists upon in Rom. 13:1–7. It was that while the subject must honour the king, the king himself is the exalted personage he is only because God has first blessed him. As outstanding personalities today must come to realize while they are still in office—if they are wise—unless they hold their office as from God, they are nothing in the eyes of men; and so as soon as they become ex-kings, retired bishops, deposed dictators, former football champions, they return to anonymity. For it is the man that counts, not the office. To quote that very biblically-minded poet, Robert Burns:

A prince can mak a belted knight,
    A marquis, duke and a' that;
But an honest man's aboon [above] his might.

Only God could make this king *love righteousness and hate wickedness*, so that his *sceptre*—his shepherd's crook of office—might dispense equal justice to rich and poor, strong and weak alike. The king *can* do the will of this God, who, as Jesus says, sends the rain impartially on the good and the bad in the world. But this is only because *God, your God*, the king's God as well as the people's, has *anointed* him to do so.

... AND QUEEN!

Psalm 45:9-17

9 Daughters of kings are among your ladies of honour;
        at your right hand stands the queen in gold of Ophir.

10 Hear, O daughter, consider, and incline your ear;
        forget your people and your father's house;
11 and the king will desire your beauty.
    Since he is your lord, bow to him;
12 the people of Tyre will sue your favour with gifts,
13 the richest of the people with all kinds of wealth.

    The princess is decked in her chamber with gold-woven robes;
14 in many-coloured robes she is led to the king,
    with her virgin companions, her escort, in her train.
15 With joy and gladness they are led along
        as they enter the palace of the king.

16 Instead of your fathers shall be your sons;
        you will make them princes in all the earth.
17 I will cause your name to be celebrated in all generations;
        therefore the peoples will praise you for ever and ever.

The Queen, verses 9–15. But before we look at her and her place in the ceremony, we should remember that she is to be united in love and loyalty (*hesed*) with an *anointed* king! In a few moments she is to become one flesh with the Lord's anointed! Note these points: (a) *Your divine throne* is to be understood in terms of 1 Chron. 28:5, "He has chosen Solomon my son to sit upon *the throne of the kingdom of the Lord* over Israel". (b) The anointing makes the king gloriously happy to do God's perfect will. This is reflected in the beauty of his royal *robes* and the majesty of the furnishings of his palace. (c) The verb behind "anoint" is the basis of the noun *Messiah*, which means simply "anointed one". In OT times kings were anointed; David was hailed while still a youth as "the Lord's anointed" (1 Sam. 16:6; and see Ps. 2:2). So were priests anointed before they could execute their office (Lev. 4:5). At Isa. 45:1 the pagan King Cyrus of Persia is called *his anointed* (or Messiah!) because God had chosen him to set free his people Israel, then in exile in Babylon, from servitude to a foreign power. So there we read, *I call you by your name, I surname you, though you do not know me.*

The king will be marked by his awesome *deeds* (verse 4), the adjective that is used to describe the kind of mighty acts which only God can do. He is to go forth *in your glory and majesty*, again words that are reserved for God alone and for the beauty of his creation. And the words *defend the right*, or better, as the RSV *ftn.* tells us, the *meekness of right*, is the word used for God's saving activity ever since he had brought Israel through the Red Sea! Such then is the meaning of the phrase *the cause of truth*! Finally (verse 6) the minister, turning to this "messianic" king before him, with his bride beside him, says " *Your throne is God's throne* [on earth], *eternal.*" The king has thus now become the sacramental sign of God's real presence as he reigns over his kingdom. In other words, God's kingdom is now "at hand".

It could be otherwise, of course. Lord Acton, the brilliant and learned historian, once wrote: "Power tends to corrupt, and absolute power corrupts absolutely." But then, what this king possesses is the power that God has given him, not his own. "The danger is not that a particular class is unfit to govern;" wrote Acton, "every class is unfit to govern." So this psalm is saying that unless any governing body accepts God as king, it cannot conceivably execute true justice.

So now the queen is introduced to this "messianic" figure as she walks in stately glory "up the aisle", as we would say today, accompanied by her ladies-in-waiting. But the poet turns first to the king, and proclaims in a loud voice: *At your right hand stands the queen in gold of Ophir* (the best gold obtainable). Only then does he turn to the bride, who was apparently a foreign princess, to give her some homely advice. He advises her to make a clean break with her old home and country. Remember how Jezebel refused to do just that, he might have explained if he were speaking after Jezebel's ugly death had become history, and how in consequence she ruined the throne she could have magnified. Rather (he might have said) be like Ruth (Ruth 1:16) who identified herself with her adopted land. That was an act which God blessed. For this foreign lass actually became the great-grandmother of King David himself! Ruth may not have been a very important person in herself, but, by her obedience, she gave the world, all unwittingly, one of the great men of all time. Thus, in surrendering your whole self to him, the king, the minister went on, as your *husband* (not *lord* as in the English), he will desire you physically. If you then form the perfectly happy couple, foreign courts will be delighted to send you wedding gifts.

We cannot disregard the fact, however, that the word *lord* or *husband* occurs here in the plural. This seems to be a kind of shorthand way of writing, and of saying that since the name of "God the divine Husband" of Israel is plural in Hebrew (as at Hos. 2:23), then God is in some sense revealing his glory in and through this human marriage. In *meekness* (verse 4 *ftn.*) God had wooed his erring Bride Israel (Hos. 2:14) all over again as in the days of the Wilderness.

The *ftn.* to RSV verse 13 provides us with both the more likely and the more theologically attractive reading. It refers to the *gold-woven* wedding dress the princess is wearing, declaring that it will be a reflection of her real self, because she was, by God's grace, *all glorious within.* Till this day a young bride is dressed in white as a symbol of her purity, that is to say, that she is a virgin being brought forward by her *virgin companions* (as here) into the presence (in church) of her husband to be. It is because she is a pure girl, then, that her ladies-in-waiting lead her in *with joy and gladness.*

The Sermon, verses 16–17. Finally we are given a short summary of the minister's sermon. The royal couple's sons, or descendants, will hold world rule; and *I will cause your name to be celebrated in all generations*, that is to say, the messianic king will be celebrated right down the arches of the years, even, as the last line puts it, to all eternity. No wonder the NT saw deep messianic significance in this beautiful poem.

GOD IS OUR REFUGE AND STRENGTH

Psalm 46:1 11

To the choirmaster. A Psalm of the sons of Korah.
According to Alamoth. A song.

1 God is our refuge and strength,
    a very present help in trouble.
2 Therefore we will not fear though the earth should change,
    though the mountains shake in the heart of the sea;
3 though its waters roar and foam,
    though the mountains tremble with its tumult.   *Selah*

4 There is a river whose streams make glad the city of God,
    the holy habitation of the Most High.
5 God is in the midst of her, she shall not be moved;
    God will help her right early.
6 The nations rage, the kingdoms totter;
    he utters his voice, the earth melts.
7 The Lord of hosts is with us;
    the God of Jacob is our refuge.   *Selah*

8 Come, behold the works of the Lord,
    how he has wrought desolations in the earth.

9   He makes wars cease to the end of the earth;
      he breaks the bow, and shatters the spear,
      he burns the chariots with fire!
10 "Be still, and know that I am God.
      I am exalted among the nations,
      I am exalted in the earth!"
11 The Lord of hosts is with us;
      the God of Jacob is our refuge.   *Selah*

Half a dozen psalms are known as Songs of Zion. In these people sing about the temple hill in the city of Jerusalem and call it *the holy habitation of the Most High*. That little citadel, with its equally little sanctuary, is evidently worth acclaiming. For these psalms tell us that there, at this one spot in all the world, God is to be found.

Martin Luther's great hymn, *Ein' Feste Burg*, "A safe stronghold our God is still" (Thomas Carlyle's translation), is based upon Psalm 46. It is said that he penned it at that moment in the year 1529 when the Turkish army turned back into the Balkans after besieging the walls of Vienna in vain. That hymn has now been translated into 183 languages. Psalm 46 was also the first psalm that John Calvin thought he ought to translate into French.

God is our personal refuge, verses 1–3. The congregation would sing these words lustily. They knew God to be a *well-proved* (see RSV verse 1 *ftn.*) *help in trouble*. God had always been their strength ever since Moses had led them out of the clutches of Pharaoh in Egypt. Consequently he could now be trusted to continue to be like that, even if the mountains below the ocean, wonderful symbols of permanency, were to shake with an unheard of earthquake, causing a consequent unheard of flood. For God is Immanuel, meaning "God is with us". Thus, if God is not moved, then, as *our refuge* is in him, we shall not be moved either.

We might have thought that deep bass voices would have been appropriate to sing these mighty words. However, in the heading of the psalm we find the word *Alamoth*. This word means "girls". Yet perhaps it may have meant "for boys'

voices". Anyway, the suggestion is made, that the light-hearted
soprano notes of young people might best hymn this thunder-
ing power of the living God. We note too that the psalm belongs
in a collection known as that of "The Sons of Korah", probably
another choir group with its own cherished repertoire of pieces.

The Gusher, verses 4–7. Last century, a German professor, in
the company of some of his students, dug his way through a
blocked-up tunnel, out of which water trickled into the Pool of
Siloam in the city of Jerusalem. Once they had cleared the long
passage of sand and mud, at its very mid-point they found an
inscription cut in the wall written in good classical Hebrew. It
told how the tunnel, which took an S-bend at one point to suit
the layers of the rock, had been started at both ends, and how
the workmen had heard each other's picks at that point where
the students were now standing. Incidentally, these old workmen must have known a good deal about both mathematics and
engineering to have perfected this feat so long ago. Probably
this is the conduit mentioned at 2 Kings 18:17, 20:20; 2 Chron.
32:30, the one beside which the prophet Isaiah took a walk (Isa.
7:3) and ruminated (Isa. 8:5–8). Jerusalem sits on the top of a
hard rocky eminence. No rivers can bring it water. But just
outside the eastern wall, high up, there was a natural spring
which they called *Gihon*, which means "gusher". But if the city
suffered a siege, the water from the spring remained beyond the
reach of the city's inhabitants. So that is why Hezekiah built (or
perhaps renovated) his tunnel, in order to feed the waters of
Gihon into the Pool of Siloam.

But the spring came gushing up out of—where? There was no
river in sight. Gihon was a marvel, a gift from God. The waters
must come, it would seem, gushing up from *the waters under
the earth*, spoken of in the Second Commandment (Exod.
20:4). Or, did they come even from the Garden of Eden with its
mighty rivers (Gen. 2:10)? Thus it would seem that the King of
the waters both above and below the earth must be the real ruler
of the *river whose streams make glad the city of God*. This
"living" water, as running water is called in Hebrew, can come
only from the living God, the giver of life. So even the wrath of

the nations cannot move the city that possesses this living water. Jeremiah, who lived a century later than Isaiah, makes good use of this "living" stream in a telling parable (Jer. 2:13), comparing God to its fountain of living waters.

He makes wars to cease, verses 8–10. See then how the living God does what a real King should do. This is what the king on the throne in Jerusalem should do also. Not *make* war, but *make wars to cease*. Yet, to do so, in the end God must surely cause great convulsions—for evil is a serious power to be reckoned with. Consequently *he breaks the bow and shatters the spear and burns the chariots in the fire*.

In quiet mood now, like the song of soprano voices, the psalm invites us (a) to *Come, behold*. This word means "Use your *in*sight to grasp the meaning of . . ." Then, (b) to stop, that is, *be still*, relax, think, learn, learn the meaning of the great events which God is performing as you look at the water gushing out of the tunnel into the Pool of Siloam. (c) Make the final discovery, that is, *know that I am God*!

In 1812 William Carey's pioneering mission printing works in Serampore, India, were burnt to the ground. At first he was dumbfounded. But the following Sunday he preached on this text, Ps. 46:10. A newspaper man who had been present wrote: "In the blaze of this fire men saw the grandeur of the enterprise." The facts were flashed out. The result was that the whole cost of the printing works was repaid in two months!

He has wrought desolations in the earth. Yes, but out of these desolations he has brought forth his loving purpose for the salvation of mankind.

The Chorus, verse 11. It proclaims, then, (a) The Lord of *hosts*, the hosts of the heavens, is *with* us— how extraordinary! (b) The God of our ancestors is still the God we have today, still *our refuge, our fortress*—how even more extraordinary!

THE ASCENSION OF GOD

Psalm 47:1-9

To the choirmaster. A Psalm of the sons of Korah.

1 Clap your hands, all peoples!
    Shout to God with loud songs of joy!
2 For the Lord, the Most High, is terrible,
    a great king over all the earth.
3 He subdued peoples under us,
    and nations under our feet.
4 He chose our heritage for us,
    the pride of Jacob whom he loves.   *Selah*

5 God has gone up with a shout,
    the Lord with the sound of a trumpet.
6 Sing praises to God, sing praises!
    Sing praises to our King, sing praises!
7 For God is the king of all the earth;
    sing praises with a psalm!

8 God reigns over the nations;
    God sits on his holy throne.
9 The princes of the peoples gather
    as the people of the God of Abraham.
  For the shields of the earth belong to God;
    he is highly exalted!

This psalm is one of those that give us the opportunity to apply the results of scholarly criticism to an understanding of the ways of God. By comparing Hebrew hymn-writing with that of neighbouring peoples, it would seem—though the theory cannot be proved beyond doubt—that once a year the king made a dramatic ascent of his throne in Jerusalem. It must have been part of a colourful and dramatic celebration. For on each annual occasion he was *re*-crowned as king, all over again. By having to be recrowned he was being reminded that a human king is only "God's silly vassal" as Andrew Melville told King James to his face. On the other hand, the human king was also and at the same time the Lord's anointed! Consequently, his action as he ascended the throne dramatized on earth the nature and purpose of God as King of all the earth. Accordingly, at an exciting moment in the drama, the people shouted the words "The Lord is King", or, "The Lord has become King". But of course, the shout reminded Israel that God was the King of all nations, and King over the forces of nature as well!

In fact, when the king re-ascended his throne in the Jerusalem temple precincts his action was just one portion of a fascinating cultic drama. It is believed that the fundamental events in the story of man's salvation were also re-enacted in this one great dramatic movement before the eyes of the assembled congregation. The mighty acts of God were thus presented to the people as a *new* event, one that was now not just confined to the past, but one which was meaningful *now* and for all God's people at the present time.

The people assemble. Pilgrims had evidently arrived from far-off lands. A cultic prophet (or "minister") would then begin the liturgy by inviting all present to *clap their hands and shout to God with loud songs of joy.* And then these songs would be sung by all. Perhaps the choir led the people line by line. We have no knowledge of how they did it. But why sing to God at all? *For the Lord, the Most high, is terrible.* He is no mere local god. He is the Creator of the ends of the earth, and the Lord of all history.

Now another voice retells the story of God's saving acts. He retells the story of Moses, of the escape from Egypt, of the manna in the Wilderness, of the giving of the Law, and of God's gift to Israel of this their Promised Land, *the pride of Jacob.* Then he spoke of the line of kings who had sat upon the throne before all eyes beginning with David the Lord's beloved son. These were all things that God had done before. That was the theme of the sermon. But God is always the same, yesterday, today and for ever. So it was inevitable, that just as God had subdued the Canaanites so long before under Joshua's feet, he would certainly keep to his plan. The day *must* therefore come when God will *subdue all peoples under our feet.* Notice the word "our". For this was to come about through "our" co-operation, "our" witness, when, in God's good time, he would conquer the hearts of all men.

The Ascension. Now would begin the royal procession, possibly from the gate of the temple right to the steps of the throne. The king would lead the column. Then came the exciting moment when the king stepped up on the dais and took his seat upon the throne, wearing the insignia of all the warrior kings passed down since the days of David

Prominent in the procession would be the Ark of the Covenant, which was carried into the city and then to the temple once again each year with joy and dancing, in memory of the time when David had brought up the Ark for the first time into "the city of David" (2 Sam. 6:12–15). Inside the Ark, of course, lay the two stone tablets on which were engraved the Ten Commandments. In this way, it was impressed upon all worshippers that the Word of God was actually present with his people in the procession, in a very literal sense.

As the human king finally took his seat upon the throne, the spokesman declared, obviously in a loud voice, *God has gone up with a shout, with the sound of a* "ram's horn". For the ram's horn had always sounded in the celebration of the New Year festival, as it is to this day in the Synagogue. And so, as their gaze fell upon the human king, the people found themselves singing praises to the divine King of all kings, because it was he, of course, and not this "son of David", who had brought them to the Promised Land.

The RSV is misleading here when it has the minister declare *Sing praises with a psalm.* For, as the *fin* to verse 7 shows, the word is not *tehillah*, a psalm, but *maskil*. As we have noted before, this word has to do with teaching. So now it probably refers to what scholarship has uncovered for us, a deliberately planned performance (compare our Nativity Plays today) that was intended to *teach* Israel the meaning of the Ascension of God. The ordinary, illiterate, unschooled peasant would surely go home after this annual festival moved to the core and thrilled not just from *watching* this "acted sermon", but because he had actually *participated* himself in acting out what was no less than a cosmic event.

The final act. The final act of the drama now takes place. The congregation makes its witness to the Covenant which God had made with Abraham so long before (Gen. 12:1-3; 17:1-14). This covenant, as we remember, was a covenant of promise. This meant that some day, in God's good time, he would use Israel to be a blessing to all the nations of the earth. That is why we can dare to say that the Church was born in promise some 1,800 years even before the birth of Christ. Israel is indeed God's "own possession" amongst all the nations (Exod. 19:5); yet, as God of all the earth, the *shields of the earth*, the lesser kings of the nations who carried these accoutrements of battle, belong to him as well.

The last words of the psalm *He is highly exalted* have led the Church over the centuries to apply this psalm to Ascension Day and its liturgy. The Church has thus used Psalm 47 to celebrate in faith the witness of the NT to the ascension of Christ to the right hand of God, where he *took his seat upon the throne of the universe.* The Church could do so, because it has always seen in that one true Israelite all the promises of God becoming incarnate in human flesh. Thus the Church long preceded modern critical scholarship in opening up the meaning of this psalm in this wonderful way. It would be helpful perhaps if, as we repeat the words of the Creed on any Sunday, "He ascended into heaven, and sits [has taken his seat on the throne] on the right hand of God", we return in thought to this impressive psalm and the help that it gives to us as we seek to understand the work of Christ.

THE CITY OF GOD

Psalm 48:1-14

A song. A Psalm of the sons of Korah.

1 Great is the Lord and greatly to be praised
 in the city of our God!

2   His holy mountain, beautiful in elevation,
        is the joy of all the earth,
     Mount Zion, in the far north,
        the city of the great King.
3   Within her citadels God
        has shown himself a sure defence.

4   For lo, the kings assembled,
        they came on together.
5   As soon as they saw it, they were astounded,
        they were in panic, they took to flight;
6   trembling took hold of them there,
        anguish as of a woman in travail.
7   By the east wind thou didst shatter
        the ships of Tarshish.
8   As we have heard, so have we seen
        in the city of the Lord of hosts,
     in the city of our God,
        which God establishes for ever.   *Selah*

9   We have thought on thy steadfast love, O God,
        in the midst of thy temple.
10   As thy name, O God,
        so thy praise reaches to the ends of the earth.
     Thy right hand is filled with victory;
11   let Mount Zion be glad!
     Let the daughters of Judah rejoice
        because of thy judgments!

12   Walk about Zion, go round about her,
        number her towers,
13   consider well her ramparts,
        go through her citadels;
     that you may tell the next generation
14   that this is God,
     our God for ever and ever.
        He will be our guide for ever.

In Psalm 47 we met with theology dramatized. It was used thus to teach a congregation about the nature of God. Psalm 48 also seeks to teach people by getting them to sing about the meaning, the "theology" of Zion, the city of God.

The theology of Jerusalem. To do this the author begins with the ways of thinking of his generation—and how sensible that is. The nations round about Jerusalem all believed in the existence of a mighty mountain that lay away far off in the north. It was a divine mountain; it was so lofty that it passed through the clouds right into the heavens, right up to the residence of those divinities who dwelt above it there in the bright blue sky. But then he takes over this generally accepted picture and applies it to that little hill-top, only 2,620 feet high, on the top of which Jerusalem sat. But what he does is to theologize about this little mountain. He calls Jerusalem *the city of our God*; it is therefore the *holy* city, *beautiful in elevation* on its cliff-top, especially as seen from the east. Yet in our psalm the city is not just beautiful in itself. As Israel's equivalent of that mountain *in the far north*, it was the highest of all the mountains in the world (Isa. 2:2). That is theology, not the science of geography! It could be seen by people right at the ends of the earth (theology again!). But in itself it was nothing. It was beautiful and it was lofty only because it was *the city of the great King*. The *theological* significance of the city is then made clear in verse 3. As Pope John Paul said when he visited Jerusalem: "This city belongs, not to any one nation, but to God" (compare Ps. 46:4–5).

At the north-east corner of the city there was a slightly higher eminence, actually the highest point, known as Mount Zion. The significance of the word Zion grew and developed over the centuries. (a) Zion was where the temple and the royal palace stood, that is to say, on it was to be found the seat both of government and of divine worship. (b) Later on, Zion became a poetic name for the people of Israel themselves. (c) Still later, after they were driven from Jerusalem in 587 B.C. by the Babylonian conquerors, Zion became the theological name even for the whole land of Israel. (d) Amongst Christians the name Zion came to be used of the whole People of God. (e) Sometimes the name was used even for the little local church building which one attended Sunday after Sunday. (f) But in the Church's liturgy Zion came to be used as the name even of the heavenly city!

More theology—an ideal hope. Verses 4–8 are a poem describing the coming Day of the Lord. As at Ps. 2:2, the kings here represent those forces of evil in the world that strive against the cosmic plan of redemption of the God whose dwelling is on Mount Zion. In this picture, then, we are told how, on drawing near to the city, these kings made the agonizing discovery that God is no mere local deity. He is *LORD*, terrible, all-mighty, controller of the winds and the waves. The *east wind* is in fact the very breath of God. It comes from the direction to which the pagan looks in order to worship the rising sun. Man's commerce on the high seas this God can shatter, even the mighty *ships of Tarshish*, or what people a hundred years ago called "Atlantic liners". But he does the same to the commerce that goes on even in the everlasting city! (compare Mark 11:15).

The interjection of the musical term *Selah* now advises us to pause before we begin a new act in the drama.

Theologizing about Zion, verses 9–11. Well then, says our orator, have you now thought as we worshipped together in the temple about what our beautiful Mount Zion stands for? In fact, its everlastingness is a symbol of Your everlasting covenant love, Your *hesed*, O God. We have looked at it in the present (verses 1–3), and in its meaning for the future (verses 4–8). Now we must think of its eternal significance. Wherever Your Name will make itself known, there Your praises will be heard, right to the ends of the earth. Your *right hand*, the one that acts for You, is filled with saving love (rather than *victory*, RSV). No wonder then that Mount Zion, along with its "daughters", Jerusalem's suburbs and Judah's villages, should be glad—for it is from Zion that the conquering love of God has gone forth to reach into eternity.

Look at her! Walk round her! Gaze in wonder at her towers and ramparts! Go right in and look at her citadel inside! What for? Just to see a beautiful city? No! But so as to be able to tell your children that *this city is God*! It is the one place in all the earth where the Creator of the universe has chosen to "embody" his purpose in bricks and mortar. But then, of course, we have seen that "Zion" also means "the People of God". Such theological thinking leads straight to the NT affirmation that "the word became flesh . . . and we have seen his glory", just as those pilgrims beheld it to the degree God intended for that period in history, as they marched together round those ancient ramparts.

Two affirmations arise from this last verse:

(1) God is the kind of God who empties himself in total humility so as to be found in one place only, and through one people only.

(2) His emptying himself is in order to come down beside his people in order to guide them right on into eternity. This couplet is then closed with the words: "He will lead us through death." The words "through death" have been omitted by the RSV, because the LXX has translated them by repeating "into eternity". Some scholars suppose that *al muth* (through death) should be *ad muth* (unto death). But why should we alter the original Hebrew? Let it stand!

THE MYSTERY OF DEATH

Psalm 49:1-20

To the choirmaster. A Psalm of the sons of Korah.

1 Hear this, all peoples!
    Give ear, all inhabitants of the world,
2 both low and high,
    rich and poor together!
3 My mouth shall speak wisdom;
    the meditation of my heart shall be understanding.
4 I will incline my ear to a proverb;
    I will solve my riddle to the music of the lyre.

5 Why should I fear in times of trouble,
    when the iniquity of my persecutors surrounds me,
6 men who trust in their wealth
    and boast of the abundance of their riches?
7 Truly no man can ransom himself,
    or give to God the price of his life,
8 for the ransom of his life is costly,
    and can never suffice,

9 that he should continue to live on for ever,
     and never see the Pit.

10 Yea, he shall see that even the wise die,
      the fool and the stupid alike must perish
      and leave their wealth to others.

11 Their graves are their homes for ever,
      their dwelling places to all generations,
      though they named lands their own.

12 Man cannot abide in his pomp,
      he is like the beasts that perish.

13 This is the fate of those who have foolish confidence,
      the end of those who are pleased with their portion.   *Selah*

14 Like sheep they are appointed for Sheol;
      Death shall be their shepherd;
    straight to the grave they descend,
      and their form shall waste away;
      Sheol shall be their home.

15 But God will ransom my soul from the power of Sheol,
      for he will receive me.   *Selah*

16 Be not afraid when one becomes rich,
      when the glory of his house increases.

17 For when he dies he will carry nothing away;
      his glory will not go down after him.

18 Though, while he lives, he counts himself happy,
      and though a man gets praise when he does well for himself,

19 he will go to the generation of his fathers,
      who will never more see the light.

20 Man cannot abide in his pomp,
      he is like the beasts that perish.

This psalm is less likely to have been sung by the temple
congregation in the first place than to have been taught in the
temple-school next door. Yet the whole-hearted and sincere
study of the Word of God can become so exciting that one is led
to sing thanks to God in joy and love. We have here a
meditation on the transitoriness of life, and on the futility of
trusting in the things that money can buy. The psalm forms a
good background to Jesus' parable of the rich farmer that we

meet with at Luke 12:13–21. Note that the language of verse 3 belongs to the "Wisdom" school of OT religious thought.

The psalm begins (remember we are in only a small classroom!) by addressing the whole world, even as the Pope does from the balcony of St. Peter's in Rome, *urbi et orbi*, to the city of Rome and to the world. For, of course, death is universal. The people of Madras and of Manchester equally are going to die. So are the rich, and so are the poor. No man can bribe the angel of death to stay away, far less bribe God.

Note that the verbs used for *trusting* and *boasting* in verse 6 occur elsewhere only with reference to God. So here they must be used in sarcasm to show that people worship their possessions as if they were gods. The verse goes on to say that since a rich man can't ever bribe God, there is no reason for people like us to be afraid of him. He is not eternal; only God is eternal. Nor can being a professor exempt you from dying, he says; the wise man (that one standing there!) is as short-lived as is the fool outside the room. There are people in every land who are called after their estates. Accordingly, along with their title there goes both *pomp* and circumstance. But even these people die in their turn, and are buried just *like the beasts that perish*.

At this point (verse 13), however, we are beginning to see that the writer uses the word "death" in two ways. He groups together all the various types of people he has mentioned so far as *those who are pleased with their portion*. By that he refers to that secularist view of life which declares that it is quite enough to enjoy your days on earth as if there were no meaning in life. When this scholarly dissertation was turned into a psalm, the editor wrote *Selah* at this point. "Stop, think! What a terrible thing to say!" is what he bids the music remind us.

He now reverses the image of God as the Good Shepherd gathering his trusting sheep into the fold. *Death* is now the shepherd of the hedonist, the Grim Reaper, the Great Leveller, and he will sweep all *his* sheep into their true home—*Sheol*! *But*—in the Hebrew this is a strong adversative—with God all things are possible (compare Luke 18:24–27). *God will ransom my soul from the power of Sheol* (something that no man, either secularist or believer, can do for himself, verse 7), *and he will receive me.* No wonder we meet with another *Selah* at this fantastic statement.

The second meaning of "death" has now become clear. To live in fellowship with God is really life itself, as we have already seen a number of psalm writers assert. Therefore to live a *self-*satisfied life, one which leaves God out, is in fact the death of the spirit. This is what Jesus meant when he said, "Let the dead bury their dead. But you come and follow me." Physical death for God's "little ones" is only a falling asleep, as Jesus said of Jairus' daughter. That simple child, we discover, did not need to be rescued from the power of Sheol.

Moreover, the verb in "he will *receive* me" is that used of Enoch at Gen. 5:24, where we read, "Enoch walked with God, and God *took* him", that is, took him home to himself. In other words, walking with God means receiving fulness of life here and now. Such real life can never be obliterated by the power of Sheol.

Verses 16-20 underline what we have already found at verses 5-9, but their message is expressed even more starkly. The rich secularist's *glory*, (perhaps meaning here his *wealth*, as in the RSV *ftn.* to verse 17) stays up here in this world; it doesn't go down into Sheol when he goes! Then, verse 18 describes the self-satisfied humanist again, perhaps to emphasize the point all the more that the praise of men is a poor substitute for the fellowship of the living God. Only God can keep a person out of the clutches of death and hell.

This psalm has a missionary purpose. It is not addressed to believing Israel alone. What we find at verse 1 is: *Hear this, all peoples*! So we hear the loving Word of God to all the simple folk on earth, especially those who do not even know that there is a Gospel at all, that there is no reason for them to go down to Sheol unless, like these rich people in this psalm, they turn their back on what knowledge of God they have received, and worship their own selfish desires.

We should note about this psalm that it has nothing to say about (a) the immortality of the soul, or (b) the transmigration of souls, such as is taught by some Indian religions. Rather, with all the rest of the OT, (c) this psalm is concerned with *this life*, and with that fulness of life which God longs to give to his children *now*. That fulness of life belongs to eternity.

DON'T DARE UNDERESTIMATE ME

Psalm 50:1–6

A Psalm of Asaph.

1   The Mighty One, God the Lord,
        speaks and summons the earth
        from the rising of the sun to its setting.
2   Out of Zion, the perfection of beauty,
        God shines forth.

3   Our God comes, he does not keep silence,
        before him is a devouring fire,
        round about him a mighty tempest.
4   He calls to the heavens above
        and to the earth, that he may judge his people:
5   "Gather to me my faithful ones,
        who made a covenant with me by sacrifice!"
6   The heavens declare his righteousness,
        for God himself is judge!   *Selah*

One aspect of the preaching at the great festivals was the stern communication of God's will. That stern warning was then sung about in a psalm! According to 1 Chron. 23:2–5 David divided the Levitical priests into four divisions, the music being the responsibility of the fourth division. This was made up of companies of 288 singers, divided in turn into twenty-four courses under three leading musicians, named Haman, Asaph, and Ethan. These three musicians led their choirs in singing with cymbals (1 Chron. 15:16). Of course, in David's day there were not enough inhabitants in Jerusalem to produce such big choirs. In the Chronicler's day, however, that is, in the period of the Second Temple, this was the way of things. For by then the numbers of priests, Levites, singers, orchestra players and so on had greatly grown and developed. So this psalm belonged to the collection of choir music named after Asaph. He was certainly a historical figure, for his name was known to King Hezekiah (2 Chron. 29:30). Yet we have no idea why this Asaph psalm was isolated from the "Asaphic collection" at Psalms 73–83. We even find that in between there is a "Davidic collection", Psalms 51–70.

The twelve *psalms of Asaph* in the Psalter all use regularly the word *ELOHIM* for God, and use Yahweh, "the Lord", only occasionally; and they also like to employ still more ancient words for "God", sometimes even piling them up two or three at a time. In most of the psalms in our Psalter people speak *about* God or *to* God. In the Asaph psalms God is frequently introduced as speaking to man, in the manner of the great prophets.

The theophany, verses 1–3. This is the technical word we use to describe the personal appearance of God to man. The first three words of the psalm are a "piling up" of names for God, to sound worthy of the Judge of all mankind, the Almighty, the Creator of the ends of the earth. Yet, God addresses mankind from that one place which he has chosen for himself, viz. Zion (Deut. 12:11,14,26, etc.). The sun rises in the east in all its majesty and beauty to shine forth for all mankind; so too God shines forth from Zion for all men. And just as the sun exerts an awesome heat, so does the "rising" of God. *Before him there are a devouring fire and a mighty tempest.* God's love is a *tempestuous, devouring* love (compare Luke 3:16). Before it all that is false and evil is consumed as by a forest fire. These two figures of speech then represent the all-righteous and unspeakably loving judgment of the Creator God who cannot be mocked.

As we saw before at Psalm 19, however, God has planned that natural revelation should not be the only means he uses to reveal himself to mankind. So he has continued to reveal himself through that special relationship which he adopted at Mount Sinai and which now goes forth from Jerusalem, God's chosen resting place on earth.

The law-court, verses 4–6. Like Isaiah and others of the great prophets, the psalmist sets the judgment scene by inviting the whole of God's creation, both heaven and earth, to come and be the jury (Isa. 1:2; Deut. 30:19). Israel is in the dock, a rebellious people (Isa. 1:2–4). What happens now? First, as we have seen, once God breaks his silence, he enters the court prepared to make a tempestuous judgment. So the mighty Judge makes the announcement: "Summon to the court all the members of my covenant people [not *faithful ones*, RSV: for this word is based on the covenantal term *hesed*], that Covenant which *I* made with *them*. Summon all those who have kept their side of the covenant with *Me* by making use of the sacrifical system which *I myself* gave them in the days of Moses." Thereupon the heavens, sitting on the jury benches, reply: "God has already saved his covenant people; he has already put them right with himself. Just imagine, their Judge is also their Advocate!"

This tremendous picture describes how God himself reminds Israel that he has been faithful to the Covenant all along, and how that means that he has saved them by grace alone. The redemption from Egypt was the outward and visible sign of that which is invisible by itself, viz., God's "prevenient grace". This last phrase describes grace which comes first, grace which is poured out upon people *before* they repent, like a torrent, like a forest fire. Once they have received this grace of God then it becomes the source of their power to repent. The biblical order is: (a) God's grace first; (b) forgiveness second; (c) repentance third; (d) change of heart and of life-style fourth; (e) joy and rejoicing at the loveliness of God.

So we see why Israel has done its human best to reciprocate, to show her *hesed* to God, by using the sacrificial system he had given her. *But*, and here is the nub, the sacrifice of a bull or a goat was also meant to be the outward and visible sign of a *heart* that sincerely sought to live by God's grace and guidance within the Covenant. The offering of these sacrifices was God's will for Israel as a redeemed people (Lev. 1:1–9); *but* they had to be performed with total sincerity, arising from the heart (Lev. 5–6). So now we are told to pause (by the word *Selah*) and take in all those words of revelation and ponder them.

THE JUDGE'S PRONOUNCEMENTS

Psalm 50:7–23

7 "Hear, O my people, and I will speak,
  O Israel, I will testify against you.
  I am God, your God.
8 I do not reprove you for your sacrifices;
  your burnt offerings are continually before me.
9 I will accept no bull from your house,
  nor he-goat from your folds.
10 For every beast of the forest is mine,
  the cattle on a thousand hills.
11 I know all the birds of the air,
  and all that moves in the field is mine.

12 "If I were hungry, I would not tell you;
  for the world and all that is in it is mine.
13 Do I eat the flesh of bulls,
  or drink the blood of goats?
14 Offer to God a sacrifice of thanksgiving,
  and pay your vows to the Most High;
15 and call upon me in the day of trouble;
  I will deliver you, and you shall glorify me."

16 But to the wicked God says:
  "What right have you to recite my statutes,
  or take my covenant on your lips?
17 For you hate discipline,
  and you cast my words behind you.
18 If you see a thief, you are a friend of his;
  and you keep company with adulterers.

19 "You give your mouth free rein for evil,
  and your tongue frames deceit.
20 You sit and speak against your brother;
  you slander your own mother's son.
21 These things you have done and I have been silent;
  you thought that I was one like yourself.
  But now I rebuke you, and lay the charge before you.

22   "Mark this, then, you who forget God,
        lest I rend, and there be none to deliver!
23   He who brings thanksgiving as his sacrifice honours me;
        to him who orders his way aright
        I will show the salvation of God."

The first pronouncement. The Judge now turns and faces his
covenant people, Israel. He tells them to *hear*, that is, really
listen, just as Jesus does so often when he says, "He that has ears
to hear, let him hear." "This time", God says, "I pass judgment
against you. You are my people; I am your God." (See the
words of the covenant-making at Exod. 19:5–6; and renewed at
Hos. 2:23.) "You are certainly punctilious in your religious
duties; you offer me burnt offerings daily. But I won't take any
more of these beasts from you—anyway all *the beasts* and *the
birds of the forest* are mine already! Do you think I need to be
fed by you? Do you really think I drink goats' blood?"

The first chapter of Isaiah tells us how God has become sick
of the smell of burning bulls, sick of the punctilious Sabbath
keeping, sick of the annual round of festivals (all of which God
himself had commanded, remember!). What God really wants
is to find in the hearts of his people love and compassion for the
helpless, the victims of greed and oppression, the orphan and
the widow (Isa. 1:17). This is because that is how God's
covenant love for Israel shows itself, so that Israel's covenant
love to God must show itself in return in compassion for one's
neighbour. Therefore, declares God, you dare not mock the
MOST HIGH! What God looks for is *a sacrifice of thanksgiving*, not the killing of bulls, or, as the RSV *ftn.* to verse 14 puts it
well, *Make thanksgiving your sacrifice to God.* If you do that,
then even as *you call upon me in the day of trouble*, then *I will
deliver you.* For it is by your heartfelt repentance and sincere
love that you will show how *you glorify me.*

The second pronouncement, verses 16–22. Strangely enough
the Judge does not turn and face the other group of people in
the court room, here called *the wicked*, a group separate from
the covenant people. This is because the wicked *are* the covenant people! It is they who had learned to recite the Ten

Commandments, and to make use of the covenant-language which God had taught them. One demand of God in the Covenant included the proviso, "If you obey my voice" (Exod. 19:5), which meant, of course, "If you keep the Law of Moses". But now the Judge declares, "*You hate discipline*" (the Hebrew word means learning through being disciplined). "*You cast my words behind you.*" "You join up with thieves and prostitutes . . . You have even created God in your own image"—the very reverse of Gen. 1:27. "You thought I was a permissive God who would let you enjoy a permissive society. Yet I now give you one more chance; don't let me have to come and *rend* you. Because, if *I* don't deliver you, there is none who will."

The Chorus; verse 23. These words sum up the double judgment we have just listened to in the last sixteen verses.

I AM GUILTY

Psalm 51:1

To the choirmaster. A Psalm of David, when Nathan the prophet came to him, after he had gone in to Bathsheba.

1 Have mercy on me, O God, according to thy steadfast love;
    according to thy abundant mercy blot out my transgressions.

Almost every word in this tremendous psalm will ask for our attention. What it has to say is timeless; it is also universal; it is a communal psalm, and yet it was composed by an individual. Its heading gives us the key we need to understand it.

With the aid of the sacrificial system available in the OT period, all sins could be atoned for except two. These were (a) murder, and (b) rape and/or incest. These two sins were equated in their heinousness by recognizing that murder leads to the death of the body, rape to the death of the soul. It is estimated that a large proportion of the young drug addicts of our time suffered from a sexual assault in their childhood days. This aberration could be mother-son, father-son oriented, although as one expert declares, the incidence of father-daughter sexual violence is probably greater. Incest in the Mosaic

Law could also involve sexual relationships between sisters and sisters, brothers and brothers, brothers and sisters, and humans and animals. "Incest rips away at the very fabric of a young person's self-esteem", adds the expert we have newly quoted. As to violence leading to murder, the offender only too often was offended against himself when young by a drunken or sex-crazed parent.

Now, it was just those two basic sins which Nathan brought home to David's conscience by his use of the parable of the little ewe lamb (2 Sam. 11:2–12:15). This great but perverse man, this "son" of God, this "sweet singer of Israel" had put himself outside of the area in which God had chosen to grant forgiveness and renewal. We understand the significance of this action of God when we realize that his special relationship with his people Israel was figured by the great prophets as a covenant of marriage. God was the divine Husband, Israel was the very human Bride. But if the Bride were actually to "go a-whoring after other gods" (or "husbands"), as she did time and time again, to the point of contracting her own divorce from her loving husband, quite simply, then, *there was nothing God could do to woo her back.* For she had broken off all relations with him, and no point of contact remained.

David, then, had "divorced" himself from God by refusing to accept God's covenant love, and by believing that he could run his own life better than God could. But now that Nathan's parable had got home to him, he saw that there was nothing left for him to do but to throw himself upon the mercy of God. This moving psalm tells us just what was in David's heart when he did so. How valuable it is that his confession should later become part of Israel's liturgy, and so have become today an element in the preaching of the Gospel, the Good News of the greatness of the love of God.

Our psalmist begins at quite a different point from that of either the psychotherapist or the social worker today. These usually begin with our inner experience. They invite us to try to face up to our moral problems, to recognize how our misdeeds affect society for the worse, in fact, how we have even broken society's laws. But our psalmist sweeps beyond all these human and moral considerations and turns our mind straight to God. Some local authorities forbid their social workers to introduce the word "God" into any of their advice to people in desperate circumstances. But Nathan had no such reservations. He helped David to appeal straight to the God whose covenant he had broken, and so to throw himself on the mercy of God who had made no provision in the Law for dealing with these "sins with a high hand", as the Law of Moses calls them. What a striking picture these words offer of deliberate intent to harm another!

David therefore appeals (a) to God's *hesed*, his unshakeable covenant love, on the ground that, even if man breaks his side of the covenant, God will never break his side. (Note that "transgression" in the Hebrew means just this, a breaking of the covenant.) Then (b) he appeals to God's "mother-love"—for what true mother would ever lose her love for the child that was once part of her very body? The word *mercy* here is derived from the noun for "womb". That then is why we translate it in this way. (See the Introduction for a discussion of the words *hesed* and "mother-love".)

WASH ME

Psalm 51:2-5

2 Wash me thoroughly from my iniquity,
  and cleanse me from my sin!
3 For I know my transgressions,
  and my sin is ever before me.
4 Against thee, thee only, have I sinned,
  and done that which is evil in thy sight,
 so that thou art justified in thy sentence
  and blameless in thy judgment.
5 Behold, I was brought forth in iniquity,
  and in sin did my mother conceive me.

Even though he knows he is guilty, even though he is aghast at the thought that he has put himself beyond the pale, yet David remembers God, or at least his court chaplain Nathan reminds him of God. This is where the task of the Church is diametrically the opposite of that of the social worker. We note the language David uses, that of man's universal experience when outside the pale. He *feels dirty*, morally leprous. It is as if the prescription in the book of Leviticus for certain washings for skin diseases of all kinds were made for him alone (Lev. 13; Jer. 2:22). The great evangelist, Dr. Billy Graham, tells us he believes that over 90% of his converts had already been baptized in their youth. That is to say, they had begun life with all the advantages of being in the Covenant. And so it was primarily they who knew where to turn now that a "Nathan" had accosted them, when those who had always been "outside the pale" were at a loss.

Once David does cry in this way, God suddenly becomes radically real to him. He now faces both God and his sins, his leprous feelings, and thus feels able to tell God all about them. He confesses (a) that he has indeed broken the covenant—oh horror! For (b) he has become blindingly aware that he has missed out on the reality of God's fellowship (as the noun in verse 3 means). So he sees that, (c) because he is now outside the bounds of the covenant his basic sin is to have sneered at God's love and to have simply turned his back upon obedience to God's offer of guidance in his life. We notice that David does not need to confess his sin against his neighbour, against that honest soldier, Uriah, a convert from paganism to the worship of the God of love, a love which David did not show to him, or against Bathsheba, a helpless female member of the people of God. It is *God* he has sinned against. For God had planned to give those two people a full life, in fact God had planned this for them from the foundation of the world. This is what verse 4 means.

It is only God who sees how evil evil really is, and what the consequences of evil actions can be. The individual who murders a man in a fit of rage has no thought of the consequences of his action in the years to come either in the psyche of the widow or in the upset equilibrium of her children. Or again, the drunken parent who has "uncovered his little daughter's nakedness" (as Lev. 18 puts it) is in fact responsible for the ruin of her children a generation later, even "unto the third and fourth generation", as the Second Commandment declares. As a fact of history, and as we can read in 2 Sam., David had infected all his children with the sins of violence and lust. In this psalm, however, he shows that he has learned two things; (a) that God, in his infinite compassion, can and does forgive even those sins that have excluded the sinner from his fellowship and have ruined the lives of others; yet (b) that the *effect* of those sins must still be felt by later generations. That is the horror of them, for in his wisdom God has ordained that his Covenant was to cover not just *us* but our children also.

At verse 4 then David confesses he has broken God's covenant which was intended to include his children, and declares that God's *judgment is blameless*. Then next he recognizes the reality of original sin. Not that the sex act is sinful. Far from it. Sex is God's good idea. For by means of it, and with God involved in it, a man and a woman together can do what God does, viz. create (see Gen. 4:1). Now, the word for God's *mercy* in verse 1 derives from the noun for "womb". So in giving birth to a child Eve would experience what we must call "mother-love". This is a special love only a woman can know for the child of her body. Eve, womankind, knows mother-love; God knows mother-love. So how could sex and human birth ever be considered sinful? Rather, what David is saying is that he was born of a sinful father and a sinful mother, and they in their turn of sinful parents, for all men and women are sinners. God's judgment upon both David and his parents is thus perfectly *justified* and *blameless*.

PURGE ME

Psalm 51:6-12

6 Behold, thou desirest truth in the inward being;
     therefore teach me wisdom in my secret heart.

7 Purge me with hyssop, and I shall be clean;
  wash me, and I shall be whiter than snow.
8 Fill me with joy and gladness;
  let the bones which thou hast broken rejoice.
9 Hide thy face from my sins,
  and blot out all my iniquities.

10 Create in me a clean heart, O God,
  and put a new and right spirit within me.
11 Cast me not away from thy presence,
  and take not thy holy Spirit from me.
12 Restore to me the joy of thy salvation,
  and uphold me with a willing spirit.

In fact, God *desires "truth" in the inward being*, that is, reality and integrity. *Therefore*, David continues, recognizing the superficiality of his previous childish individualistic confession, *teach me wisdom in my secret heart*. In other words, he virtually begs, "Give me a new personality, one that is aware of my relationship to You and to other people within the Covenant."

In self-loathing he uses once again the language of the Law. See Lev. 14 for the regulations for the cleansing of skin diseases, Exod. 12:22 for sprinkling as a protection at the first Passover, and Isa. 1:16 for another moral application of the need for washing. "I feel filthy, O God", he is saying. "Cleanse me, for I cannot do it for myself. *Let me hear* [verse 8 *ftn.*] the *joy and gladness* of the worshipping people once again." That is, "Bring me home into the redeemed covenant fellowship again. Let my physical body be renewed" (not just my "soul") "and *blot out all my iniquities*" (or, better still, my "perversions").

So he makes three points in his prayer. (a) *Create for me* a new personality, he begs. He dares to pray thus, for God is he who makes all things new. The verb is one that is used of God only, never of man's work; it is the verb we find at Gen. 1:1. The miracle is, then, that forgiveness is in fact *re*-creation! (b) He continues, *Renew a steadfast spirit in me* (verse 10, RSV *ftn.*). That is, he asks God to give him back what he had once possessed but had later spurned, the spirit he had received from

God at his circumcision, when he became a limb in the body of the Bride of God.

The word *spirit* occurs here three times. We find it (a) in verse 10, where it is used in parallel with "personality". In verse 11, next (b) we read, "Don't take Your Holy Spirit from me". As a repentant sinner David knew his God well enough to be aware that God had never really left him, even though he had undoubtedly left God. So he still had the right possessed by all Israelites to declare "The Spirit of the Lord is upon me ..." (Isa. 61:1). How far David's experience of God's grace is, then, from some people today, who suppose that one must be baptized twice before one can receive the Holy Spirit! But then, David knew what *hesed* is all about. So he can declare: "Don't take away from me your gift to me of Your Holy Spirit." (c) Then may my own spirit voluntarily respond to Your gracious lead.

A forgiven sinner dare not rest on his laurels. He must let himself become God's servant to the world. That then is why (d) David asks God to give him a spirit that, like God's own, will provide him with the strength, the power to live a life of love and service, though not forgetting to witness to what God has done for him in forgiving him and renewing his life. This psalm, being of course the Word of God itself, helps us to understand that other and very important event of the coming of the Spirit that we meet with in Acts 2:1–36. We should always ask the Old Testament to help us interpret the New.

LET ME SHOW MY GRATITUDE

Psalm 51:13–19

13   Then I will teach transgressors thy ways,
       and sinners will return to thee.
14   Deliver me from bloodguiltiness, O God,
       thou God of my salvation,
       and my tongue will sing aloud of thy deliverance.

15   O Lord, open thou my lips,
        and my mouth shall show forth thy praise.
16   For thou hast no delight in sacrifice;
        were I to give a burnt offering, thou wouldst not be pleased.
17   The sacrifice acceptable to God is a broken spirit;
        a broken and contrite heart, O God, thou wilt not despise.

18   Do good to Zion in thy good pleasure;
        rebuild the walls of Jerusalem,
19   then wilt thou delight in right sacrifices,
        in burnt offerings and whole burnt offerings;
        then bulls will be offered on thy altar.

That then is why David declares (verse 13) "I will teach to those
who, like me, have broken the Covenant, the ways that lead
people back to thee (NEB), so that *sinners will return to thee*."
For in repentance there are two steps: (a) The first step is to be
sorry and repent and receive pardon. (b) The second is to act in
love towards others, in obedience to God, and help to lead them
home.

There are three words in verse 14 we must not gloss over,
thinking that we already know what they mean.

(1) One is *bloodguiltiness*. This word does not apply merely
to murder, though it may, as it did with David. But verse 14 *ftn.*
("death") suggests that there is more to it, as does Isa. 1:15.
There it refers to the death of our social conscience. Bloodguiltiness is that sense of guilt that we ought to feel when we eat a
good meal knowing that the society of which we are a part
allows to exist without a thought the misery of millions of
children who are dying of starvation; or, nearer home, it is what
it means to look away when little children are battered by a
drunken parent.

(2) The second word is in the phrase *Thou God of my
salvation*. This is the feminine term that we have met before (see
the Introduction). So it means "Thou God who hast given me
power to do something about the hungry masses and those
battered babies". It does *not* refer to my own personal salvation.

(3) The third word is *deliverance*. It means, My tongue shall

sing aloud about this power I now have, now that I have been
delivered from servitude to my own egotism, to love and to
serve God's orphans and his destitute people everywhere (Isa.
1:17).

Probably we have now reached the end of David's psalm. In
that case the last five verses have been added later to bring his
personal appeal to God into the worship of the believing
community. We often use verse 15 today (as did the Second
Temple) as an opening sentence in public worship. The words
remind us that we need God's grace even to be able to praise
God!

My sacrifice, O God, is a broken spirit (see verse 17 *ftn.*).
Twice we meet with the word "broken". A "whole" heart
implies an element of egotism, and a sense of self-confidence
and self-righteousness in approaching God. But a repentant
sinner must first sacrifice his egotism, and be "stricken, smitten
and afflicted" (three words found together at Isa. 53:4) just as
was the Suffering Servant; for such, *O God, thou wilt not
despise.* The servant of Isa. 53 was indeed despised and rejected
of men, but not of God. The "tax-collector" in Jesus' day was
one who had put himself "beyond the pale of the Covenant".
Yet even this outcast was accepted because he beat his breast
and said "God be merciful to me a sinner" (Luke 18:13).

Finally (verses 18-19) the re-creation of even one individual
human being, such as David the king, through confession,
forgiveness and the receiving of power to do what God does, is
bound up together within the purpose of the whole creation,
that is, with the re-creation of Israel at that point in history. I
would suggest that these last two verses were penned between
the years 538 B.C. and 520 B.C., between the return from exile in
Babylon and the commencement of the rebuilding of the
temple. The rebuilt temple was completed in 516 B.C. Thereafter
there was a great Passover service held to *dedicate the house of
the Lord with joy* (Ezra 6:16). At that moment, then, the
Covenant was renewed, and God—once again—dwelt in the
midst of his people in the Holy Place. This took place exactly at
the end of the seventy years that Jeremiah had predicted the

exile would last. Though they had come back home to Jerusalem physically some years earlier, after fifty years in exile, only now with the dedication of the temple did there take place the end of their separation from God in a spiritual sense. Consequently, the whole sacrificial system that atoned for the sins of Israel could now be re-instituted, and Israel could live once again as the Holy People in continually renewed fellowship with the Holy God. And so we have a continuity from this point to the fulfilment and completion in the New Covenant of that Holy Communion with God which he has offered to us through the one and *right sacrifice* in which *thou wilt delight*.

HOW STUPID CAN YOU GET?

Psalm 52:1-9

To the choirmaster. A Maskil of David, when Doeg, the Edomite, came and told Saul, "David has come to the house of Ahimelech."

1 Why do you boast, O mighty man,
    of mischief done against the godly?
2 All the day you are plotting destruction.
  Your tongue is like a sharp razor,
    you worker of treachery.
3 You love evil more than good,
    and lying more than speaking the truth.   *Selah*
4 You love all words that devour,
    O deceitful tongue.
5 But God will break you down for ever;
    he will snatch and tear you from your tent;
    he will uproot you from the land of the living.   *Selah*
6 The righteous shall see, and fear,
    and shall laugh at him, saying,
7 "See the man who would not make God his refuge,
    but trusted in the abundance of his riches,
    and sought refuge in his wealth!"

8 But I am like a green olive tree
    in the house of God.
  I trust in the steadfast love of God
    for ever and ever.

9 I will thank thee for ever,
   because thou hast done it.
 I will proclaim thy name, for it is good,
   in the presence of the godly.

How greatly the psalms can differ from each other! How very different Psalm 52 is from Psalm 51! We see why it requires 150 psalms to range over the whole gamut of human emotions, hopes and fears, and to express a truly "ecumenical" response to God's continual offer of grace. Yet although all the psalms are valid for all kinds of people in all ages, the editors very wisely applied each of the Davidic psalms, at least, to a moment in the experience of this one particular man—both saint and sinner at the same time. The heading tells us of the particular moment in question—see 1 Sam. 21:7–22:23—in David's experience into which the psalm could fit. Then, as a well-known scholar puts it: "Through the mouth of David the man they become a personal word from God in each individual situation." Consequently, the title does not tie the psalm to the past, but releases it to be our contemporary. And so, as a *maskil*, it has something to teach us even now. This psalm is in three parts.

Part I. Sarcasm. How stupid you are, you "he-man", to boast of your own destructive ideas in face of God's faithful love (see RSV *ftn.*). Do you really think your evil plotting can win against God's creative plan? One way of showing your contempt for God is in the *deceitfulness of your tongue.* A terrible description of an evil bully such as this man seems to be is to be found at Mic. 3:2–3.

Part II. Malicious laughter. Our bully is stupid because he does not realize he can't win against God. The Deity (*el*) will simply demolish you—*for ever! God will tear you from your tent* (the language of Israel's journey on its march to the Promised Land), *and he will uproot you from the land of the living* (reflecting the life of the community now settled in their land). Then, speaking for those who have now been put right with God, that very human character David—here more sinner than saint!—declares that God's people will laugh at the "he-man", this bully type, on three counts:

(1) His ego is too big to admit his need of God.

(2) He trusts instead in the power of his bank balance.

(3) He seeks refuge, not in God, but in his own lusts, as the Hebrew has it.

We too, like David, are sinners. Therefore we can understand his malicious laughter at this poor fool of an egotist.

Part III. Deep satisfaction. Verse 8 reverses the tone of verse 5. Instead of breaking down and tearing up, here we have a picture of a quiet growth. This is because *I* (David) (a) worship in the house of God, and (b) trust in God's *hesed*, his unchanging, steadfast and loyal covenantal love. David is therefore not boasting here of his own faith and commitment to God as against the stupidity of the great egotist. He is boasting, like St. Paul (1 Cor. 1:31) in the unchangeableness of God. And so, all he can do, since it is *God who has done it*, who saved him from the company of stupid *workers of treachery* (verse 2), is to *thank* him *for ever*. "I have trusted in his unchanging love," he adds. Consequently we can now give a deep content to the last couplet:

(1) God is as gracious to this gleeful, gloating poet, whether he be David or me, in all his narrow-mindedness, as he is to the most generous-hearted of believers.

(2) In the light of this wonderful reality, he can say, "I will wait expectantly till all eternity for God to reveal himself to his covenant people [as the Hebrew says]—for that will be good for us indeed!"

GOD IS IRRELEVANT

Psalm 53:1–6

To the choirmaster: according to Mahalath. A Maskil of David.

1 The fool says in his heart,
    "There is no God."
  They are corrupt, doing abominable iniquity;
    there is none that does good.

2 God looks down from heaven
    upon the sons of men
to see if there are any that are wise,
    that seek after God.

3 They have all fallen away;
    they are all alike depraved;
there is none that does good,
    no, not one.

4 Have those who work evil no understanding,
    who eat up my people as they eat bread,
    and do not call upon God?

5 There they are, in great terror,
    in terror such as has not been!
For God will scatter the bones of the ungodly;
    they will be put to shame, for God has rejected them.

6 O that deliverance for Israel would come from Zion!
    When God restores the fortunes of his people,
    Jacob will rejoice and Israel be glad.

The phrase *according to Mahalath* probably means "set to a sad melody". For this psalm is about a very sad fact of human life, that many people take it for granted that God doesn't matter. They say: "Oh yes, I suppose there is a God—but what difference does that make?"

This fallacy is both ancient and modern. In OT times virtually nobody was an atheist. Life was too mysterious for them to make that foolish mistake. So the words, "*There is no God*", must be looked at from within the Bible, and not from a modern secularist standpoint. In the OT nowhere do we find that God just "is", or "exists". Always he is "doing". Gen. 1:1 (RSV *ftn.*) runs: "When God began to create." So now we know him by his actions, for loving, saving, redeeming, and so on are all creative actions. This fool spoken of here simply cannot see God *in action*. He is the "absentee landlord" in the world. Consequently, "when the cat's away, the mice do play". Since God seems to be away, then *men do abominable iniquity*.

The psalmist, however, asserts that such a view of God is nonsense. God *is* concerned for his world. *God looks down* (that in itself is an action) *upon the sons of Adam*, all of whom God has *made* (another divine activity) in his own image (Gen. 1:27). And since these sons have rebelled against the divine image (compare Isa. 1:2–3), that is, against God's saving action in so creating them, God must necessarily become their Judge. *All have fallen away. There is none that does good, no, not one* (see Gen. 6:5; Jer. 5:1; 17:9; Rom. 3:9–12).

We are told at verse 6 that God's people Israel are now in exile in Babylon. Their sin has brought them to this disastrous situation. Only God therefore can *act* to save them and bring them home, since it is only God who can redeem a sinful people.

At this point, however, we should ask ourselves—"Does this psalm not sound a familiar chord?" Of course it does. For it is almost identical with Psalm 14. So we should go back and see what comments were made there. Psalm 14 is a *Yahweh* (the Lord) psalm. Psalm 53 belongs in the *Elohim* (God) collection, being in Book II that began at Psalm 42. Why should we not ask ourselves the meaning of the slight changes from Psalm 14 that we find here? And why should sensible men include this psalm in their Book II when it has already appeared in Book I? Evidently the reason is to emphasise that God is no mere philosophical idea, but is the living and loving God, the Creator God, in whom so few people really believe.

Finally, since this is a "Study" Bible we are reading, we might well challenge ourselves now with a second translation (slightly paraphrased) of the last verse. This new translation makes full use of those basic terms we have noted so often, differentiating between their occurrence in the masculine and the feminine forms: "Would that out of Zion [that is to say, from God present in Israel's midst], once God has re-established his people in Jerusalem, Israel might again receive the strength to seek the salvation of the world! Then Jacob would rejoice and Israel would be glad." These are the two names of the ancestor of God's people, and so of the people themselves in the psalmist's day, and to fit with the rules of poetry in Hebrew they are set down in parallel, though referring to one and the same man.

GOD'S ABSOLUTE FAITHFULNESS

Psalm 54:1-7

To the choirmaster: with stringed instruments. A Maskil of David,
when the Ziphites went and told Saul, "David is in hiding among us."

1 Save me, O God, by thy name,
 and vindicate me by thy might.
2 Hear my prayer, O God;
 give ear to the words of my mouth.

3 For insolent men have risen against me,
 ruthless men seek my life;
 they do not set God before them. *Selah*

4 Behold, God is my helper,
 the Lord is the upholder of my life.
5 He will requite my enemies with evil;
 in thy faithfulness put an end to them.

6 With a freewill offering I will sacrifice to thee;
 I will give thanks to thy name, O Lord, for it is good.
7 For thou hast delivered me from every trouble,
 and my eye has looked in triumph on my enemies.

If we wonder why the cry we hear in this psalm should occur so frequently in the Psalter, we should take a look at ourselves. For each new day as it dawns we face life all over again. The old doubts return, the old sins obsess us, the desperate need of grace is upon us once again. The editors knew that David, that very human person, must have felt the need to cry to God frequently, simply because they felt it themselves. For comment on the heading see 1 Sam. 23:19. Ziph was three miles south-east of Hebron.

The first two verses each begin, in the Hebrew, with "O God". That is how one prays. Then the poet puts content into the *name* "God". He is not a distant Spirit. He is "our Saviour God", for that is what his *name* means (compare Matt. 1:21). Moreover, he is *mighty* to save. Despite God's greatness,

however, the poet has the courage to begin his second line with
"O God" once again, and then to offer a very short prayer,
"Listen, please, God". What is his plea? Foreigners (see RSV
verse 3, *ftn.*), that is, people outside the Covenant, are acting
violently against me, naturally so, for they know nothing about
the God of forgiveness, compassion and saving love. The God
whom we know and worship is naturally kept in the centre of
our lives. We should note that this is actually Isaiah's terrible
indictment, not of foreigners in general, but of God's own
people. He declares that by their rebellious lives they have
turned themselves into foreigners who live their lives outside
the Covenant (Isa. 1:4)!

The psalmist here faces the same problem as we do today.
The violence in our cities is occasioned by people who do not
belong in the New Covenant. Unwittingly, they worship Baal,
the biblical god of violence, and Ashera, the biblical goddess of
sex. Their heart and mind are regulated and controlled by the
object of their faith. People become similar to what they
worship, whether their God be Yahweh or Baal, as Elijah
pointed out to the excited crowd on Mount Carmel (1 Kings
18). Or again, "Choose this day whom you will serve, Yahweh
or the god of foreigners", shouted Joshua to the Israelites who
had now entered Canaan (Josh. 24:14–18). Our problem with
the ruthless youth of our cities is that we may have lost contact
with their minds, for we worship different gods.

This man, whose God is the Lord, confesses that he is helpless
in face of the effect that the worship of false gods has upon their
followers. Of course he does not know the answer which was
still to come, and which was to be given during the exile, that it
is suffering love, crucifixion if you like, which alone can break
through the barrier that exists between the "gods" and their
respective adherents. But Israel's God remains utterly faithful
to his own; and so, says the psalmist, I can leave *him* to handle
the problem of the "gods".

The Chorus begins at verse 6. The congregation now adds its
joyous voice as it takes to itself the significance of God's
absolute faithfulness. The *freewill offering* mentioned is de-

scribed at Lev. 7:11–18; 22:18–30, and at Num. 15:1–10. It was an extra-ordinary one, not a routine offering. It was given only when the worshipper wanted to say an extra-special thanks to God for his gracious, saving love. Note that it must be offered to God "with a whole heart", that is, in complete sincerity of purpose. The animal to be sacrificed must be itself perfect, with no blemishes, not diseased in any way, but the best beast one can afford to give.

Then, says the congregation, *I will give thanks to thy name, O Lord*, for, as we saw at verse 1, God's *name*, the very essence of his being, is Saviour. As Saviour, *thou hast delivered* (saved) *me from every trouble*, including the discomfiting of my enemies. *Thy name is good.* Good, indeed, "*for*" me, as we have seen this word "good" really means. The name of Saviour can be nothing less.

In this psalm, then, we don't find any gloating over the fate of the wicked as we have seen before. This psalmist leaves the wicked in the hands of God. Since God is the power to help, he must also be the power to deal with evil. The emphasis, rather, is upon the wondrous nature of Israel's God. For he is the Saviour God. That then is why we want to praise him, says the congregation, not only in word but also in deed.

"DON'T ROCK THE BOAT"

Psalm 55:1–14

To the choirmaster: with stringed instruments. A Maskil of David.

1 Give ear to my prayer, O God;
    and hide not thyself from my supplication!
2 Attend to me, and answer me;
    I am overcome by my trouble.
3 I am distraught by the noise of the enemy,
    because of the oppression of the wicked.
For they bring trouble upon me,
    and in anger they cherish enmity against me.

4 My heart is in anguish within me,
    the terrors of death have fallen upon me.

5 Fear and trembling come upon me,
and horror overwhelms me.
6 And I say, "O that I had wings like a dove!
I would fly away and be at rest;
7 yea, I would wander afar,
I would lodge in the wilderness, *Selah*
8 I would haste to find me a shelter
from the raging wind and tempest."

9 Destroy their plans, O Lord, confuse their tongues;
for I see violence and strife in the city.
10 Day and night they go around it on its walls;
and mischief and trouble are within it,
11 ruin is in its midst;
oppression and fraud
do not depart from its market place.

12 It is not an enemy who taunts me—
then I could bear it;
it is not an adversary who deals insolently with me—
then I could hide from him.
13 But it is you, my equal,
my companion, my familiar friend.
14 We used to hold sweet converse together;
within God's house we walked in fellowship.

There is much to comment on in this psalm, for it rises up out of the depths of a *distraught* heart. And while few of us live continually in such a state of soul, all of us have experienced at least momentarily a terrible awareness of blankness. This experience has been called "The Dark Night of the Soul". The Germans have a word for it; it is *Angst*, a word meaning very much more than our English word anxiety. The psalm teaches us (in the heading it is called a *maskil*, a teaching psalm) to turn back to God alone if we do ever have such a brush with hell—if only, adds the psalmist, if only God would listen and answer! The psalm tells us why there are times when God does not seem to answer. Evil is, of course, not a mere philosophical idea; evil is incarnate in human flesh; it is found in people who can turn themselves into the enemies of God's people, simply because the latter seek to show forth to others the grace and love of God. Evil is the actions of people. The NEB brings this out well; verse 3 runs: "I am panic-stricken at the shouts of my enemies, at the shrill clamour of the wicked."

All people fear death (verse 4). The horror of its inevitability may hit us quite suddenly, especially if an "enemy"—whether he be an individual person, a group, a cancer, a fire, a flood— overwhelms us unawares. It is said that the basic cause, usually quite unexamined and not faced up to, of much mental illness in our hospitals today is the experience of this basic *Angst*. Any kind of person may suffer from it. It may lead eventually, even, to suicide. Job knew about it (Job 21:6); so did Isaiah (Isa. 21:3–4), and Ezekiel saw it all around him when the people of Judah finally realized the fact of the coming destruction of their beloved capital city (Ezek. 7:18).

It is natural human instinct to run away from trouble (verse 6). This is shown when people declare defiantly, "Why does God allow this and this to happen?" They do so because they do not accept the fact that they are living in a world where good and evil cohabit, and where the kingdom of God "is not of this world", as Jesus said. For God's kingdom emerges and grows out of the creative tension between the two. In flying away from the tension and seeking for *rest* from having to live in that tension, this psalmist would be willing to alight even in *the wilderness*. There at least there would be no tension, only what is negative, no *raging wind and tempest*. In fact, the psalmist shows a terrible misunderstanding of the purpose and plan of God for us his children in this world he has created. A silly young man once said to the great philosopher, Thomas Carlyle, "I accept the universe." To which Carlyle replied, "Gad, sir, you had better."

The beautiful poetic lines "O for the wings of a dove . . . " have haunted men and women over the centuries. But one notices that they have been repeated only by those of little faith, as, for example, Lord Byron, the poet, who frequently suffered fits of depression. Unfortunately, today a whole generation of youth is seeking to "stop the world—I want to get off", or opt out of what they call the rat race and seek the simple life. They remain unaware that unless they contribute to the cost of our communal medical services, sewerage, transport, and so on, they have no right to make use of them in their need; nor do they realize that faithful people stay in the rat race deliberately in order to contribute their mite to the common good.

It is true that one can look out at the ills of society with despair (verse 9). "God made the country, man made the town", with all its deep social problems arising from ignorance, greed and selfishness, especially, as our poet says, in *its market place*. It is an aspect of our deep depression therefore if we beg God to destroy the vast cities of Jakarta, Calcutta, Tokyo, Lagos and Los Angeles. "*Split their tongues, Lord*", the psalmist says, just as today the self-righteous cry: "Horsewhip them all!" Greed and sweated labour, he says, are never absent from the city's business life.

Our writer even comes down to personalities. Not only is the market-place ("Wall Street", if you like), or the social system under which we live, riddled with evil; the structures of society, he declares, are being bolstered by people who have been "my personal friends and fellow-worshippers". So it is a case of "*Et tu, Brute*" (*Julius Caesar*, Act III, Scene 1, line 77). These so-called friends now consider me a fool for questioning the system at all, or as we say today, for "rocking the boat". Plaintively, then, he sighs, "There is no one left to love me." Consequently, what follows is a complete and horrible reversal of the will of God.

CAST YOUR BURDEN ON THE LORD

Psalm 55:15–23

15 Let death come upon them;
    let them go down to Sheol alive;
    let them go away in terror into their graves.

16 But I call upon God;
    and the Lord will save me.

17 Evening and morning and at noon
    I utter my complaint and moan,
    and he will hear my voice.
18 He will deliver my soul in safety
    from the battle that I wage,
    for many are arrayed against me.
19 God will give ear, and humble them,
    he who is enthroned from of old;
    because they keep no law,
    and do not fear God.   *Selah*

20 My companion stretched out his hand against his friends,
    he violated his covenant.
21 His speech was smoother than butter,
    yet war was in his heart;
    his words were softer than oil,
    yet they were drawn swords.

22 Cast your burden on the Lord,
    and he will sustain you;
    he will never permit
    the righteous to be moved.

23 But thou, O God, wilt cast them down
    into the lowest pit;
    men of blood and treachery
    shall not live out half their days.
    But I will trust in thee.

Those self-centred, influential people whom the social reformer, the environmentalist, the thoughtful economist oppose for being destructive of society, our poet now begs God, not to confront, but to destroy! In the same way there are people today who would do just what this psalmist wants done—"Shoot the lot!"; "Bring back capital punishment!" In fact, the psalmist shows a double tragedy of soul:

(1) He himself would like to take wings and fly away from the world's problems; but

(2) If he had the power, he would quite simply get rid of the trouble-makers by sending them all to hell.

But I! In his present mood of self-righteousness our writer declares, "*But I*, unlike those evil people, *I call upon God.* So I know that *the Lord will save me.*" So he keeps on pounding at God's door with his self-righteous prayer, morning, noon and night, confident that God will lift him out of *the battle that I wage*, the tensions in which I am living, the tensions, in fact, in which all mankind must live. He reminds us of the specious nursery rhyme "Little Jack Horner". That objectionable small boy "put in his thumb and pulled out a plum, and said 'What a good boy am I'". *God will give ear to my prayer*, he continues, *and humble them*, *because* they never change (see RSV verse 19, *ftn.*), *and they do not fear God.* For evil has now become their second nature.

Now he pin-points the disloyalty of one particular friend, though the word *companion* does not occur in the Hebrew. The word "covenant" in the OT is used in two ways. (a) There is the Covenant of Sinai when the living God entered into a special relationship with sinful Israel. It was a covenant imposed by grace. (b) But there was also the equal covenant, such as that between David and Jonathan, or today such as that between husband and wife. It is this second meaning of the word that is referred to here. This sworn friend, however, had turned out to be completely false within.

The Chorus, verses 22–23.

(1) The first part of the psalm described how distraught the writer is.

(2) The second part described the wickedness of the city.

(3) The third part pointed a finger at the psalmist's friends.

(4) The fourth began with "But *I* call upon God . . . " in great self-righteousness.

(5) The fifth part again describes an individual who has been disloyal to the covenant he made with the psalmist. And there the poem suddenly ends.

(6) But now the editors prepare an answer to all the above agonizing situation for the congregation to sing, and at last we meet with a worthy declaration of faith.

Cast your "lot" (RSV verse 22, *ftn.*) *on the Lord, and he will sustain you.* That is the first (a) possible meaning of the word in inverted commas. God will never permit those whom he put right with himself to be upset. God takes you as you are, vengeful thoughts and all. Our lot is to live somewhere in this world, wherever God has decided to put us; but wherever that may be there will certainly be tension arising from *the raging wind and tempest* (verse 8), which is part and parcel of life on God's earth.

However (b) there is a second possible meaning to this rare and peculiar word. It may refer to those talents you have which you could employ in service to the world. If you would only do so, then "he will feed you" is how we can interpret the following verb. But (c) the phrase may mean quite simply "He *loves* you, and he will care for you".

However we are to understand this phrase, then, we are to tell God all about things, all about the problems, the tensions, the pain and sorrow of our life. Let him carry your burden for you; he is able to do it (see 1 Pet. 5:7). And then, remember (as Paul puts it at Rom. 12:19), vengeance is God's prerogative, not yours. Leave him to deal with the wicked.

Finally, in the last line we return to the "But I" of verse 16. This time, however, we find it pointing straight in the opposite direction. *But I will trust in thee.* A worthy ending to the psalm, one that truly answers one of the great hindrances to the life of faith.

THE DOVE ON FAR-OFF TEREBINTHS

Psalm 56:1-13

To the choirmaster: according to the Dove on Far-off Terebinths. A Miktam of David, when the Philistines seized him in Gath.

1 Be gracious to me, O God, for men trample upon me;
    all day long foemen oppress me;
2 my enemies trample upon me all day long,
    for many fight against me proudly.
3 When I am afraid,
    I put my trust in thee.

4 In God, whose word I praise,
      in God I trust without a fear.
   What can flesh do to me?

5 All day long they seek to injure my cause;
      all their thoughts are against me for evil.
6 They band themselves together, they lurk,
      they watch my steps.
   As they have waited for my life,
7   so recompense them for their crime;
      in wrath cast down the peoples, O God!

8 Thou hast kept count of my tossings;
      put thou my tears in thy bottle!
   Are they not in thy book?
9 Then my enemies will be turned back
      in the day when I call.
   This I know, that God is for me.
10 In God, whose word I praise,
      in the Lord, whose word I praise,
11   in God I trust without a fear.
   What can man do to me?

12 My vows to thee I must perform, O God;
      I will render thank offerings to thee.
13 For thou hast delivered my soul from death,
      yea, my feet from falling,
   that I may walk before God
      in the light of life.

The heading as a whole helps us understand how elastic the psalms are, that is to say, how they can fit as many occasions and as many persons as need the love and forgiveness of God.

(1) The psalm is a *miktam*. Thus it is here to teach us something about God. The word probably means "containing pithy, expressive sayings". But at Ps. 16:1 we noted another scholarly suggestion as to what the word means.

(2) The psalm could well fit the occasion reported in 1 Sam. 21:10–15.

(3) It was evidently one of a collection kept in a cupboard of the temple, to which the choirmaster held the key. Some archaeologists believe that such cupboards were built into the

outer wall of the temple where were stored the various accoutrements for the sacrifices and for the services of worship. The name of the tune to which it was to be sung means either (a) To the Dove of (on) Far-off Terebinths (a kind of oak tree), or, (b) To the Dove of (amongst) far-away gods. Now, the word "dove" in Hebrew is Jonah. We remember that, just as the Fish was the symbol used by the early Church for Christian believers, so the Dove in the late Second Temple period signified the people of Israel. In our biblical book of Jonah that individual fled from the God who dwelt in Zion and found himself amongst the gods of the pagan crew of sailors on a ship going very far off, to Tarshish in fact. This town lay beyond the Straits of Gibraltar on the west coast of Spain, and was thus right out of "civilization" altogether. Under the judgment of God, however, Jonah ended up on the bottom of the sea with sea-weed in his hair (Jon. 2:5). That sea was not the Mediterranean, however. Rather it was the ocean of chaos in which swam that "far off" and destructive goddess Tiamat, the monster of the deep. At Creation God had "put her in her place". Like the devil in the NT, however, she was not destroyed. God used her to discipline his loved ones; she still had to do God's will. God's will was that this monster of the deep should spew Jonah out again, back onto *Yahweh*'s land. God planned in love to give this foolish man, this representative of all Israel, this Jonah, this dove, a second chance to be his missionary to the nations of mankind.

When we see this fascinating parabolic tale as referring to Israel-Jonah-Dove, we realize that while the forgiveness of God comes out of Israel's failure and "descent into hell", their calling to be a light to lighten the Gentiles still stands as God's purpose and plan. Jonah, Israel, was called to preach God's Word to Nineveh, that huge city that symbolized the great population of the Near East. Israel was to *be* (as Isa. 49:6 has it in the Hebrew), to incorporate, to embody, God's saving love to those lands afar off where there were already many gods, now that the exiles had been rescued from the "belly" of the monster of the primal ocean (Jer. 51:34).

As the people sang this psalm, then, to the tune that brought their mind back to what the Covenant was all about, and why God had chosen them at all, they were reminded that God's forgiveness and renewal were not ends in themselves, but only the end of the beginning.

IN GOD WE TRUST

Psalm 56:1-13 *(cont'd)*

Just as Jonah, when he sank spluttering in the sea, cried to God, *When I am afraid, I put my trust in thee*, so also does the psalmist. The American people have put this assertion upon their coins. Yet we should ask, Is such a statement enough? In the petty spirit that we see in Jonah we note how this psalmist begs God to take vengeance on *all humanity* (see the last chapter of Jonah). What a distortion of justice! "They" have waited for *my* life, he says, therefore let the whole world perish! So we note how the perspicacious writer of the Jonah parable puts his finger on Jonah's (and Israel's, and the psalmist's) problem (Jon. 4:1-3). There Jonah shows himself to be as small-minded as the speaker here shows himself to be. It is not enough to say: "*I know that God is for me.*" Of course he is; for I belong in the Covenant. Of course *I have no fear what man can do to me*. But is that the whole reason why God has given me life? Is it just that I should *praise him without fear*? Is this all that it means to belong to "the Servant People of God"?

But before we look for an answer to this, make a note of God's personal care for "narrow-minded me", in preserving *my* tears in *his* bottle, and writing up even *my* midnight hours in *his* book. Yet even this picture furthers the purpose of the psalm by means of a pun. For the words for *tossings* and for *bottle* are two different spellings of the one word that we find at Gen. 4:16. There Cain *wanders* off to the land of *Nod*, that is, to the land of *wandering* away from God.

The book of Jonah deals with the manner in which the God of grace gives Israel a second chance to be his Servant to the nations. God's compassionate love and care, which he offers to Israel, is not meant for her to clutch to her own breast. It is indeed a joyous reality that *God is for me*; but it is for me as his "missionary" and not as his selfish seeker after my own private salvation. Is it sufficient, then, as we find at verse 11, merely to repeat what we have already heard at verse 4?

The Chorus, verses 12–13. The tune the congregation are using has now reminded the worshippers of their proper relationship to God. So each here declares:

(1) I will *pay my vows to thee, O God*. The heathen sailors had of course done as much to their gods. But Jonah had refused to do so (Jon. 1:16).

(2) *I will render thank offerings to thee*, even as Jonah did eventually (Jon. 2:9) when he came to his senses.

(3) *For thou hast delivered my soul* (my whole being) *from death*. This is what God had done for Jonah when the latter was actually in Sheol, the abode of the dead. It was from there that God had rescued him (Jon. 2:2). For flight from the living God means flight into death, the death of the spirit.

(4) God had done all this for a purpose—*that I may walk before God in the light of life*. "To walk" here, as we saw at Ps. 1:1, means "to go about one's daily life".

So the congregation now confesses that God has forgiven his people. For that they are whole-heartedly grateful. They will therefore let "Nineveh" see the Light of life reflected from their human faces as they live their lives and go about their daily calling before the eyes of the vast host of the heathen in this world. The heathen will then see that this Light is of God (see Job 33:30; Isa. 9:2; 58:8; Mal. 4:2; John 8:12).

"SOMETIMES A LIGHT SURPRISES..."

Psalm 57:1–11

To the choirmaster: according to Do Not Destroy.
A Miktam of David, when he fled from Saul, in the cave.

1 Be merciful to me, O God, be merciful to me,
    for in thee my soul takes refuge;

in the shadow of thy wings I will take refuge,
  till the storms of destruction pass by.
2 I cry to God Most High,
    to God who fulfils his purpose for me.
3 He will send from heaven and save me,
    he will put to shame those who trample upon me.   *Selah*
God will send forth his steadfast love and his faithfulness!

4 I lie in the midst of lions
    that greedily devour the sons of men;
  their teeth are spears and arrows,
    their tongues sharp swords.

5 Be exalted, O God, above the heavens!
    Let thy glory be over all the earth!

6 They set a net for my steps;
    my soul was bowed down.
  They dug a pit in my way,
    but they have fallen into it themselves.   *Selah*
7 My heart is steadfast, O God,
    my heart is steadfast!
  I will sing and make melody!
8   Awake, my soul!
  Awake, O harp and lyre!
    I will awake the dawn!
9 I will give thanks to thee, O Lord, among the peoples;
    I will sing praises to thee among the nations.
10 For thy steadfast love is great to the heavens,
    thy faithfulness to the clouds.

11 Be exalted, O God, above the heavens!
    Let thy glory be over all the earth!

Unlike Psalm 56 this psalm is a cry to God for help, made by one who knows God will answer, for God has already done so. For the heading, see 1 Sam. 22 and 24. A number of Christian Churches recite this psalm on Easter morning.

The Cry, verses 1–4. These verses contain the cry. It comes from the lips of one who knows that *God fulfils his purpose for me*, that is, gives my life a meaning. His purpose for me is based on his *hesed, his steadfast love and his faithfulness which he will send forth.* Note that there is no such thing as love and no such thing as faithfulness; these are merely abstract ideas. Only a living person "sends forth love". In other words, God sends *himself*, full of steadfast love and loyalty to his own faithfulness, that is, to his unchangeableness within the Covenant. The phrase *storms of destruction* (verse 1) could be "gusts of greed". *God Most High* is the name of the deity who spoke with Abraham on the first occasion that Jerusalem is mentioned in the Bible (Gen. 14:18, where it is called Salem). The poet remembers that Yahweh, (the Lord), is the God both of the Covenant and of Creation.

The language of verse 4 is intentionally grotesque. The oldest bridge in the city of Prague, the Charles Bridge, spans the river Vltava in a number of graceful arches. Hollowed into the top of each of the columns where they meet the parapet, and at eye-level, there are mythological scenes which the pedestrian cannot help but look at. One of them is a grotesque peep into the flames of hell, the damned being prodded by the devil's fork. "It makes you think," said my companion on the bridge. That then is what this verse is meant to do. Literally it reads: "My soul, my whole being, is lying amongst lions." Thereupon the next verb could mean either "as they scorch", or "as they swallow up" human beings. Either idea, of course, sounds fearsome, as it is meant to do.

The Chorus, verse 5. The congregation bursts in at this point with this *Te Deum*.

The Picture continues, verse 6. "They set a net in front of me; they fell in." The practice in those days was to dig a hole on the track that wild animals were accustomed to follow, place a net over it, and camouflage it with boughs and leaves. The animal would then fall in, get entangled in the net, and so not be able to climb out again. But this trap was now a man-trap! The poet's enemies had fallen into their own trap, he declares, just as today a terrorist may inadvertently blow himself up with his own hand-grenade. Then comes *Selah*, the burst of music to make one pause and think.

Faith triumphant, verses 7-10. The poet's faith is total. The old Hebrews did not know that the brain is situated inside the skull; they supposed that one thought with one's heart. So, in the psalms, "heart" should be understood to mean "brain" or "mind". Then he says, *Awake, my "liver"* (not soul at all!). He might instead have invited his kidneys to praise God as other writers do; see Jer. 11:20, for example. What he means, of course, is that he must worship God with the whole of his being. How far we are here from the Greek and the Indian notion that the "soul" is the imperishable part of man, and that his body is of no importance, that, in fact, the body is evil—*soma sema*, "the body is a tomb", as one ancient Greek philosopher declared. Paul says that the body is the Temple of God, and so is holy, not evil (1 Cor. 3:16–17).

Our psalmist's lovely phrase, *I will awake the dawn*, reminds us how Bonhoeffer, Hitler's special prisoner, in his Berlin jail, did just that as he awaited the firing squad at dawn. For he too believed utterly that God's *hesed*, his steadfast love, and God's *emeth*, his faithfulness, reach both down into a prison cell and up to the highest clouds in the sky.

The Chorus, verse 11. After such a grand declaration of faith, is it any wonder that all present want to shout their faith in the words they had used at verse 5? This is because the object of their faith is not "religion", but God's *faithfulness*, or, as we might say today, the ultimate living reality behind all that we can see and touch.

THE FATE OF EVIL POWERS

Psalm 58:1–11

To the choirmaster: according to Do Not Destroy.
A Miktam of David.

1 Do you indeed decree what is right, you gods?
   Do you judge the sons of men uprightly?

2 Nay, in your hearts you devise wrongs;
   your hands deal out violence on earth.

3 The wicked go astray from the womb,
   they err from their birth, speaking lies.

4 They have venom like the venom of a serpent,
   like the deaf adder that stops its ear,
5 so that it does not hear the voice of charmers
   or of the cunning enchanter.

6 O God, break the teeth in their mouths;
   tear out the fangs of the young lions, O Lord!
7 Let them vanish like water that runs away;
   like grass let them be trodden down and wither.
8 Let them be like the snail which dissolves into slime,
   like the untimely birth that never sees the sun.
9 Sooner than your pots can feel the heat of thorns,
   whether green or ablaze, may he sweep them away!

10 The righteous will rejoice when he sees the vengeance;
   he will bathe his feet in the blood of the wicked.
11 Men will say, "Surely there is a reward for the righteous;
   surely there is a God who judges on earth."

The tune recommended for this psalm is entitled "Do Not Destroy". That seems odd, when, at first glance, it would appear that the psalmist is imploring God to do the very opposite. But what this psalm offers us is a deep insight into the meaning of God's provident rule.

Address to the gods, verses 1–5. What a plethora of gods there were in those days! The Egyptians worshipped over eighty gods and goddesses, some in the shape of animals, some half-animal, half-human beings. There were Canaanite, Arabian, Babylonian, Cretan, Greek, Ammonite, Edomite gods, and scores more. The psalmist does not deny that they exist, just as we do not deny that there are many religions and ideologies today other than our own. The difference between the gods and Israel's God is this, however. The gods all behave like human beings do. They fight, they quarrel, they murder, they copulate, they like to be wheedled, because every one of them is a copy of mankind. This is because from earliest times men had created their gods in their own image. Men and women are sinners, however, even from birth (verse 3). Thus, if they create their gods in their own image, then the gods too are bound to be evil. This is a point to which the secularist humanist of the nineteenth century was entirely blind, when he declared that men always create God in their own image. But, of course, the reverse is true of the God of the Bible. At Gen. 1:27 we learn that God created men-and-women, male and female together, in *his* image. Judaism and Christianity alone in the thinking of the whole world regard this as the truth.

One of the OT's favourite pictures of these theological ideas is that of an assembly or parliament of the gods of the nations sitting in the sky. There they legislate for what human beings are to do on earth, for man has created them to do what man wants done. Our psalmist begins with this picture; but then he goes on to ask sarcastically how the gods suppose they can legislate anything good at all when they themselves reflect the mind of man! The movement is two-way, for the gods above are now the cause of the violence on earth from which mankind has always suffered. A telling mythological picture of the reality of the powers of evil, shown here to be no mere abstractions, but as alive and vicious beings, is given us at Gen. 6:1-4. Following it we come to the words, *God saw that the wickedness of man was great in the earth.* But while God permits the powers of evil to exist (the NT likewise speaks of God permitting the devil to be active amongst humankind), God—to continue with our picture-theology—is in the chair at those assemblies (see Ps. 82:1), and so is able to keep a rein on the activities of the gods.

This all means that God gives evil freedom to act. He has created man free to obey himself or to listen to the gods. But the subtlety of their wiles is such that poor humans let themselves become slaves without knowing it. This is obvious in the realm of economics and big business, in the case of drug-taking or of sexual licence. Faceless, beastly powers now have such people in their grip.

That, then, is why in verse 6 the psalmist calls upon God—the Chairman of the group—to *break the teeth* of these doers of evil, and to *pull out the fangs of these young lions.* "Annihilate them, Lord!" he cries. Pour them away like water, tread them down like grass in a hot, dry summer, let them dissolve like a snail in its own slime, let them be like an abortion that never becomes a human child. And quickly too! Quicker than the time it takes to heat water on an open fire, using either nice dry sticks or wet green ones.

Such a prayer is often in the heart of the honest political or religious dissident when he is hauled before a kangaroo court, one in which justice is seldom dispensed, because the judges have made up their minds in advance that the dissident is guilty (see verse 1 again). This unjust court on earth, the psalmist means, is merely carrying out the decision of the court of the gods, a decision which human beings have created first in the minds of the gods, or, as Paul would express it, of *the principalities and powers in the heavenly places* (Eph. 3:10). What we find here then is a deep theological issue expressed in picture-theology.

The Chorus, verses 10-11. *The righteous will rejoice when he sees the vengeance.* This vengeance must only be what the Chairman of the divine court can execute overruling the committee of gods; for it is he who up till now has allowed evil to persist "in the heavenly places". On earth, however, it is otherwise. Amongst humanity God *judges*, which is not the same thing as condemns. The righteous must rejoice on the day when God vindicates their faith. For unless God triumphs in the end, then God himself is not just and true. The picture of *the righteous bathing his feet in the blood of the wicked* is a drastic one. But then God is dealing with the drastic power of evil. Accordingly it is no more of a drastic statement than are the NT words, "Washed in the blood of the Lamb".

Little did the congregation know that God's final act of vengeance against the powers of evil would actually be to allow these powers to win the victory over himself, and that that seeming victory would actually be God's judgment of destruction upon those same powers. What we have here, then, is the reality that lies behind Paul's amazing language in Col. 1:13-20, a reality that was embodied later on in the thinking of the Church in the title *Christus Victor*—for Christ on the Cross!

I AM IN TROUBLE

Psalm 59:1-9

To the choirmaster: according to Do Not Destroy. A Miktam of David, when Saul sent men to watch his house in order to kill him.

1 Deliver me from my enemies, O my God,
   protect me from those who rise up against me,
2 deliver me from those who work evil,
   and save me from bloodthirsty men.

3 For, lo, they lie in wait for my life;
   fierce men band themselves against me.
   For no transgression or sin of mine, O Lord,
4   for no fault of mine, they run and make ready.

   Rouse thyself, come to my help, and see!
5   Thou, Lord God of hosts, art God of Israel.
   Awake to punish all the nations;
   spare none of those who treacherously plot evil.   *Selah*

6 Each evening they come back
   howling like dogs
   and prowling about the city.
7 There they are, bellowing with their mouths,
   and snarling with their lips—
   for "Who," they think, "will hear us?"

8 But thou, O Lord, dost laugh at them;
   thou dost hold all the nations in derision.
9 O my Strength, I will sing praises to thee;
   for thou, O God, art my fortress.

David, or whoever the psalmist is, always seems to be in trouble. David certainly was during the incident mentioned in the heading (see 1 Sam. 19:11-17). That incident provides a romantic story. But the psalmist is speaking here rather of national enemies, as is implied at verse 5. Yet in verse 6 we are in the situation rather of the wild hooliganism that keeps people off the streets of our present-day large cities after dark. But the genius of the psalmist is to cover all such dangerous situations, even those that we ourselves must face.

Protect me is really "lift me high up above their reach", an interesting picture. It is as when a parent lifts his child on to his shoulder high above a snapping dog. Then in verse 3 the emphasis is laid on the way in which a gang of hooligans can plot to attack an innocent pedestrian. Today *bloodthirsty men* (verse 2) could be harsh slum landlords or loan sharks in the West, or pitiless money-lenders in the East. So our psalmist begs God to come and see for himself. When such as these behave like a pack of wild dogs they can be terribly frightening.

Swords are in their lips (see RSV verse 7, *ftn.*). What a vivid Semitic picture this is! And just as dogs don't consider that anyone can see or hear them, neither do these thugs and troublemakers. Then he adds, *Thou, Lord God of hosts.* Thus he reminds himself that God is Lord of all, of the hosts of stars, that is to say, of the heavenly powers, but also of the hosts of Israel, the hosts or armies (for these are the one word) whom God helped to fight their way into Canaan, the God of the Red Sea as well as the God of the revelation at Sinai.

The Lord does see these cruel men, declares the psalmist, thus reaffirming his faith, and God just laughs at them. Such laughter is not so much *in derision*, as in peace of mind and in a sense of security For God knows he is going to win his war. In the psalmist's day God is going to win against every evil individual, gang, or nation that can ever arise to defy him. Consequently, here on earth, I, in my turn, can address God as *my Strength*, and can then add (as does RSV verse 9, *ftn.*) *I will watch; be on the look out for thee*, knowing that I can place my whole confidence in this God who is going to win. Amazingly the word "watch" here is that which is normally used for God's watching over *us*! It is used in the sense of his keeping us safe. How many a prisoner in a prison camp has maintained his faith with these words. Meanwhile God, like my father does (see verse 1), picks me up and keeps me safe in his fortress.

BUT I WILL SING

Psalm 59:10–17

10 My God in his steadfast love will meet me;
      my God will let me look in triumph on my enemies.

11 Slay them not, lest my people forget;
      make them totter by thy power, and bring them down,
      O Lord, our shield!
12 For the sin of their mouths, the words of their lips,
      let them be trapped in their pride.
    For the cursing and lies which they utter,
13   consume them in wrath,
     consume them till they are no more,
    that men may know that God rules over Jacob
      to the ends of the earth.   *Selah*

14 Each evening they come back,
      howling like dogs
      and prowling about the city.
15 They roam about for food,
      and growl if they do not get their fill.

16 But I will sing of thy might;
      I will sing aloud of thy steadfast love in the morning.
    For thou hast been to me a fortress
      and a refuge in the day of my distress.
17 O my Strength, I will sing praises to thee,
      for thou, O God, art my fortress,
      the God who shows me steadfast love.

The psalmist is now using here the language we have so often met before, that it is not my faith that counts, it is God's faithfulness that is everything. The latter always goes in front of me (rather than *meets me*; see the task of the Angel of the Covenant at Exod. 23:20). But not in front merely of "me". There is no room for a selfish satisfaction about one's own salvation in our biblical faith. It is "all Israel" (verse 11) for whom he seeks God's aid. By the way, the old Prayer Book version of the psalm uses *prevent* for "go in front". This is what the verb means in Latin. That is why we have in the well-known prayer, "Prevent us, O Lord, in all our doings with thy most gracious favour . . . "

But the psalmist is only too human. *Slay them not* he begs of God; "don't kill them outright—let them suffer first before they die". Let *my people* first see your justice as you deal with them. Only after that *do thou consume them till they are no more.*

Let us now put verse 13b in its proper perspective: *That men may know to the ends of the earth that God rules over Jacob.* Justice must be *seen* to be done, according to the saying we use today, for as Jesus declares, "That which a man sows, so shall he reap" (see Matt. 7:2). In verse 13 then we find an expression of the grim truth that (a) every man is working out his own judgment, (b) all pride and arrogance will one day be humiliated. *Pride* is what is emphasized here specially (verse 12). "Pride goes before destruction" says Prov. 16:18, "and a haughty spirit before a fall." Pride is the deadliest of the seven deadly sins. Even the pagan Greeks regarded *hybris*, as they named it, the reason for the fall, not just of man, but of the *gods!* Let us then put it in today's terms: If you arrogantly choose to make use, for example, of drugs for your own greedy pleasure, these will, in the end, *consume you.*

The Chorus, verses 16-17. Using the keywords of the psalm up to this point, the congregation now responds by shouting: *But I . . .* : and then it acknowledges that God's *might* is in fact God's "mightiness to save".

Perhaps we may have lived sheltered lives all our days, and never had any experience of persecution. But Orthodox Christians have known it endlessly for the last 1,500 years. In the Eastern Churches the idea of "mission" is completely parallel with that of "martyria", i.e. martyrdom, witness. Eastern Christians also read the psalms, of course, just as we do.

The Psalter has much more to say to the world of suffering humanity than you and I can ever grasp in our own small corner in the history of mankind. Narrow-mindedness, ignorance, and

self-centredness are emotions that a study of the psalms themselves can help us to overcome, and in their place give us a
concerned, thoughtful and prayerful view of the kind of life that
many of our fellow human beings are condemned to face.

But then, we should also be aware that while we may be living
in peace and security, our ancestors did not. We should
remember that the characteristic state of the ordinary man in
any European country in the Middle Ages was one of fear—of
(a) the plague, (b) disease, (c) invasion, (d) the tax-collector, (e)
witchcraft and magic, (f) the unknown, (g) an early death.

AN APPEAL TO GOD FOR HELP

Psalm 60:1–5

*To the choirmaster: according to Shushan Eduth. A Miktam of David; for
instruction; when he strove with Aram-naharaim and with Aram-zobah, and when
Joab on his return killed twelve thousand of Edom in the Valley of Salt.*

1 O God, thou hast rejected us, broken our defences;
     thou hast been angry; oh, restore us.
2 Thou hast made the land to quake, thou hast rent it open;
     repair its breaches, for it totters.
3 Thou hast made thy people suffer hard things;
     thou hast given us wine to drink that made us reel.

4 Thou hast set up a banner for those who fear thee,
     to rally to it from the bow.   *Selah*
5 That thy beloved may be delivered,
     give victory by thy right hand and answer us!

Aram-naharaim is the Hebrew for the area and the people of
Mesopotamia. *Aram-zobah* was one of the Aramaean states
nearer Palestine. The *Valley of Salt* was the *Ghor*, the low flat
area to the south of the Dead Sea. The figure of 12,000 killed
must have been taken from an historical source not used by the
compilers of 2 Sam. 8, where we get information about this
heading. There at verse 13 and at 1 Chron. 18:12 we are given

the figure of 18,000. It is thought that there may be some confusion in our sources about who was slain. In Hebrew the word EDOM differs from ARAM (Hebrew uses square block characters like our capital letters) by only a tittle, the name given to a corner of one such letter; so it would have been easy enough for some scribe when copying a manuscript to transcribe the wrong name of the people concerned. The tune is called "A Lily is the Testimony"—whatever that may mean. Probably it was the name of a popular song.

In verses 1-3 what defences has God broken through? Is this a reference to an actual battle? Was the tramp of enemy soldiers the earth-like shuddering that the Holy Land, God's gift to Israel, had just sustained? Had Jerusalem been actually besieged? Had its people been forced to drink contaminated wine? Or are all these statements to be regarded as metaphorical?

The last statement, in verse 3, seems to hold the key that we need. Firstly, all these horrors had been God's doing, not man's, we are told. Secondly, *wine that makes us reel* is a phrase used quite frequently by the prophets. See for example Jer. 25:15-29, where we have a vivid picture that shows how God allows sinners to bring about their own punishment. Paul refers to the same reality at 1 Cor. 11:27-29. So, while the description above could of course be that of an actual enemy invasion, the enemy could also be a person's own "staggering", "reeling" self-deception and folly.

Verses 4-5. But, just as in a battle, *thou hast set up a banner* for thy faithful followers. The picture is like the famous Pacific war photograph showing American soldiers in the heat of the battle on Iwojima, pushing up the standard bearing the Stars and Stripes to act as a rallying point for their stricken comrades. For this is the pennant flag of the Lord of hosts that is referred to here. It is the sign of victory, of triumph and rejoicing. The God-fearers are to hold on in faith despite the seeming defeat which they are facing, as described in verses 1-3. For they are still the covenant people. They still belong to the God who can be relied on to be utterly faithful. And that God is certainly going to win in the end. This idea is expressed by the words *thy right hand*. For this phrase is often used of God's victory becoming visible in the human situation. As in the illustration from Iwojima the troops here are to congregate round God's standard and find shelter from the arrows fired at them by the bowmen. If you wonder how the word *truth* occurs at all as an alternative to *bow* (RSV verse 4, *ftn.*), it is because the two words sounded alike in Hebrew. *Those who fear thee*, where fear means awe and reverence rather than terror, are God's people Israel, for in verse 5 they are also called *thy beloved*. We note with joy therefore that God has evidently not abandoned them to the enemy.

GOD HAS SPOKEN BY HIS HOLINESS

Psalm 60:6-12

6   God has spoken in his sanctuary:
      "With exultation I will divide up Shechem
      and portion out the Vale of Succoth.
7   Gilead is mine; Manasseh is mine;
      Ephraim is my helmet;
      Judah is my sceptre.
8   Moab is my washbasin;
      upon Edom I cast my shoe;
      over Philistia I shout in triumph."

9   Who will bring me to the fortified city?
      Who will lead me to Edom?
10   Hast thou not rejected us, O God?
      Thou dost not go forth, O God, with our armies.
11   O grant us help against the foe,
      for vain is the help of man!
12   With God we shall do valiantly;
      it is he who will tread down our foes.

We get our title from reading the *ftn.* to verse 6. In the book of Leviticus, after each divine utterance, we meet with God's signature, so to speak, seeing it in such a phrase as "I am the Lord", or as "You shall be holy as I am holy". That is what is meant here. God can swear only by his own self, or his own holiness. He cannot swear "by heaven", or "by earth", for he has made them (Gen. 22:16). So now he swears to his deep concern for his own people, Israel. When God first brought up the tribes into Canaan, he apportioned them each an area to settle in. This task he will now continue. Although God's people, it would appear, had fallen from grace, and in consequence God had to allow them to suffer defeat, that made no difference to the reality of his steadfast love. According to Deut. 31:10-13 after every seven years' period the people met together in assembly, and listened to the word of the Law being read out to them once again. One clause in that Law which they listened to was "The land is mine, says the Lord"; so of course it was his to apportion as he chose. But he had already divided it up amongst the twelve tribes; so they only had the *use* of it, and only if they kept their side of the bargain (Deut. 8:11-20). But even then, God's *hesed*, his covenant love, was greater than any bargain that Israel failed to keep.

Shechem was near Samaria, *Succoth* was east of it. Both places were Patriarchal settlements (Gen. 33:17-20), and both of them were on Joshua's route when the tribes arrived in Canaan. *Gilead* and half each of *Ephraim* and *Manasseh* lay east of the Jordan. But though all these places were so far away from the Temple, God is saying that they are not forgotten. The western half of *Ephraim* later became the general name for the northern tribes, the area that came to be ruled, after Solomon's death, by the line of northern kings. Yet *Ephraim* was still *my helmet*, the covering for God's head (!). Then again, *Judah* became the general name for the southern kingdom with Jerusalem as its capital; the latter was where David (and his line) held the *sceptre* of *my* (!) *rule* (see Gen. 49:10).

But God owns the lands of all the nations of the earth and of their peoples (Exod. 19:5)! He makes use of *Moab* to be his instrument for washing unclean Israel (Lev. 11). (Moab lay to the east of the Dead Sea.) God can call upon *Edom* to clean his sandals, after God has "set foot" in the midst of his sinful people, Israel. (Edom lay to the south-east.) He then adds,

"You Philistines, shout in triumph, for I am your King," whether you know it or not.

Verses 9–11 seem on balance to be Davidic. For here another voice, perhaps one of David's army generals, or perhaps even the king himself, proclaims to the assembled people: "I hope we have learned our lesson; we cannot win without God. Petra, the *rock-city*, capital of *Edom*, is inaccessible without God's help. So next time we sally forth, *O grant us help against the foe, O God!*"

The Chorus, verse 12. The people thereupon make this cry their confident hope and prayer. We can tell from the Hebrew in the last line that they were in fact calling upon the living God, for God alone can *tread down* the enemy. Is this what this psalm then, has taught us to grasp? Is it that, while God's people deserve punishment for disloyalty to God's plan, yet God will never let them go; and since he rules all nations of men, he can use foreigners and strangers as instruments of his judgment upon his own people, Israel?

ROCK OF AGES

Psalm 61:1–8

To the choirmaster: with stringed instruments. A Psalm of David.

1 Hear my cry, O God,
   listen to my prayer;
2 from the end of the earth I call to thee,
   when my heart is faint.

   Lead thou me
   to the rock that is higher than I;
3 for thou art my refuge,
   a strong tower against the enemy.

4 Let me dwell in thy tent for ever!
   Oh to be safe under the shelter of thy wings!   *Selah*
5 For thou, O God, hast heard my vows,
   thou hast given me the heritage of those who fear thy name.

6   Prolong the life of the king;
     may his years endure to all generations!
7   May he be enthroned for ever before God;
     bid steadfast love and faithfulness watch over him!

8   So will I ever sing praises to thy name,
     as I pay my vows day after day.

Where was our psalmist crying from when he said *from the end of the earth*? Today we think perhaps of the Antipodes or of China. Probably he thought of Babylon as being "the end" of everything. There he felt himself to be in Sheol, the land of the dead. Here he was, a single Israelite, plucked up and away from amongst the fellowship of his people and cast all alone amongst blaspheming foreigners. In Babylon there was no meaning to life. He was now beyond the bounds of the Covenant, which alone gave meaning to existence. Yet, wherever this poor man was, he could only cry: "Do more than hear me, God, listen!"

In the language of the ideology of his day the *Rock* was the antipole of the bottomless world of chaos. This mystical language that was common throughout the Near East, however, had a basis in fact for Israel. For David had purchased from the self-employed farmer, Araunah, the rock on his property on which he had trained his bullocks to tread out the grains of his barley and wheat. This incident is to be found at 2 Sam. 24:18-25. Later on David's son, Solomon, built his temple over this rock. The rock is visible to this day as it stands within the great Mosque of Omar, which is known now as the Dome of the Rock. During the period of the temple, it was on this rock that the sacrifices were slaughtered in preparation for the altar holocaust. Again in the mythical thinking of the day (the equivalent of the scientific thinking of our time) a shaft plunged straight down vertically from under the rock into Sheol (or into the Hell of later Christian thinking), the rock forming a kind of stopper at the mouth of the shaft, keeping the powers of evil from bursting up into this world of human society.

The psalmist, however, brushes aside such mythical thinking

(even though it continued right on into the Middle Ages) and claims defiantly that this Rock is God! He develops his allegory in language we have met already in Psalm 18 and elsewhere. The purpose of Solomon's Temple was of course to continue the place of sacrifice that the Tent in the Wilderness had been prepared for in earlier generations in the days of Israel's pilgrimage. Yet, since Israel was still on pilgrimage, the language of the camp is retained. So we have, *Let me dwell in thy tent for ever*, where God the Rock still kept control over the powers of evil that always sought to burst up into the human soul.

But how could you be on the march and yet remain at this rock which was a fixture? How could you take refuge on this rock when you were in exile in Babylon? It is interesting that Paul, drawing upon this ancient mythology, seeks to answer this paradox; and in doing so gives it a theological, rather than a mythical interpretation. He pushes his allegory *back* from David to the rock which Moses struck (Exod. 17:1–7), and then *forward* to Christ (1 Cor. 10:4). In this way he passes *through* the significance of this psalm and others like it, since they were written between the times of Moses and Christ. The psalmist, however, brings out the never-ending significance of the Rock by using the term *for ever* in the plural. Thus he makes it mean "for all eternity". We notice that it is after that great statement that there follows the liturgical command *Selah*!: Lift up your voices, your chords, your hearts! No wonder we must stop, and think at this point, and then shout in praise!

Under the shelter of thy wings is a reference to the wings of the cherubim that touched each other over the mid-point of the Ark of the Covenant that resided in the Holy of Holies in the temple. The psalmist can therefore end his plea with the same certainty that Jesus expects from us when he says, "Knock and it shall be opened unto you." For *Thou hast given me* my heritage—I don't need any more. It is all I want and need.

We have seen before that the king was meant to show forth on earth the very qualities of the heavenly King whom he represented (e.g. Ps. 45). Because of that, a new voice, perhaps that of a courtier, prays now for the king. For the king ought to show his people what God is like. Yet, of course, this poor human being needs our prayers, for he is utterly dependent upon the love and faithfulness to him of the living God.

The Chorus. Each "I" in the assembly of the "saints" finally responds, saying, "I will faithfully uphold this prayer by turning daily to God in praise and worship." Since the whole ceremony has now been "chaired" by the king himself, the "head" of the "body" of Israel, the whole congregation is now welded into one living and worshipping community. We should not forget that to praise God daily is the business, not just of each "I", but of the whole Church in both earth and heaven.

PEACE IN TROUBLE

Psalm 62:1-12

> *To the choirmaster: according to Jeduthun. A Psalm of David.*

1 For God alone my soul waits in silence;
     from him comes my salvation.
2 He only is my rock and my salvation,
     my fortress; I shall not be greatly moved.

3 How long will you set upon a man
     to shatter him, all of you,
     like a leaning wall, a tottering fence?
4 They only plan to thrust him down from his eminence.
     They take pleasure in falsehood.
   They bless with their mouths,
     but inwardly they curse.   *Selah*

5 For God alone my soul waits in silence,
     for my hope is from him.
6 He only is my rock and my salvation,
     my fortress; I shall not be shaken.
7 On God rests my deliverance and my honour;
     my mighty rock, my refuge is God.

8   Trust in him at all times, O people;
         pour out your heart before him;
     God is a refuge for us.   *Selah*

9   Men of low estate are but a breath,
         men of high estate are a delusion;
     in the balances they go up;
         they are together lighter than a breath.

10   Put no confidence in extortion,
         set no vain hopes on robbery;
     if riches increase, set not your heart on them.

11   Once God has spoken;
         twice have I heard this;
     that power belongs to God;

12   and that to thee, O Lord, belongs steadfast love.
     For thou dost requite a man
         according to his work.

Six different times in this poem a line begins with the little word
akh, a strong guttural expression. It is something like the
German word *doch*. We have no English equivalent for it. It
means something like: "O yes, that may be so, but . . ." or, "I
don't care what you say, but I am sure that . . ." and then
follows a strong positive assertion. So our writer begins with
"Say what you like, but unto God—my whole being—in
silence". There is no verb in the sentence. We don't need one.
Any verb would spoil the holy mystery of the psalmist's total
commitment to God.

Then he continues with his second *akh*: "No matter what
objections you like to raise", *he only* (very emphatic) *is my rock,
and from him comes my power to love*, not "the salvation of my
soul" (using the masculine noun we have previously noted), for
that is something that had happened long before. In his
marvellous closeness to God, that God of love had given him
what results from his personal salvation. This new thing may
perhaps be explained by Paul's word "sanctification". This is a
Latin word meaning "being made into a saint", that is, into a true
loving member of the redeemed people of God (see 1 Thess.

5:23; 2 Thess. 2:13). Because this is now happening to him our psalmist is experiencing a deep sense of peace, even when things go wrong. Of course, he is still a human being; he can still be upset when troubles come his way, or *moved*, as the word is here—yet not *greatly*, that is, not beyond his strength.

At verse 3 he gives us an instance of the kind of trouble that assails him. He paints a picture of a badly-built brick wall, with a gang of toughs pushing it and pushing it, *until finally it collapses* over the top of him—just one poor man all alone. With another *akh* he then declares, "Don't you believe me? Oh yes, but in fact, like king David, I have reached a position of eminence in the community. So it is that out of sheer jealousy 'they' now want to make this poor Humpty Dumpty have a great fall."

At verse 5 the fourth *akh* repeats what we heard at verse 1: "I don't care what they do to me", *for unto God alone—my whole being—in silence; for my hope is in him.* One cannot hope in a god of whose very existence one is in doubt. But one dares to hope in the living God whom one knows absolutely to be *there*. Then he repeats his verse 2: "No matter what you say . . . " *He only is my rock . . .* We note that *I shall not be shaken* uses the same verb as in *not be moved* at verse 2.

The psalmist goes on to make a change in verse 7. Now he declares, *my deliverance* (this time the masculine form of the word *salvation* that he used at verse 2) *rests on God.* God rescued me, he says, saved me, in the first place. We should understand the words *my glory* in the same way, rather than as the RSV says, *my honour.* With this word he refers, first, at the lowest level, to one's reputation as a good man; but the meaning of the term probably goes deeper than that. When Moses came down from the mountain after meeting with God in the great silence— the silence the psalmist now shares with Moses— what we read is that "Moses did not know that the skin of his face shone because he had been talking with God" (Exod. 34:29). Moses had brought back with him, and was actually displaying it in the radiance visible on his face, something of the very glory of God.

ALL-POWERFUL LOVE

Psalm 62:1-12 *(cont'd)*

It looks as if we had reached the end of the original psalm at verse 7—a magnificent end. The following verses, therefore, turn the psalm as it is into a hymn to be used in public worship. First, verse 8 invites "us" to trust God in the same way as the original psalmist did, that is to say "No matter what . . . ", by using *akh* once again. Then it teaches us that *men of low estate*, or the proletariat, as we might say today, *are but a breath*. But then he adds, so are *men of high estate*, the bosses, the government, *they are a delusion*.

The great prophets have much to say about God's judgment upon those who "grind the faces of the poor in the dust". Looking at it the other way round, however, the psalmist encourages these very poor folk to hold on to their faith by reminding them that the activities of the rich and of the powerful, not being in tune with the will of God, will simply not weigh at the judgment. Only something positive can do so, never what is negative (compare the phrase, *lighter than a breath*). So a man wastes his life if he puts his confidence in what is purely negative. Wealth breeds only wealth. *Extortion*, or robbery with violence, is in the same category. "Surely oppression makes the wise man foolish" (how many people believe that today?) "and a bribe corrupts the mind" (Ecc. 7:7). Yet we dare not merely take sides in this issue against the rich. At Ezek. 22:29, where *the people of the land* are becoming ever more prosperous at the expense of their poorer neighbours, Ezekiel denounces them for not listening to the Word of God such as this psalm proclaims.

All this addition to the psalm appears in the Wisdom style of writing, none more so than the last two verses. We have now been reminded of the passage at Isa. 40:6-8: "All flesh is grass . . . the grass withers, the flower fades, when the breath of the Lord blows upon it . . . but the word of our God will stand for ever." So, as in a class-room, where the teacher bids her class repeat after her *once*, *twice*, the congregation must now make the emphatic declaration not just once, but twice, about what God himself has said about himself, viz. that *power belongs to God*. Yet, as if asking the teacher questions in the class-room, we may ask next, What is the nature of infinite power? To this we are given the amazing answer, one that is to be found in the Bible, and in the Bible alone; it is, "God's infinite power is God's infinite love. You, God, infinitely loving, You actually make up for, You complete [not *requite*, as the RSV] what is lacking in a person's actions"—for, being a mere breath, he cannot do it for himself.

What a God this is, the God we meet with here! And all knowledge of this wonderful God can be reduced to two little sentences! Never again need a poor human mind ask the question: "If God is all-powerful, then why does he not do this and this?" Nor need he pose the questions, "Can God do anything he wills to do? Can he send a man to Hell?" The only answer that we can now give, based on the conclusion of this psalm, is to say, "Being all-powerful love, as an act of justice God can only send himself to Hell—in the person of a Man."

THIRSTY FOR GOD

Psalm 63.1-11

A Psalm of David, when he was in the Wilderness of Judah.

1   O God, thou art my God, I seek thee,
      my soul thirsts for thee;
  my flesh faints for thee,
      as in a dry and weary land where no water is.

2   So I have looked upon thee in the sanctuary,
      beholding thy power and glory.

3   Because thy steadfast love is better than life,
      my lips will praise thee.

4   So I will bless thee as long as I live;
      I will lift up my hands and call on thy name.

5 My soul is feasted as with marrow and fat,
     and my mouth praises thee with joyful lips,
6 when I think of thee upon my bed,
     and meditate on thee in the watches of the night;
7 for thou hast been my help,
     and in the shadow of thy wings I sing for joy.
8 My soul clings to thee;
     thy right hand upholds me.

9 But those who seek to destroy my life
     shall go down into the depths of the earth;
10 they shall be given over to the power of the sword,
     they shall be prey for jackals.
11 But the king shall rejoice in God;
     all who swear by him shall glory;
     for the mouths of liars will be stopped.

What an extraordinary idea! Can you imagine an ancient Greek philosopher thirsting for that horrible divinity Zeus? Or a Canaanite contemporary of the psalmist thirsting for that bloodthirsty god, Baal? Or a present-day New Guinea Highlander thirsting for one of his gods of whom he lives in continual mortal fear? We should not take the Psalms for granted, though we have sung them since our youth. Let them speak to us again with a glad surprise!

People suggest that physical thirst can lead to spiritual thirst. That is as may be. But travellers in the desert dying of thirst have been known to curse God and then die. A more suitable background to this verse is to place the writer far from Jerusalem and in the midst of unbelievers, such as find their soul satisfied by what they can see and hear and feel—in fact much like the secular society of the West today. If so, then this psalm could also be the background of Jesus' Beatitude: "Blessed are those who hunger and thirst . . . " (Matt. 5:6).

My soul here is the word *nephesh*, meaning the whole person, the liver and the kidneys included, as we have lately seen. That is why *my flesh* too *faints for thee*. But faints is not quite an accurate translation. The word seems to mean "has gone blind", or "gone dark". How vivid Hebrew poetry is! Then *seek* is a most revealing verb. Basically it means longing for the first light of the dawn. So here our friend gets up at first light after perhaps a sleepless night eager to "see" his Lord.

Previously he had *looked* upon God in the sanctuary when he had had a visionary experience, *beholding thy power and glory* just like the young Isaiah (Isa. 6:1–8). The verb *looked upon* has this meaning; it does not describe what one sees with the physical eye. So now he makes his great statement of faith: (I declare) *that Your covenant love is better than life itself.* Let this declaration of faith hit us hard! For don't we say that life comes first? Don't we suggest that everything else depends upon our having life in the first place? No, our friend replies, the love of God is even better than the gift of life God has given us! How far we are here then from the religions of the Greeks, the Indians, the New Guineans, the Marxists, and all others.

One's *lips* are part of a person. In consequence I praise and bless God through them, because I am a person, not an automaton, not a hand in a factory, a government statistic, or a cypher on a computer. Mine are the lips of a person made in the image of God, who uses his lips (the OT would dare to say) to speak to me. Then again, when one person *blessed* another, he used not only his lips to speak, but his hands, which he placed on the head of the other. Here then is the daring picture of a man actually laying his hands on the head of God! Yet in what other way could he have expressed the utter humility of this God of steadfast love? Finally, God's *name* is his essential Being. The psalmist has discovered, through the experience of membership in the Covenant people, that that name is love.

The *marrow and fat* of a sacrificial victim were the best bits of the flesh. These were offered to God in love and gratitude (Lev. 3:16). But here our poet suggests that he experiences God's friendship as deeply as God enjoys man's offerings! So that is why he (a) *praises* God, (b) *meditates*, thinks through the meaning of things, theologizes, if you like, (c) ever recognizing that everything he thinks, knows and experiences is already a gift from God. His is a total experience, one that he maintains both by day and by night. So all he can do in response is to shout for joy. Remember that for his generation the darkness of night could be quite terrible. For (i) at three in the morning one's vitality is at its lowest—and he was trying to sleep in a mud hut with the domestic animals puffing and blowing around his feet; (ii) it was under the cover of darkness that all kinds of demons crept forth from that Wilderness that he has mentioned in verse 1. (Quite probably we are meant to see Jesus' temptation in the wilderness in the light of this psalm—Mark 1:12-13). Yet our friend concludes his declaration of faith with a most daring analogy: My *nephesh*, that is my body too, *cleaves to thee, thy right hand upholds me*. Note that this last phrase employs the same words as those used by the young girl as she holds her lover tight to her, when he embraces her with his right hand around her (Song of S. 2:6; 8:3). Such is indeed the enchanting picture of the meaning of the Covenant. For God is the Husband of Israel, and Israel is his Bride (Hos. 2:16-20).

With these great words (verse 8) the psalm seems to end. Then two appendices have been added to turn this tremendous soliloquy into a hymn for public worship. (a) Two verses are added to show up the horror of *not* knowing the joy of the Lord. All destructive types will go down into that Sheol which is their natural home. (b) A third verse is added to allow the king to act as representative of the assembled congregation. As the "head" of the "body" that is Israel, he can speak for all those with whom God has made his covenant of love.

SECRET POLICE

Psalm 64:1-10

To the choirmaster. A Psalm of David.

1 Hear my voice, O God, in my complaint;
    preserve my life from dread of the enemy,
2 hide me from the secret plots of the wicked,
    from the scheming of evildoers,
3 who whet their tongues like swords,
    who aim bitter words like arrows,

4   shooting from ambush at the blameless,
        shooting at him suddenly and without fear.
5   They hold fast to their evil purpose;
        they talk of laying snares secretly,
    thinking, "Who can see us?
6   Who can search out our crimes?
    We have thought out a cunningly conceived plot."
        For the inward mind and heart of a man are deep!

7   But God will shoot his arrow at them;
        they will be wounded suddenly.
8   Because of their tongue he will bring them to ruin;
        all who see them will wag their heads.
9   Then all men will fear;
        they will tell what God has wrought,
        and ponder what he has done.

10 Let the righteous rejoice in the Lord,
        and take refuge in him!
    Let all the upright in heart glory!

The heading tells us that this psalm is of the Davidic type, and so could have fitted into David's situation around 1,000 B.C. But the Bible is not dead print. Nor should we suppose that it is only "the original text" (which in fact we don't possess and never have possessed) that we are to regard as the inspired Word. The Word of God is (a) alive, just because God is the living God. (b) So we need not worry about all the variant readings and corruptions in the Hebrew text some of which are shown as footnotes in the RSV. (c) Psalm 64 in fact echoes the cry of countless men and women down the centuries who live in terror in the police states of the world. And so (d), just because the psalm is alive, such people gain new hope and new strength on reading it.

The Hebrew text of this psalm is full of corruptions. The various modern translations reveal this by the way they differ so much from each other. Note, for example, how different the NEB is from the RSV. Yet these differences in detail are not important. It is what the psalm says as a whole that is important. Such, anyway, is Paul's understanding of the OT. He seldom quotes it accurately, sometimes he even seems to quote from memory. For, of course, you couldn't carry around a pocket Bible with you in those days, for an OT filled several large scrolls too big to carry. Moreover, more often than not, Paul quoted from the Septuagint Greek text rather than the Hebrew, though of course it is the Hebrew which is the original.

The poet succeeds in conveying to us a real sense of horror, so that we can identify with him in his fear and dread of the secret police, his political enemies, or whoever these ruthless persons are. They evidently operate under a cloak of secrecy, believing that no one knows what they are scheming. *They lay snares secretly.* We might say that they install listening devices by bugging the homes of their prey. Then, like partisans or revolutionaries in any age they act quickly, *shooting at the blameless suddenly and without fear. For*, adds the psalmist with great insight, *the inward mind and heart of a man are deep*! Jeremiah thinks strongly on this strange fact in his earlier chapters.

Taking a grip upon his faith, however, the poet quickly turns the language he has been using to another purpose. *God* will suddenly *shoot his arrow at* such people, he declares. God will let them bring ruin upon themselves, when their own declared plans will find them out, or show them up even to people who live in distant places. The result will be what they had not intended to happen, that *all men will fear, they will tell what God has wrought.* That is to say (a) God acts for me when I can do nothing for myself; (b) God actually acts *in* the evil-doers by letting them overstep their authority; (c) the result is unexpected. Instead of destroying the innocent, they lead the latter to a new grasp of faith! (d) People then lose their fear of man, but discover a new fear of God. (e) Such people then *ponder*, or think their way through, theologically, the acts of God. For God is not known just through speculative or rational thought; you cannot find faith in God merely with the help of the so-called "proofs" of God that theologians have produced. You can know God only as you "see" what he has *done* both in history and in your own private life. For the work of evil-doers is secret, but the work of God is in the open for all to understand.

The Chorus at verse 10 brings the thoughts of the poem home to the worshipping congregation. These are the *righteous*, that is to say, those whom God has brought into a right relationship with himself.

THE ONENESS OF GRACE

Psalm 65:1–13

To the choirmaster. A Psalm of David. A song.

1 Praise is due to thee,
    O God, in Zion;
  and to thee shall vows be performed,
2   O thou who hearest prayer!
  To thee shall all flesh come
3   on account of sins.
  When our transgressions prevail over us,
    thou dost forgive them.
4 Blessed is he whom thou dost choose and bring near,
    to dwell in thy courts!
  We shall be satisfied with the goodness of thy house,
    thy holy temple!

5 By dread deeds thou dost answer us with deliverance,
    O God of our salvation,
  who art the hope of all the ends of the earth,
    and of the farthest seas;
6 who by thy strength hast established the mountains,
    being girded with might;
7 who dost still the roaring of the seas,
    the roaring of their waves,
    the tumult of the peoples;
8 so that those who dwell at earth's farthest bounds
    are afraid at thy signs;
  thou makest the outgoings of the morning and the evening
    to shout for joy.

9 Thou visitest the earth and waterest it,
        thou greatly enrichest it;
     the river of God is full of water;
        thou providest their grain,
        for so thou hast prepared it.
10 Thou waterest its furrows abundantly,
        settling its ridges,
     softening it with showers,
        and blessing its growth.
11 Thou crownest the year with thy bounty;
        the tracks of thy chariot drip with fatness.
12 The pastures of the wilderness drip,
        the hills gird themselves with joy,
13 the meadows clothe themselves with flocks,
        the valleys deck themselves with grain,
        they shout and sing together for joy.

In the days of the temple the Harvest Thanksgiving Service and
the celebration of New Year were conjoined in an eight-day-
long festival. This also included remembrance of how God had
re-created Israel when he brought them out of servitude in
Egypt. This long ceremony took place about the end of our
September. This was because, once the grape harvest (the last to
be brought in) was finally gathered, the farmer must necessarily
begin to prepare all over again for the new cycle of the
agricultural year. This psalm puts together two aspects of God's
grace:

(1) God is all-grace in rescuing his people from Egypt and in
forgiving their sins. Forgiveness re-creates a person and lets
him be a "new man".

(2) God is all-grace in controlling the powers of nature, and
so in giving his people a good harvest of their crops. At New
Year then God is again about to create a new cycle of nature. In
other words, the psalm here expresses the people's gratitude
that God had fed them spiritually, and that he had also fed them
materially. That is why this is a harvest song, and is addressed
to God as Creator. It takes into account the reality that all
creation is one whole, and that God is ever re-creating Creation
in all aspects of it, both human and material.

At the heart of the psalm we find the word *God*, not man. Man "owes" God praise, and man simply must pay up to God what he owes, the vows he promised he would perform once he had discovered God's goodness to him in forgiving him and re-creating his whole being. *All flesh* means all mankind, and so not just Israel.

Then we read (literally in the Hebrew) "Iniquitous deeds have been too much for me; yet, our acts of rebellion—thou hast atoned for them", or, as some scholars prefer to translate, "thou hast wiped them away". Between the lines then we read astonishment expressed at the grace and goodness of God. Yet it is just such forgiven sinners whom God *chooses*, *brings* into the place of worship so as *to dwell in thy courts*! More astonishment! Such generosity on God's part offers us total satisfaction derived from just being there in the temple along with the God of all grace. Yet, as Jesus declares, while many are called, few are chosen. This psalm, then, helps us understand what we are chosen *for*.

The second part of the psalm, beginning at verse 5, proceeds to discuss this matter. *By dread deeds*, that is, great acts of redemption such as when he brought Israel out of Egypt, God "put us right" with himself. *Thou dost answer us with deliverance*—we who are sinners! No wonder we exclaim that God is *the God of our salvation*. But not of us alone, but also of *all the ends of the earth and of the farthest seas*! Clearly that *hope* shows the reason why the ordinary believer has been chosen; it is that he may invite Gentiles to come right in to the Holy of Holies, as Isa. 56:6–8 looks forward to seeing happen.

What connection is there, though, between the salvation of all mankind and the workings of nature as we see it in the ongoing agricultural year? It is that (a) since God is God, then he must be the God of all men. (b) Therefore he is also the God of all nature. "When God began to create the heavens and the earth ..." is how the RSV *ftn.* translates Gen. 1:1 correctly. God has never ceased to create. This is clearer to us today than ever before. In earlier centuries the Church was prone to regard God as an "absentee landlord", in that he had created in the beginning, but had now gone away. But today we live in an expanding universe and among an expanding humanity.

Thus even the new generations and the far-off heathen, the unknown inhabitants of the earth beyond the Pillars of Hercules where the Land of Atlantis was thought to lie, even they would see the creative power of the *one* God. For they too see the *signs* in the heavens, such as the sun, moon, and stars, and as the rainbow (Gen. 1:14; 9:17) by which God had promised so long ago to regulate the seasons and to give all men their food in due times. That is why God becomes the "object of trust" (*hope* in the RSV) even of the heathen, as they learn to put their trust in him, and so are heathen no longer!

At verse 9 there follows a lyrical description of how God has always kept this covenant of his that he made with Noah. He has done so by *visiting* his creation, each visit being an act of re-creation—the blade of wheat from the seed, the bird from the egg, the butterfly from the caterpillar, the sheep from the lamb, the bird evolving from the fish, the dog from the wolf, and so on. So all nature shouts together with the joy of its annual re-creation.

This re-creative activity is finally summed up in the metaphor of *the river of God* being *full of water*. Right throughout the OT, from the story of the Garden of Eden onwards, this river is regarded as the symbol of God's actions as he fructifies the life of this world with his creative grace. (See particularly Ezek. 47:1-12 for this picture.) But nothing God has done is more wonderful than when he visits a man, woman or child, and, by forgiving them, re-creates them in his own likeness as a child of God.

COME AND SEE—COME AND HEAR

Psalm 66:1-7

To the choirmaster. A song. A Psalm.

1   Make a joyful noise to God, all the earth;
2   sing the glory of his name;
        give to him glorious praise!

3   Say to God, "How terrible are thy deeds!
     So great is thy power that thy enemies cringe before thee.
4   All the earth worships thee;
     they sing praises to thee,
     sing praises to thy name."   *Selah*

5   Come and see what God has done:
     he is terrible in his deeds among men.
6   He turned the sea into dry land;
     men passed through the river on foot.
     There did we rejoice in him,
7   who rules by his might for ever,
     whose eyes keep watch on the nations—
     let not the rebellious exalt themselves.   *Selah*

What a strongly "evangelical" psalm this is! The temple minister speaks first. He invites not just believing Israel, but *all the earth* (!) to make a joyful noise to God. Evidently man, the creature, is not meant to keep his praise of God tucked up in his heart. There is a missionary element in his praise. The shouting can become a form of attack against the powers of evil. It is like a Maori *haka* which a rugby team can use to scare the opposing team out of its wits before the game begins. We find it used in this way by Joshua at the siege of Jericho (Josh. 6:20). *Sing* (or, better, sing to the accompaniment of a musical instrument) *the glory of his name*. As we shall see, as the poem proceeds, God's glory is to be equated with his power. This is the equation that Paul uses in his Letter to the Romans. And God's *name*, as we have seen, is the very essence of his being.

But of course we do not and cannot know the essence of God. "No man can see God and live." But we can know and we can see what God has *done*. The deeds he has done are *terrible*, because they are performed by him to whom all power belongs. Those who oppose him find that he opposes them. So they feign submission, or *cringe before thee*. But those who willingly submit to him are glad to "bow with their face to the ground" before him. This last verb should be noted, for there are several words for *worship* in Hebrew. The physical position here is that employed to this day by the Muslim when he is at prayer. He spreads his prayer-mat on the ground, kneels down on it, then touches the ground in front of him with his forehead. Neither Jews nor Christians, however, have kept up this position, probably because in cold and wet Europe there are easier ways to bow down! What happened was, as time went on, that people either (a) stood to pray, or (b) knelt on the ground—not on a kneeler or on a nice soft cushion as is common today, or else (c) remained seated in a chair or pew. All three positions have survived to this day. Naturally the physical position is not important to God. This great invitation then ends with a clash of cymbals, shown by the word *Selah*.

Come and see what God has done. Not, "Come and let us have an argument about the existence of God". Rather we remember the simple NT cry: "This one thing I know", as the man born blind exclaimed, "though I was blind, now I see" (John 9:25). What God has done is awe-inspiring, *terrible. He turned the sea into dry land.* Israel remembered her escape from Egypt. *Men passed through the river on foot.* They remembered the crossing of the river Jordan (Josh. 4:23). But, theologically speaking, the river here means also the waters of chaos, shown as the power of sickness and death. We have kept that idea alive to this day in the hymn, "One more river, and that's the river of Jordan, one more river to cross", meaning, of course, the river of death.

There then in those historical moments of crisis *did we rejoice in him*—without seeing him, remember, without arguing about his existence, for all we saw was what God had done. So we can now take the next three steps of faith: (a) We can declare that *God rules by his might*; (b) that *God rules for ever*; and we can declare that (c) *God rules over all nations.* So then, warns the psalmist, you who rebel against his rule—watch out!

THE TRAINING OF THE SERVANT

Psalm 66:8–12

8   Bless our God, O peoples,
        let the sound of his praise be heard,

9   who has kept us among the living,
         and has not let our feet slip.
10 For thou, O God, hast tested us;
         thou hast tried us as silver is tried.
11 Thou didst bring us into the net;
         thou didst lay affliction on our loins;
12 thou didst let men ride over our heads;
         we went through fire and through water;
         yet thou hast brought us forth to a spacious place.

The Good News is meant for all peoples. The poet invited the
heathen to *bless* or lay their hands on the head of *our* (Israel's)
God (as we have seen the action means literally; see at Ps. 63:4).
What an extraordinary invitation to the heathen! He goes on:
God has kept us, (Israel), *among the living*—why? *He has not
let our feet slip*—why? Yet Israel already knows why, already
knows the answer. Our poet need only hint at it here, because he
has already suggested the answer as given above.

   The next three verses describe what it means to *pass through
the river*, and so to be *tested and tried* by God. Here we must
recall the familiar language of the great prophets. As we have
now seen twice in this psalm, God is *terrible*. The prophets
therefore dare to declare, again and again, that "Our God is a
consuming fire" (e.g. Deut. 4:24; Isa. 10:17; 33:14, etc.). That is
why God speaks to man *out of* the fire, for that fire is himself
(Exod. 3:2; 24:17; Deut. 4.12, etc.). No wonder later generations pictured Hell in terms of flames of fire; for "it is a fearful
thing" (as Heb. 10:31 puts it) "to fall into the hands of the living
God", this God who is terrible in his deeds.

   But there is another aspect to fire. A metal can be refined only
if it goes through the furnace, be melted, and then be re-created
in a new form. Before it entered the flames it was of course a
precious commodity, even though it was still mixed with dross.
Yet the dross in it simply must be burned away (see Job 23:10;
Isa. 1:25; Zech. 13:9; Mal. 3:2–3). But the "evangelical" element
in all this is the proclamation that God too goes through the fire
and through the floods *with* his people Israel (e.g. Isa. 43:2), a
reality that is made clear to us in a memorable parable (Dan. 3).

It may be that the parable, written some centuries later than the exile in Babylon, was actually intended to interpret our passage here as well as such others as Isa. 43:1–2. If such a parable does not offer us "good news", then what does? Our passage, then, ends with *thou hast brought us forth* (not "sent us out", but "led us out" thyself) to full satisfaction (see RSV verse 12, *ftn.*). This last word covers the idea we find at Ps. 23:5, where we meet with the phrase "my cup runs over"; for the cup is so full that it cannot hold any more, just as a sponge can be so full that it is "satiated" (the word in Hebrew here); and so one becomes totally satisfied, and made ready for service to God.

TWO STEPS TO SALVATION

Psalm 66:13–20

13 I will come into thy house with burnt offerings;
  I will pay thee my vows,
14 that which my lips uttered
  and my mouth promised when I was in trouble.
15 I will offer to thee burnt offerings of fatlings,
  with the smoke of the sacrifice of rams;
  I will make an offering of bulls and goats. *Selah*

16 Come and hear, all you who fear God,
  and I will tell what he has done for me.
17 I cried aloud to him,
  and he was extolled with my tongue.
18 If I had cherished iniquity in my heart,
  the Lord would not have listened.
19 But truly God has listened;
  he has given heed to the voice of my prayer.

20 Blessed be God,
  because he has not rejected my prayer
  or removed his steadfast love from me!

We have to note here how well this psalm expresses the deep recesses of biblical theology. Let us therefore begin by remem-

bering the two words we have met before, *yesha* (masculine
form), *yeshuah* (feminine), both of which, unfortunately, are
translated in the RSV by the same word, "salvation" (see the
Introduction). *Yesha* tells us what God *has done* to save us, as
we found the psalmist considering above. God had delivered
them, rescued them, saved them, had brought them out of
slavery into his life in *a spacious place* (verse 12), that is, into
their land flowing with milk and honey. In the same way, we
today can "know" what God has done for us when he rescued us
from the powers of evil, whether these be greed, or lust, or
alcohol or drugs, or just sheer emptiness of life, and gave us a
place in his spacious Kingdom. Thus we "know" what *yesha*
means. Yet in the passage we cited above, Isa. 43:1-4, the
prophet makes the event of salvation even more clear, for there
God goes on to address Israel *after* he has redeemed her and
after he has claimed her as his people, using the lovely words,
"You are mine . . . and I love you". This is because God's
redemptive activity is not complete in his act of *yesha*. None of
us, for example, dare declare "I am saved" and do no more
about it. We have got to get into the act of "saving" others. We
have to enter upon the second step in God's plan of salvation.
For until we do so then we are not saved ourselves. In the Bible
a person is "saved" only when he or she has accepted the whole
new way of life of love and compassion that is a reflection of the
essential nature of God himself. We recall how, after Jesus had
said to Peter "You are my disciple", he went on to challenge him
with the words, "Take up your cross and follow me" (see also
Matt. 10:38-39; 16:24-25).

Paul interprets what this psalm is referring to in his Letter to
the Romans. In the first eleven chapters he expounds *yesha*,
what God's salvation means as it comes to us from his free
grace. Till that point he has dealt with God's plan at its Stage I.
But he begins chapter 12 with the word *therefore*, and then
leads us his readers to discover the essential nature of Stage II.
This second Stage is described in terms of the OT word
yeshuah, which speaks of God empowering a person who has
now been "saved" to take up his own cross, and so to present his

body as a living sacrifice. For sacrifice is God's chosen way of changing the world, and both the psalmist and the Christian must necessarily share in the act. It is not for nothing that the theology of sacrifice is laid out for us in the book of Leviticus. (See the study of this in the *Daily Study Bible* volume on *Leviticus*.)

Thereafter Paul spells out in detail what presenting your body as a living sacrifice means for ordinary people, how it means costly giving, costly hospitality, carrying the spite of one's enemies without retaliating, and so on."The new man" is learning to live in the Kingdom of God where the accent is not upon progress from one event to another; but upon the reality that good comes out of evil, love out of hate, but only at the expense of the Cross that is always there in the heart of God (Hos. 11:8-9). When we follow God's command then we find that he is always *with* his servant who is being prepared for service to the world; consequently since we must carry our cross, we discover that God shares with us in carrying it. The pure metal spoken of in this psalm is an intimation of the "Kingdom of God" that can emerge only once God *didst lay affliction on our loins* (verse 11), and *didst let men ride over our heads*.

It is because God has been through the fires with "me" that "I" consider no offering to be too costly to make to him in responsive gratitude. This God of ours is extraordinary. He has actually invited this "I" to share in the cost of the world's redemption with himself. But in the meantime he has brought us into *a spacious place*, the place where our cup runs over.

Verses 16-20. Earlier on in the psalm we heard the words "Come and see what God has done" (verse 5). Now we meet with the words, "Come and hear . . . " The Church has always needed a ministry. Someone, trained to do so, has always interpreted by word of mouth what God has *done*. Yet here the speaker is his own interpreter—*I will tell what he has done for me*, in fact, how he went through the fires with me.

John Bunyan immortalized these very words for us, writing from prison, in his famous book *Grace Abounding*. Surely he of all people knew all about the fires of suffering. *He was extolled "under"* (literally) *my tongue*, that is, I kept my story there, ready to tell it to any who would listen to me. When *I cherished iniquity in my heart, the Lord would not listen*, but instead, *he has given heed to the voice of my prayer.*

Blessed be God, then. Despite the sin in my heart (for though redeemed I am still a sinner) which I myself have noticed, he has chosen neither to *reject my prayer*, nor to take away his *steadfast love from me.*

THE POWER OF GOD'S BLESSING

Psalm 67:1-7

To the choirmaster: with stringed instruments. A Psalm. A song.

1 May God be gracious to us and bless us
   and make his face to shine upon us,   *Selah*
2 that thy way may be known upon earth,
   thy saving power among all nations.
3 Let the peoples praise thee, O God;
   let all the peoples praise thee!

4 Let the nations be glad and sing for joy,
   for thou dost judge the peoples with equity
   and guide the nations upon earth.   *Selah*
5 Let the peoples praise thee, O God;
   let all the peoples praise thee!

6 The earth has yielded its increase;
   God, our God, has blessed us.
7 God has blessed us;
   let all the ends of the earth fear him!

Obviously this psalm was composed for public worship. Perhaps it belonged particularly to the autumn harvest festival (see verse 6). Moreover, it was used antiphonally, first one group singing their verses, than a second group answering them.

Choir I, verses 1-2. The psalm begins by placing the Aaronic Blessing of Num. 6:24-25 in the mouths of one of the two choirs. Perhaps we are helped to grasp the full meaning of the word *gracious* when we envisage the idea rather of graciousness, that lovely ingredient that can appear in a person's character. We see it here then in God's *shining face*, shining with love, not *upon* us (as RSV) but *with* us—sharing our life with us, and giving us light to restore relationships with other people that we had smirched or even destroyed. Such is the power of his blessing.

God plans that people may know his *way* for them; this is explained in poetic parallelism by *saving power*. These two words in English are the one Hebrew word *yeshuah* whose meaning we studied in Psalm 66. God's blessing conveys to us, whom he has now rescued, the power to "save lives". For, if we "take up our cross", that action releases God's saving power for the redemption of others. No doubt that is why the new young Church, not having any other name for itself, called itself for a number of years just The Way (see Acts 9:2; 18:25). Christianity was not of course a religion, a new religion amongst the welter of religions at that time. It was "the Way of the Lord", revealed through the crucified and risen Christ.

Choir II, verse 3. God blesses his people, then,—why? *That thy way may be known upon earth*. In other words God blesses them with a missionary purpose in view. Otherwise how could *all the peoples praise thee*?

Choir I, verse 4. Israel is chosen to serve, *that my salvation may reach to the end of the earth* (Isa. 49:6). Thus *God judges the peoples with equity*, that is, with even-handed justice, for all men are equal in his sight. He is not like one of the ancient gods, nor is he like a modern dictator. He sends the rain on the just and on the unjust alike. Rabbi Joshua b.Hananya, in the second century A.D., asked the question: "At what time are all men equal?" Then gave the answer: "When the rain comes down, and all rejoice and praise God." And *he guides all the nations upon earth* in the same way, just as a shepherd leads (this is the Hebrew word) *all* his sheep alike. We recall the words of Jesus: "I have other sheep; I must bring them also" (John 10:16).

Choir II, verse 5. This choir responds in the same words as we find in verse 3. Praise is our first human *re*-action to God's action; dependence upon him is our second one (Acts 17:28).

All the people together, verses 6–7. The whole congregation now concludes this act of praise which has reminded them of their duty as the people of God when they came to the point of thanking God for harvest-home. The mystery of growth is something no man dare forget. Why should the acorn grow into an oak, and not into an elm? Why should the tiny ear of a cereal grow into a stalk of barley and not into one of wheat? It is, of course, the Lord's doing and his alone, the God of power and might. But he is also the God of love! And this God has blessed us. But why us? Because he has work for us to do for him. The Lord is the God *both* of the powers of Nature *and* of saving power amongst men. *Therefore let all the ends of the earth fear him!*

THE LORD OF HOSTS

Psalm 68:1–4

To the choirmaster. A Psalm of David. A song.

1 Let God arise, let his enemies be scattered;
   let those who hate him flee before him!
2 As smoke is driven away, so drive them away;
   as wax melts before fire,
   let the wicked perish before God!
3 But let the righteous be joyful;
   let them exult before God;
   let them be jubilant with joy!

4 Sing to God, sing praises to his name;
   lift up a song to him who rides upon the clouds;
   his name is the Lord, exult before him!

How different this psalm is from those immediately preceding it! In fact, it does not seem to be one psalm at all, but a collection of "psalm material" coming down from a very early period, some of it even from David's day. Parts of it may be compared to the style we find at Exod. 15:1–18; 15:21; Num. 21:27–30; Judg. 5. The poem at Num. 21:27 is headed by the words *Therefore the ballad singers say*, just as they might have "said" at the battle recorded at 1 Sam. 4:1–11.

This is not a "genteel" psalm. But were David's warriors, as we read of them in 1 Sam., educated gentlemen? They were surely wild characters, most of them—yet they had all been circumcised. Consequently they were all God's children. They belonged in his covenant people and so had been called to be his servants. God had chosen to use them just as they were, even as he uses young children today who have not yet grasped the Faith intellectually, or have not yet made a deliberate response of faith. It is useful to have such a psalm as this in our Bible. It reminds us that the Church is not made up merely of the spiritually élite.

In later years the final editor has taken the various sections of the psalm and made them into one string of beads for use at one of the festivals in temple worship. In fact, we notice traces of how the psalm may even have been acted by people who were in procession, while a priest declaimed parts of it in a loud voice. In this way he was teaching the unlettered the greatness of God and of his rule.

Arise, O Lord, verses 1–3. This is a quotation from the cry used in the Wilderness (Num. 10:35) when, each morning, the Ark was carried forward one day's journey. The Ark was the cultic sign of the presence of the warrior Lord of hosts. The enemy in those Wilderness days were usually the Amalekites; but here they are now all God's enemies anywhere. As we have noted, at this very early period there were only two kinds of people—the "goodies" and the "baddies"; or at least David's warriors would take such a distinction for granted. But so do millions of ordinary folk today who, in their hearts, think of "us" and "them". But the people of God certainly grew in faith over the years, discovering ever more of the depths of the mysteries of the purposes of God. David's warriors were, we might suggest, still at the school-boy stage of declaring that "My school is better than your school".

A pearl in the string of beads, verse 4. Someone else, or possibly the whole congregation, responds with this little chorus. In it they use very ancient wording. (a) *Lift up a song* uses a word like that found in Isa. 40:3, where the noun from this root is translated by "highway". What we have then is a beautiful idea; we picture Israel's song of praise rising up like a highway to God. (b) *Him who rides upon the clouds* is in the first place a description of the god Baal. We read in the poems discovered at Ugarit that he did just that (see at Ps. 18:10). These poems were already ancient even in David's day. Someone unknown to us has adapted the phrase to describe, instead of Baal, Israel's Lord of hosts. (c) We are to understand the last line as: *His name Yah* shows his real being, his very essence. *Yah* is the ancient short form of the name Yahweh. It is found in the old shout of praise "Hallelujah", as well as in the ancient poem we have already noted, at Exod. 15:2.

But the writer wants the congregation to *exult before*, not a mere Baal, but the *Lord* who has been there from the beginning of creation, and who has brought Israel herself into being. These lines, then, say in a primitive sort of way what Isa. 51:16 declares in more sophisticated language centuries later: "While I was stretching out the heavens/ and laying the foundations of the earth,/ I was saying to Zion,/ You are my people."

THE GOD OF THE POOR

Psalm 68:5-14

5 Father of the fatherless and protector of widows
     is God in his holy habitation.
6 God gives the desolate a home to dwell in;
     he leads out the prisoners to prosperity;
     but the rebellious dwell in a parched land.

7 O God, when thou didst go forth before thy people,
     when thou didst march through the wilderness,   *Selah*
8 the earth quaked, the heavens poured down rain,
     at the presence of God;

yon Sinai quaked at the presence of God,
　　the God of Israel.
9　Rain in abundance, O God, thou didst shed abroad;
　　thou didst restore thy heritage as it languished;
10　thy flock found a dwelling in it;
　　in thy goodness, O God, thou didst provide for the needy.

11　The Lord gives the command;
　　great is the host of those who bore the tidings:
12　"The kings of the armies, they flee, they flee!"
　　The women at home divide the spoil,
13　though they stay among the sheepfolds—
　　the wings of a dove covered with silver,
　　its pinions with green gold.
14　When the Almighty scattered kings there,
　　snow fell on Zalmon.

The great contrast. Yet this *Yah*, this mighty Warrior, the Origin of all things and Creator of Israel herself, is also *Father of the fatherless*, and *Protector of widows*; in fact he is the God of the masses of the poor of this world. We remember the famous quotation: "God must love the poor very much because he has made so many of them." Here then is an understanding of God made long before even the great prophets spoke. And yet there are self-righteous Christians today who believe that they are amongst the "saved", while the masses will perish for ever. The judgment here is otherwise. It is the rebellious, those who do not *want* love, who *will dwell in a parched land*, meaning of course the opposite of the green pastures of those who love the Lord that we met with in Psalm 23.

The Warrior God, verses 7–10. Here is a snippet of the kind of pre-Davidic poetry we have already noted. For verses 7–8 are almost word for word what we find at Judg. 5:4–5. This passage speaks of the ancient concept of a "theophany", that is, God presenting himself before the eyes of his people through the forces of nature, even as he did to Moses when, in a great electrical storm, he thundered from Mount Sinai (Exod. 24:15–17).

Yon Sinai may employ a pre-classical Hebrew term, to be

found also in the Ugaritic poems. If so the phrase means "The One of Sinai" and is a title of God (see NEB). Perhaps our psalmist remembered how, one year, the autumn rains that Israel had prayed for came as a deluge and swelled up the brook Kishon, and carried away the enemy's horses and chariots (Judg. 5:4-5, 21).

Plentiful rain is a sign of God's blessing. The poem seems to suggest that the land of Canaan was not originally particularly productive until God chose it (*thy heritage*) for Israel to occupy. Then he poured on it *rain in abundance*, and it became the land flowing with milk and honey. But then, this is poetry, so we are not to take such pictures too literally. The main stress is on the fact that God gave the land to a people that was both poor and *needy* (see Ps. 34:2).

Another poem about the Warrior Lord, verses 11-14. In Gen. 1 we read that God created all things by uttering his Word. This theological statement is echoed at Ps. 33:6. In line with this idea we are told that God creates victory also by the power of his Word. But a new element is introduced here not easily seen from the English text. *The great host* that *bears the good tidings* is a host of women! On the one hand, the army of male soldiers does the task on the battle-field of routing the enemy. The women on the other hand remain at home. There they do their own quiet job of dividing up the booty as *God* would do it, that is, *evenly*, impartially (Ps. 67:4). Thereafter it is the task of God's huge army of female evangelists to gossip the good news (this is the same word as "evangel") amongst the folk at home, or at work with the sheep. The Hebrew of verse 13 is corrupt. Remember, it is ancient poetry, and was probably passed down by word of mouth for centuries before it found written form. But the verse seems to describe the women's elegant articles of attire or the wall-hangings that they were working at together. In fact, it describes what they had actually *created* together, when the men were out "destroying" each other in a snowstorm that had fallen right at the mid-point of the Holy Land, on Mount Zalmon in Ephraim (Judg. 9:48).

The ancient nature of Israel's faith is once again emphasized by the use of the name *the Almighty*, because *shaddai* is a name for God that goes back into the mists of history. But the important point to note about the whole of this ancient fragment is, in the words of a recent commentator, "The Almighty has just to utter one word of command, and a great army of women-evangelists comes into being". From the description we have in this poem these seem to be a good mixture of Martha and Mary (see Exod. 15:20)!

POEMS ABOUT ZION

Psalm 68:15-20

15 O mighty mountain, mountain of Bashan;
       O many-peaked mountain, mountain of Bashan!
16 Why look you with envy, O many-peaked mountain,
       at the mount which God desired for his abode,
       yea, where the Lord will dwell for ever?
17 With mighty chariotry, twice ten thousand,
       thousands upon thousands,
       the Lord came from Sinai into the holy place.
18 Thou didst ascend the high mount,
       leading captives in thy train,
       and receiving gifts among men,
     even among the rebellious, that the Lord God may dwell there.

19 Blessed be the Lord,
       who daily bears us up;
       God is our salvation.   *Selah*
20 Our God is a God of salvation;
       and to God, the Lord, belongs escape from death.

The mountain range called *Bashan*, probably what we know today as the Golan Heights, with their *many peaks*, was much higher than little Mount Zion. And yet, says the poet, it was envious of the hill which God "*desired* passionately" for his abode, that little hill where Yahweh (the name of the God of the Covenant) dwells to all eternity. What he is saying in poetic form is that Natural Revelation ought indeed to be jealous of

Special Revelation, for it is through the latter particularly that God has chosen to make himself known to men.

Another poem about Zion, verses 17–18. With wonderful poetic licence the ancient author speaks of the dispirited army of ragged Israelites, men, women and children, entering Canaan as a mighty army of chariots, led by the Lord himself. Then the poem telescopes 150 years of history, and proceeds to picture what David did in capturing Jebus and in making it his capital; and what Solomon did in building the temple there. Finally it pictures God entering into the *holy place*. By the way, 10,000 was the largest figure ancient languages could handle. Those nations had no word for millions. That is why this figure of 10,000 recurs right through the Bible into the book of Revelation.

Yet RSV verse 17 *ftn.* maintains the original reading. *The Lord is in them, Sinai is in the holy place.* At Isa. 45:14 the Gentiles, looking at Israel, declare explicitly that "God is *in* you only" (not, as RSV, "with"), the Saviour God hides himself *in* Israel. When the festal procession reaches the gates of Zion, the people, who are about to march through them themselves exclaim: "Be lifted up, O ancient doors, that the King of glory may come in" (Ps. 24:7). Evidently God goes through the gates *in* the motley throng, wearing their shoes, as we put it at our commentary on Psalm 24. Then, *Sinai* is the name of the mountain from which God uttered his Word to Moses. Consequently, our poet, by means of his vigorous language, is actually declaring that Sinai has "moved into" Zion, so to speak, so that it is from there that God now utters his Word and reveals himself (see Ps. 50:2; etc.).

Without warning, however, the poet ceases to speak *about* God, and turns to speak *to* him. *Thou didst ascend on high*, he says. The words *the high mount* in the RSV are not there in the original. For the ascent is "eschatological", and not literal. The ascent is not just to the top of Zion, it is to the heights of God on high. Paul knew this well when he "updated" the poem to refer it to the resurrection of Christ (see Eph. 4:8; Col. 2:15). For he too *led a host of captives* to the place were God dwells for ever

(Eph. 4:8). Yet here it is to Zion at the moment that God is *leading* this host of *captives* in his train (that is to say, converts from amongst the nations) *and receiving gifts*. He does so "as the price of", "as the ransom for" (not *among*) men, even including *rebellious* Israel, that is, *Yah*'s people (the word is used again here) who had rebelled against him, and he does so in order to *dwell there* in their midst.

Blessed be the Lord, then indeed (verses 19–20), sings the choir. For "day after day he carries the load for us". He does this in two ways: (a) He gives us the power to enter into and share in his redemptive purposes (the word is plural, "salvations"); and, (b) He himself provides the "ways out of" (again plural) death. Surely these two plural nouns, being found in parallel, refer to the same thing; for, to OT man, death meant separation from God and from his loving purposes; so that life meant the opposite of that; it meant doing along with God what God himself delights to do and to be—*the God of salvation*.

A POEM ABOUT VICTORY

Psalm 68:21-35

21 But God will shatter the heads of his enemies,
　　the hairy crown of him who walks in his guilty ways.
22 The Lord said,
　　"I will bring them back from Bashan,
　　I will bring them back from the depths of the sea,
23 that you may bathe your feet in blood,
　　that the tongues of your dogs may have their portion from the
　　foe."

24 Thy solemn processions are seen, O God,
　　the processions of my God, my King, into the sanctuary—
25 the singers in front, the minstrels last,
　　between them maidens playing timbrels:
26 "Bless God in the great congregation,
　　the Lord, O you who are of Israel's fountain!"
27 There is Benjamin, the least of them, in the lead,
　　the princes of Judah in their throng,
　　the princes of Zebulun, the princes of Naphtali.

28 Summon thy might, O God;
  show thy strength, O God, thou who hast wrought for us.

29 Because of thy temple at Jerusalem
  kings bear gifts to thee.

30 Rebuke the beasts that dwell among the reeds,
  the herd of bulls with the calves of the peoples.
  Trample under foot those who lust after tribute;
  scatter the peoples who delight in war.

31 Let bronze be brought from Egypt;
  let Ethiopia hasten to stretch out her hands to God.

32 Sing to God, O kingdoms of the earth;
  sing praises to the Lord,   *Selah*

33 to him who rides in the heavens, the ancient heavens;
  lo, he sends forth his voice, his mighty voice.

34 Ascribe power to God,
  whose majesty is over Israel,
  and his power is in the skies.

35 Terrible is God in his sanctuary,
  the God of Israel,
  he gives power and strength to his people.

  Blessed be God!

If this part of the long psalm was really enacted before the eyes of the worshippers, then it must have produced a bloody spectacle. But we have already said that this is not a "genteel" psalm. Nor, of course, is redemption through the Cross of Christ a "genteel" subject for enactment. The Bible, fortunately, is concerned with reality, not gentility.

The episode begins with the word *akh*: Yes, indeed, *God will certainly shatter the heads of his enemies*; these are those who have grown old *in their guilty ways*. They have had a whole lifetime to repent, but have consistently refused to do so. There are of course many old scoundrels to be found. Not all old men are nice and saintly.

To understand what follows we are to recall the ideological thinking of the whole Near East in those days, and recollect the bas-reliefs from both Egypt and Assyria that pictured such thinking as we meet with here. In the beginning the Divine

Being had done battle with the goddess of chaos and had relegated her to the underworld. *Bashan* seems to be a misreading of a very similar word meaning "belly", in the sense of "the belly of Hell", or, "of Sheol" (see Jon. 2:2), the word thus being one of the biblical titles of the Serpent, or Leviathan, the very symbol of Hell. This Hell was also pictured as being the depths of the Ocean ("Ocean" being originally a god himself). Now, these white-haired old men and women had evidently deliberately chosen thus to "descend into Hell"! But God could fetch them out even of those depths to stand in judgment before him. Verse 23 then paints a cosmic picture, similar to what we have at Ps. 58:10, where we have a kind of Last Judgment. The wicked can be ransomed from their Hell only at the cost of blood. Here it is at the cost of their own blood. But the psalmist, surely without realizing it, expresses the truth, or perhaps rather the principle, that is brought forward in Isa. 63 at a later date, and finally in the NT, that since rebellion from God is such a terrible thing, the cost of redemption too must be terrible, to the degree that it can be paid for only by the shedding of the blood of God himself. At this point, however, it is the king, the representative of God on earth, who is to *bathe* his *feet in blood*.

The solemn procession, verses 24–27. This is a snippet, describing part of the great procession we have met in previous psalms, and which is now coming into view. The king leads the throng, but, being in the Davidic, messianic line, he represents the King of kings. Again, note how women have their full place in the ceremony; in proportion to their numbers in the community they must, in fact, have been seen to be a huge army. For *the great congregation* occurs here in an unusual plural form, and so must mean something like "all possible congregations"—(everywhere? and, at all times?).

Israel's fountain was the spring of water called Gihon which provided the only source of drinking water for the city apart from the roof-drainage that Jerusalem possessed. So the phrase spoke of the very water of life in a risky world. What an interesting picture our poet paints of God's life-giving presence in the midst!

Benjamin was the youngest son of Jacob, and the clan of that name occupied the smallest territory. Next to it lay *Judah*, much larger in extent; it was represented in the procession by members of its nobility. *Zebulun* and *Naphtali* lay away to the north of Palestine. Mentioning them specially thus meant that all the tribes whose territories lay in between would also be present.

The mighty God, verses 28-31. From the point of view of the condition of the Hebrew text of this snippet, it is the most notorious in the whole Bible. You might try the experiment of laying side by side all the versions of the Bible you can discover, the AV (or KJV), the RV of a century ago, Moffatt, Knox, NEV, TEV, the Jerusalem Bible, and more. Then you will note how much these all differ from each other. Yet the text of the RSV that we have before us is probably the best rendering of them all. There is no need for us, however, to seek here to reconstruct the text. The passage as a whole is a cry to God to *show his strength* over (a) the wild *beasts*, that is, the heathen nations, with special mention of *Egypt*, as well as (b) the *bull* worshippers (Baal was conceived in the form of a bull, as the symbol of sexual prowess, among the neighbouring Canaanites); (c) also over those pagan armies that destroy their neighbours merely in order to get booty; and (d) all other warmongers. Rather, he asks God (e) to have the great nations bring their offerings peacefully and willingly. By the way, the very ancient *Ethiopian* or Abyssinian Church (of which the late Emperor Haile Selassie was the Head) is very proud of this verse, for they regard it as a proof-text and symbol of their country's passionate adherence to the Orthodox faith.

Summary, verses 32-35. The congregation sings in conclusion a summary of this long psalm, inviting the whole world to join in. It began with a call to Israel to praise God; now it ends in a wild crescendo by inviting the whole world to join in. No wonder there sounds the clash of cymbals (*Selah*) at this point. The heathen are to take note that (a) God's *majesty* lies over Israel like a crown of glory, while (b) God's *power* is to be seen in the forces of nature. Then the poet seems to reverse his statement! He says, (c) God's *terrible* acts issue *from the sanctuary* (see RSV verse 35, *ftn.*), as he turns and speaks *to* God. Then he adds (d) The God of Israel, *he gives power* and deeds of *strength* (plural) *to* (his) people—not, in this case, to the forces of nature! No wonder the acclamation ends with *Blessed be God!*

The whole poem, in the edited form we have, is a tremendously vital *Te Deum* that cries out to be sung. It brings in (a) the faith of the ancestors in Wilderness days, (b) the central place of David in the worship of God, (c) the centrality of temple worship. (d) It gives us a glimpse of the vitality of Israel's festal worship, sometimes in the form of (e) narration, sometimes (f) as acted prayer. (g) Some references are historical, others are (h) eschatological, so that the final blessing is given *for all time*! Is there any reason why we today should not have just such an exciting and comprehensive faith as our ancestors had 3,000 years ago? Again, is it any wonder that the Russian Orthodox Metropolitan read out this psalm triumphantly in Moscow Cathedral on the day when Napoleon's armies began first to retreat and then to flee away back to where they had come from?

UP TO MY NECK

Psalm 69:1–15

To the choirmaster: according to Lilies. A Psalm of David.

1 Save me, O God!
   For the waters have come up to my neck.
2 I sink in deep mire,
   where there is no foothold;
   I have come into deep waters,
   and the flood sweeps over me.
3 I am weary with my crying;
   my throat is parched.
   My eyes grow dim
   with waiting for my God.

4 More in number than the hairs of my head
    are those who hate me without cause;
mighty are those who would destroy me,
    those who attack me with lies.
What I did not steal
    must I now restore?
5 O God, thou knowest my folly;
    the wrongs I have done are not hidden from thee.

6 Let not those who hope in thee be put to shame through me,
    O Lord God of hosts;
let not those who seek thee be brought to dishonour through me,
    O God of Israel.
7 For it is for thy sake that I have borne reproach,
    that shame has covered my face.
8 I have become a stranger to my brethren,
    an alien to my mother's sons.

9 For zeal for thy house has consumed me,
    and the insults of those who insult thee have fallen on me.
10 When I humbled my soul with fasting,
    it became my reproach.
11 When I made sackcloth my clothing,
    I became a byword to them.
12 I am the talk of those who sit in the gate,
    and the drunkards make songs about me.

13 But as for me, my prayer is to thee, O Lord.
    At an acceptable time, O God,
    in the abundance of thy steadfast love answer me.
14 With thy faithful help rescue me
    from sinking in the mire;
let me be delivered from my enemies
    and from the deep waters.
15 Let not the flood sweep over me,
    or the deep swallow me up,
    or the pit close its mouth over me.

We saw that at least sections of Psalm 68 come from a very early period, some parts even from the days of the Judges. Psalm 69 has perhaps been placed next as a contrast. For it seems to have been composed after the destruction of Jerusalem in 587 B.C., and so to be contemporary with the Book of Lamentations. It contains the outpouring of a heart broken by the horrors of the exile. Jerusalem has been destroyed by the armies of Nebuchadnezzar, and the intellectuals and artisans of Israel have been taken off to Babylon to do forced labour alongside many other subjugated peoples, all speaking a babble of strange tongues. No wonder it is a very emotional psalm. Part of it reminds us of the cry of Jeremiah who lived through that terrible siege. It is interesting to note (a) that the NT quotes or makes reference to Psalm 69 more than any other psalm except Psalm 22, and (b) that it has been read traditionally on Good Friday. We might ask ourselves why this has been so.

Up to my neck, verses 1–3. This is not an instance of modern slang. For the word for *neck* here is translated elsewhere as "soul", though the RSV usually has "me", "myself" or such like. But in the very early days of the language the seat of life was reckoned to be in the throat, probably because life could so easily be extinguished by squeezing it. There are two much more important points to note, however, about the speaker.

(1) He is in absolute despair, as we would surely be if we found ourselves in a forced labour camp in a land where no one had any idea that the God we served is a loving, caring, and compassionate God. For in that strange land it was normal for people to treat each other as ravening wolves, simply because their gods behaved like that to each other.

(2) It is difficult to determine whether he is an individual, or whether the *I* means all the exiles, or at least a section of them taken as one body. Of course it is not the king now who speaks. The last of the line of David is now languishing in a filthy dungeon where he remained for the unbelievable period of thirty-seven years (see 2 Kings 25:27–30; Jer. 52:28–34), after which Evil-Merodach, king of Babylon, finally took pity on him. News of his release and pardon acted as a great symbol of hope for the exiles. They were then encouraged to believe that God would rescue them all. It is possible that this hope is reflected in the last paragraph of our psalm.

The waters, then, whose significance we have discussed

before, are those powers of evil that can take shape as both
personal troubles or as national disasters; yet here it seems that
the two are intertwined. The psalmist, however, refuses to give
up praying to God. We see that he never desists from believing
that God is actually hearing him.

Is it fair?, verses 4-8. I am a sinner, he says. That I confess.
The wrongs I have done are not hidden from thee. But this
catastrophe that has befallen us far outstrips the punishment
any of us deserves. Let me give You two examples, Lord: (a)
Am I expected to pay back, not only the value of the thing
stolen plus 20% (see Num. 5:7), when I didn't even *steal* the
thing at all? That would not be fair, Lord. (b) Would You want
to destroy the faith of those who hope in You by letting them see
how You are not answering their prayers? It would seem that
individual Babylonian work-overseers were behaving abomin-
ably to our complainant, with the result that their actions
merely emphasized the horror of the whole national catastrophe. Yet our tortured Israelite, *by God's grace!*, is now
drawing nearer to discovering (verses 7-8) the great secret of
God's ways with man that another unknown exile set down in
writing in the passage we call Isa. 53.

I have really tried, verses 9-12. In these verses, at any rate, it
is an individual who is speaking, like in Job 19:13; Jer. 12:6. His
zeal means that total commitment which he showed to the
worship at the temple, and which he has brought with him into
the exile. But people sneer at me being like this, he declares,
and the drunkards make songs about me. Just a few words, but
what a vivid picture they paint!

But they can't get me down, verses 13-15. "I keep on praying
to You, Yahweh, Lord of the Covenant, even when it might
seem that the Covenant is dead and buried." So it is in just such
"impossible" circumstances that this psalmist along with others
makes a real "breakthrough" in matters of faith. He discovers
that (a) God does not answer prayer that is offered flippantly.
He waits until a person is truly humbled and at his wit's end.
Jeremiah makes this plain at Jer. 14:19-22. (b) God answers
prayer, not when we think he ought to, but at what we today

would call the psychological moment, but which the psalmist regards rather as the eschatological moment, God's *acceptable time*. (c) That right moment will happen only in conformity with God's great *hesed*, his *steadfast*, unswerving, *faithful love* and *help*. And that *acceptable time* can be at any moment, even up till the moment of death.

GOD'S STEADFAST LOVE

Psalm 69:16–36

16 Answer me, O Lord, for thy steadfast love is good;
    according to thy abundant mercy, turn to me.
17 Hide not thy face from thy servant;
    for I am in distress, make haste to answer me.
18 Draw near to me, redeem me,
    set me free because of my enemies!

19 Thou knowest my reproach,
    and my shame and my dishonour;
    my foes are all known to thee.
20 Insults have broken my heart,
    so that I am in despair.
    I looked for pity, but there was none;
    and for comforters, but I found none.
21 They gave me poison for food,
    and for my thirst they gave me vinegar to drink.

22 Let their own table before them become a snare;
    let their sacrificial feasts be a trap.
23 Let their eyes be darkened, so that they cannot see;
    and make their loins tremble continually.
24 Pour out thy indignation upon them,
    and let thy burning anger overtake them.
25 May their camp be a desolation,
    let no one dwell in their tents.
26 For they persecute him whom thou hast smitten,
    and him whom thou hast wounded, they afflict still more.
27 Add to them punishment upon punishment;
    may they have no acquittal from thee.

28 Let them be blotted out of the book of the living;
   let them not be enrolled among the righteous.

29 But I am afflicted and in pain;
   let thy salvation, O God, set me on high!

30 I will praise the name of God with a song;
   I will magnify him with thanksgiving.

31 This will please the Lord more than an ox
   or a bull with horns and hoofs.

32 Let the oppressed see it and be glad;
   you who seek God, let your hearts revive.

33 For the Lord hears the needy,
   and does not despise his own that are in bonds.

34 Let heaven and earth praise him,
   the seas and everything that moves therein.

35 For God will save Zion
   and rebuild the cities of Judah;
   and his servants shall dwell there and possess it;

36 the children of his servants shall inherit it,
   and those who love his name shall dwell in it.

We have seen before that *good* often means "good for". This verse comes alive when we realize this to be so. For, of course, God's *steadfast love* is indeed good for me! Then the phrase *turn to me* becomes a good parallel to "good for me". God's *abundant mercy* is, literally, "the multitude of Your acts of compassion to me". This last noun is built from the word for "womb". So its basic emphasis is on the mother-love for the child of her body that only a woman knows and can know. The OT is careful to depict God in both male and female categories of love. He is the Father, of course, but he is also the Mother. It is God's child, then who cries, *Redeem* "me" (the word translated "neck" at verse 1), "ransom" me (or, *set me free* in the RSV) out of this total situation of evil I am now in.

Is verse 21 to be taken literally? Had he to suffer a Borgia trick? No wonder he asks God to guard him, as today, in their personal helplessness in a corrupt society, men are driven to call upon God as a kind of last resort.

Vengeance!, verses 22–29. So he calls upon divine aid to do for him what he would like to do for himself but cannot. He does not realize that he has no right to *use* God in this way, or that it is just because he does so that God has not as yet answered his prayer. One very nasty wish is that when his enemies offer to God a peace-offering, to "make-up", literally, for their offence, it should turn into a *trap* such as God might use to catch them instead of to forgive them.

The succeeding clauses are equally nasty. But at verse 26 we meet with a new element in the situation. It is that the psalmist is well aware that the suffering he is enduring in Babylon has been brought on him by God as part of what is both the punishment he deserves and the education that that punishment produces. These enemies of his now seek to add to God's *just* punishment their own vicious acts of punishment! Thus, since he is being punished twice, he asks God to punish them twice! If God were to do so, he hopes, it would lead to their total annihilation, to their being *blotted out*, to their *not being enrolled* amongst the *righteous* (i.e. those who belong to the covenant people). We meet with this idea of being blotted out at Exod. 32:32; Neh. 13:14; Ps. 109:13, copied in the NT at Rev. 3:5; 13:8. In contrast to them, he says (using a pun), *I am afflicted and in pain.* Yet I recognize that this has been God's doing to me, because he wants to use me as his servant. "Therefore let the creative love You have fostered in me through suffering, O God, lift me to new heights." These heights are, of course, the heavenly places. What he is saying is that the saving love for others with which God has empowered him through suffering unites him with God himself who dwells on high, thus enabling him to be God's true servant. And God grants all these requests of his despite his cry for vengeance! Truly God is the God of grace.

Thanks be to God, verses 30–36. For that is what he is, the God of grace. Consequently he prefers grateful and loving hearts to big money donations—the equivalent today of a highly expensive stud bull! Obviously they are not in a position any more to offer sacrifices of thanksgiving (Lev. 1) as they had been able to do at the temple. Now they are *in.bonds*, that is, treated as prisoners of war.

All life is one, that of man and that of nature together, in that all is God's creation. So the natural world is to rejoice too when God finally sets free his imprisoned people, brings them back home to Zion, and *rebuilds the cities of Judah*; then *his servants shall re-inherit* the land, and their children's children *shall dwell in it* once again.

This hope implies two things: (a) God is faithful. In his *acceptable time* (verse 13) he will act and rescue his people from Babylon. (This is the theme of Isa. 40–55.) (b) In his wisdom God has decided to use one particular place on this earth where he may work out his cosmic plan of redemption (see Mark 10:32–34; Luke 18:31), and that is the Holy City of Jerusalem.

I NEED YOU GOD

Psalm 70:1–5

To the choirmaster. A Psalm of David, for the memorial offering
1 Be pleased, O God, to deliver me!
   O Lord, make haste to help me!
2 Let them be put to shame and confusion
   who seek my life!
   Let them be turned back and brought to dishonour
   who desire my hurt!
3 Let them be appalled because of their shame
   who say, "Aha, Aha!"

4 May all who seek thee
   rejoice and be glad in thee!
   May those who love thy salvation
   say evermore, "God is great!"
5 But I am poor and needy;
   hasten to me, O God!
   Thou art my help and my deliverer;
   O Lord, do not tarry!

This is an odd little psalm. Except for half of one verse, it is identical with Psalm 40, verses 13–17. Psalm 40 is the second last psalm of Book I. Psalm 70 is the third last psalm of Book II.

Psalm 40 belongs in the collection that prefers to use *Yahweh*, "the Lord", as the divine name. Psalm 70 is in the collection that prefers to use *Elohim* for God.

Why has it been repeated here in this second Book? Its heading contains one addition not found in Psalm 40, viz., *For the memorial offering*. We have seen that this one word in Hebrew is more likely to mean "to act as a reminder". And this is what the psalm does in fact do for us. It reminds us once again that we are all poor *and needy* creatures (verse 5), so that our only hope is in God.

GROWING OLD WITH GOD

Psalm 71:1–8

1 In thee, O Lord, do I take refuge;
      let me never be put to shame!
2 In thy righteousness deliver me and rescue me;
      incline thy ear to me, and save me!
3 Be thou to me a rock of refuge,
      a strong fortress, to save me,
      for thou art my rock and my fortress.
4 Rescue me, O my God, from the hand of the wicked,
      from the grasp of the unjust and cruel man.
5 For thou, O Lord, art my hope,
      my trust, O Lord, from my youth.
6 Upon thee I have leaned from my birth;
      thou art he who took me from my mother's womb.
   My praise is continually of thee.

7 I have been as a portent to many;
      but thou art my strong refuge.
 8 My mouth is filled with thy praise,
      and with thy glory all the day.

Psalm 71 also begins as a duplicate, for verses 1–3 are the same as Ps. 31:1–3a. But here the writer goes on to develop his cry to God in a different way. This is because he tells us he is an old man, with an old man's long memory of the years.

But his memory is really of a long life of grace. He has lived through the experience of the "two steps to salvation" we discussed at Psalm 66, yet he is aware that the second stage is a never-ending one. So we find that verse 2 means for him, "Deliver me and rescue me, incline Your ear to me and save me by continuing to give me Your power to love others". Of course he has already experienced "step 1". In fact, he actually tells us so at verses 5-8. But he still needs to be delivered from his continuing selfishness and self-centredness: "You have uttered the divine directive when You came to me again and again in my life, with the command to fill me with your caring, understanding, saving love" (see RSV verse 3, *fin.*). "Moreover, You continue to do so, because You are *to me a rock of refuge, a strong fortress.*"

This old man has lived out his days safe in that fortress, and with his feet firmly planted upon that rock. But being satisfied with stage 1 of salvation can actually be a mark of selfishness. So he is glad to receive from God the power to accept the second stage. In the same way, when Jesus named Peter as Rock, he was speaking of this stage 2. For, of course, Peter could be the rock on which the Church would arise with its Gospel for the whole world only if he had, by faith, first found that his feet were firmly resting upon the Rock that is God, and thus found that the experience of stage 1 is real. So Jesus was now summoning Peter to do exactly what God does, viz. he was to become a rock to others.

But our old friend is being given a bad time. Is the *unjust and cruel* man here scheming to get hold of his heritage? All that we read here is very human. Yet, he tells us that God is still his *hope.* (This is the word *ha-tikvah*, the name of the national anthem of modern Israel.) A famous heart specialist once declared: "Hope is a medicine I use more than any other medicine." Our old friend had leaned upon God ever since he was a little boy. How human and how sincere his language is here! The next line means actually: "You cut my umbilical cord when you brought me forth from my mother's womb." Since then he had never ceased to praise God, as only a little boy could, then as only a teenager could, and finally as a man with a long memory of God's grace was able to do.

Then he makes a most interesting statement. He declares (a) that *I have been as a portent to many*, and (b) that it was God who gave him the strength to be this portent. This word *mopheth* is often found along with *oth* (a sign). It means an occurrence that is something out of the ordinary, almost "not of this world", and so one that is "impressed with a divine purpose". This, of course, is what any believer should be like. He is meant to witness to the rock-like nature of God by showing forth through his faith and life a similar rock-likeness to those around him. People would then see that *my mouth is filled with thy praise, and with thy glory* (perhaps meaning "beauty" here) *all the day*.

BECOMING PART OF GOD'S PLAN

Psalm 71:9-24

9   Do not cast me off in the time of old age;
      forsake me not when my strength is spent.

10 For my enemies speak concerning me,
      those who watch for my life consult together,

11 and say, "God has forsaken him;
      pursue and seize him,
      for there is none to deliver him."

12 O God, be not far from me;
      O my God, make haste to help me!

13 May my accusers be put to shame and consumed;
      with scorn and disgrace may they be covered
      who seek my hurt.

14 But I will hope continually,
      and will praise thee yet more and more.

15 My mouth will tell of thy righteous acts,
      of thy deeds of salvation all the day,
      for their number is past my knowledge.

16 With the mighty deeds of the Lord God I will come,
      I will praise thy righteousness, thine alone.

17 O God, from my youth thou hast taught me,
    and I still proclaim thy wondrous deeds.
18 So even to old age and grey hairs,
    O God, do not forsake me,
  till I proclaim thy might
    to all the generations to come.
19 Thy power and thy righteousness, O God,
    reach the high heavens.

    Thou who hast done great things,
      O God, who is like thee?
20 Thou who hast made me see many sore troubles
    wilt revive me again;
  from the depths of the earth
    thou wilt bring me up again.
21 Thou wilt increase my honour,
    and comfort me again.

22 I will also praise thee with the harp
    for thy faithfulness, O my God;
  I will sing praises to thee with the lyre,
    O Holy One of Israel.
23 My lips will shout for joy,
    when I sing praises to thee;
  my soul also, which thou hast rescued.
24 And my tongue will talk of thy righteous help
    all the day long,
  for they have been put to shame and disgraced
    who sought to do me hurt.

Despite his continuing witness he still suffers. So did Paul; Paul never got rid of his thorn in the flesh. So now that he is old and weak our old man pleads with God to let his enemies see that God has not just dropped an old man from his plan. "Unless You hold me close," he says, "rancour may enter my soul."

Then after this very human cry he begs God to deal with his *accusers*. Have these people now brought him into court over his inheritance? But he regains his confidence in God at once. For he realizes that his confidence is not in any mere "Supreme Being", but in *the Lord*, the God who acts, day in day out, in creative love in people's lives, so much so and so often that his *mouth* cannot *tell* of all his deeds; in fact they are even beyond his understanding. Such changes in the lives of people, when God turns them from slaves (not now in Egypt, but slaves to their passions) into loving personalities—these are God's *mighty deeds*. It is these I want to talk about, he adds, not about any mere acts of human kindness. And this is because he himself is actually one of these *mighty deeds* of God. The consequence therefore is that he knows he has been caught up into God's great cosmic plan of redemption. In that great movement he now has a place! His little life now actually possesses eternal significance! He has become an instrument of the living God!

Even in old age he is still learning (verses 17–21), or rather, he is still being *taught*. He doesn't tell *us* about this here, rather he tells *God* about it. For in his case, one aspect of prayer is conversation with God. So he tells God "I can now do all things" *in* the power of the plan. The gods of Canaan too were powerful. But they were "power-drunk" in the way that some petty officials can become. The Lord's power, on the other hand, is to be seen, not merely in the awesome ways of nature, but more surely in the way he creates love in sinful human hearts.

So what I tell about God's deeds, he says, will now affect the lives of *all the generations to come*, both here on earth, and will *reach to the high heavens*. This is simple English for our theological expression, that God's love made known in human lives has "eschatological significance". This line of verse is clarified when we follow the Hebrew, and not the RSV; for the former goes on to explain that great things are great simply because no one else but God could do them.

It is just because he has fought his way to such a mighty faith, therefore, that our old man can now make the great biblical confession that occurred centuries before his day and which is to be found at Deut. 32:39. It is that we are not to lose faith when God lays suffering upon us, because God will certainly "bring us back to life" again, even if we have gone down into the depths of Hell. For, of course, God can "descend into Hell"— the words of the Apostles' Creed—if need be. This is because

God may choose to make use of suffering as an essential element in his plan of redemption.

Then *thou wilt increase my honour*, he declares, a word that is used virtually only of God himself and of his mighty deeds. But then this old man *is* now one of God's mighty deeds! This has happened, not in his own strength, but through God's countless acts of *comfort* to an old and feeble man. This word *comfort* entails within it ideas of strengthening, bracing, sometimes of rebuking, but always with the delicate intuition of a mother.

God's faithfulness, verses 22–24. It is that which once again is the key to all else. He is "*the Holy One of Israel*", the God who, being holy, seeks to make Israel holy too, yet in order that Israel in her turn may make the whole world holy. What a high calling for the people of God! No wonder our dear old friend wants to *talk of thy righteous help* (*tsedaqah*) in all this. Here then is another good instance of the use of this feminine noun, for which we have no English word at our disposal. This old man knows more about the mystery of his being than any of the ancient Greek philosophers. These all separated a man's "body" from his "soul", the latter alone being immortal. Not so, believes our "covenant" old man. He will praise God with his *lips*, with his *tongue*, and with his *soul* impartially. What did he mean by that last word? Throat (see Ps. 69:1)? More likely he meant "my whole being", our idea of "body, soul and spirit". We are to remember that when *the acceptable time* did finally come (see Ps. 69:13) the Word did in fact become flesh and dwell among us. Jesus was no mere phantom spirit, no mere immortal soul. He was Son of *Man*, a phrase he devised about himself meaning "a real human being"; and he was Son of David, that very human being, who had been chosen to spearhead the mission of God's people everywhere and in all ages. If the OT had not thought in the way this psalmist has learned from God how to think, then men would not have been able to recognize either the Incarnation to be what it was, or the Resurrection to signify something very different from the survival of the soul.

People who have only a superficial knowledge of the OT only too often hopelessly misunderstand the Christian faith. Many such declare that Jesus gave the world an ethical way of life that has never been surpassed, but that it was Paul who invented a religion around Jesus. Actually, as we discover from a reading even of the Psalms alone, the theology which Paul offers us in his Letters, and which puts Christ at the centre, he takes over wholly from the OT; while the Gospel writers themselves consistently claim that what they are reporting on is fulfilment of what God has already done in and through the OT covenant people whose songs and prayers we meet with in the Psalter.

GOD SAVE THE KING!

Psalm 72:1-14

A Psalm of Solomon.

1 Give the king thy justice, O God,
  and thy righteousness to the royal son!
2 May he judge thy people with righteousness,
  and thy poor with justice!
3 Let the mountains bear prosperity for the people,
  and the hills, in righteousness!
4 May he defend the cause of the poor of the people,
  give deliverance to the needy,
  and crush the oppressor!

5 May he live while the sun endures,
  and as long as the moon, throughout all generations!
6 May he be like rain that falls on the mown grass,
  like showers that water the earth!
7 In his days may righteousness flourish,
  and peace abound, till the moon be no more!

8 May he have dominion from sea to sea,
  and from the River to the ends of the earth!
9 May his foes bow down before him,
  and his enemies lick the dust!
10 May the kings of Tarshish and of the isles
  render him tribute,
  may the kings of Sheba and Seba bring gifts!

11 May all kings fall down before him,
      all nations serve him!

12 For he delivers the needy when he calls,
      the poor and him who has no helper.

13 He has pity on the weak and the needy,
      and saves the lives of the needy.

14 From oppression and violence he redeems their life;
      and precious is their blood in his sight.

How very varied the psalms are! What a great range of human experience they cover! This last psalm of Book II very rightly brings to a climax the hope of God's people that through their king the whole nation may some day possess the strength to extend the kingdom of God. The psalm bears the name of Solomon, rather than that of David. For Solomon greatly expanded and consolidated his father's rule. For his reign see 1 Kings 1-11.

The chief emphasis of this poem is on God's concern for social justice, the relief of the needy, and the crushing of the oppressor. This programme is to be carried out by God's "son" (2 Sam. 7) on God's behalf. But since the king is the headstone of the edifice that is all Israel, it is the whole people of God who are to bring the divine plan of love to fruition.

Using the word *justice*, the RSV hides the fact that the word is plural. Justice, of course, is an abstract idea only. But here at the enthronement festival of Israel's king an orator prays God to give the king the power to do *acts of justice*. These will, in their turn, create acts of justice in his people's relationships one with another.

Next comes a prayer that the king might *judge*, that is, rule over, God's people with *tsedeq*. This means that the king is to organize God's gift to Israel of an ordered and just society.

Verse 3 contains a reference to Lev. 26:3-6. There we read of God's promise that if his people should live together lovingly under God's rule, then the blessings of nature would follow. This whole state of *prosperity*, or better, of "well-being", is what *shalom* means rather than the modern idea of "peace". So the verse conveys a wonderful biblical truth. It is that God's purpose is that there should be a fellowship between nature and man, the hills even contributing to man's attempts to love his neighbour. His neighbour, of course, is likely to be a poor man. As Jesus puts it, "The poor you have with you always". He may not necessarily be poor financially, but he may be poor in terms of ability, physical health, strength of character and much else. Such "also-rans" in Israel's society are actually God's special care. Accordingly, God's anointed king (see Psalm 2) is to ensure that they are especially given the opportunity to live full lives, no one saying them nay. Clearly, prosperity can be a reality only when we share our love and concern with those who need it.

How many British people today, when they reach the fourth line of verse two of the British National Anthem, are aware that the words of that line are taken from here? We may well ask— Do people today really understand that the prayer in that verse, where the Sovereign should *defend our cause*, is in fact the cause of the underdog everywhere, for "we" are the ordinary folk of the world. Do we realize that the prayer is not for an expanding trade, or for military power, or for influence amongst the nations? "God save the king" means we are asking God to give the Sovereign just this particular power and ability; and the phrase "Confound their knavish tricks" is a poetic way of saying "*Crush the oppressors* of the poor and needy" (verse 4).

Again, while we are on the subject of National Anthems, we should note that the noun "Dominion" (which appears as a verb in the Hebrew) in the phrase "dominion from sea to sea" (verse 8), was first taken over from the AV of the Psalter by Canada and used by that nation as a description of its strategic nationhood.

The lovely poetry of verses 5–14 echoes the court-style used by many nations of the ancient world. But when Israel borrowed from others, she was in the habit of putting her own unique meaning upon the words she took over. As we see at Ps. 89:36 Israel applied these ideas here to the Covenant King, and in a unique way. These verses thus speak of a special divine blessing upon Israel's king beyond anything we could apply to any ordinary king in any land.

The world in those days was thought to be an island, the earth being surrounded by "Ocean", the name originally of a god. The prayer here therefore was that the messianic king might rule all nations right from the farthest east to the far west of earth's "island". Before modern scholarship made us aware of the significance of "Ocean", to the psalmist it was supposed that *the River* was the Euphrates. But today we see that it referred to the river of God that, first flowing out of Eden, then flowed right round the Earth (Gen. 2:10). Thus Israel's king would, under God, become King of Kings and Lord of Lords.

It is hardly credible that the orator who was addressing the throne with these words expected them to be taken literally. That is why later generations recognized he was under the pressure of the Holy Spirit, so that he was saying, as we might put it, much more than he knew. We would say that he had a vision of what lay behind history and beyond the moment of this act of enthronement. Yet we are not given a picture of a world dictator, such as Nebuchadnezzar was in the days of Jeremiah. For of course it was Nebuchadnezzar who applied this particular title to himself, that of king of kings and lord of lords. Strangely enough what we have is a picture of a kind and just man, a man of compassion and of concern for the poor and weak, and for all those who are oppressed and who suffer violence. Verse 12 begins in Hebrew with *(I declare) that he delivers the needy when he calls*; that is to say, God informs us that the king actually has a responsibility to the poor! This king might in fact have sat as the model Shakespeare used in *The Merchant of Venice* (IV.1,184): "The quality of mercy is not strain'd,/ It droppeth as the gentle rain from heaven [see verse 6, where we have "gently sprinkle"]/ Upon the place beneath . . . " It is a picture, no less, of "our gracious King (or Queen)". That is why the British people have adopted these verses as an ideal description of the royal family.

A MISSIONARY HOPE

Psalm 72:15-20

15 Long may he live,
     may gold of Sheba be given to him!
   May prayer be made for him continually,
     and blessings invoked for him all the day!
16 May there be abundance of grain in the land;
     on the tops of the mountains may it wave;
     may its fruit be like Lebanon;
   and may men blossom forth from the cities
     like the grass of the field!
17 May his name endure for ever,
     his fame continue as long as the sun!
   May men bless themselves by him,
     all nations call him blessed!

18 Blessed be the Lord, the God of Israel,
     who alone does wondrous things.
19 Blessed be his glorious name for ever;
     may his glory fill the whole earth!
         Amen and Amen!

20 The prayers of David, the son of Jesse, are ended.

But there is more to this vision of the future than that. This psalm is actually expressing a missionary hope. *The kings of Sheba and Seba bring gifts.* The Queen of Sheba was the first to do so when she visited King Solomon around 950 B.C. But now the nations of the earth have become voluntary subjects, not of the king in Jerusalem, but of the divine King whose "son" the Jerusalem king is. Such a hope can be expressed in the tenth century B.C. only in the language and thought-forms of the period. If this hope had been expressed in A.D. 1930 in central Europe, then we might have supposed that the orator was referring to Hitler's desire for *Lebensraum*, room for his Nazi youth to strut in Tarshish (this town was as far west as you could go, since it lay on the west coast of Spain), or in the Arabian desert, as the *ftn.* to verse 9 in the RSV indicates may be the meaning, or in Seba, that is, away somewhere in the far south on the sea route to India. But no, what we have here is a description of what later generations learned to call "The Kingdom of God", which, as Jesus said, "is not of this world". In summary, then, three kings are to come bearing tribute to this gentle and compassionate king in Jerusalem. We remember how the Church saw the fulfilment of this hope when three kings came to pay homage to a gentle baby king lying in a manger in Bethlehem.

Precious is their blood in his sight (verse 14). We are to remember that to OT folk the blood was not just the seat of life, it was actually the life itself. You could see a man's life ebb away as you watched his blood flow out of his wound into the soil. When sacrifices were made at the altar, the blood was first drained from the carcass and only then was the flesh given to God (Lev. 1·5, 11, etc.). This showed that the blood was important to God. The blood of those who suffered violence was especially *precious*. (See how this idea is expressed at Rev. 6:9-10.) We recall that the OT has no word for "soul" in the sense understood by the eastern religions. Perhaps, however, the idea of it can best be visualized under the word "blood". How important all these ideas are to Paul, as he theologizes upon the death of Christ.

Verses 15-17. We can't draw a line between nature and man. Both belong to the realm of God's creation. Both are to give of their produce under his rule. Both are to *blossom* under his reign. Mountains are to be fruitful right up to their tops. Human beings are to *blossom forth from the cities*! Because God has blessed the king, people will find God's blessing in the community life he creates, not as mere lone individuals, but as members of the redeemed fellowship that is Israel.

And to God be the glory! No wonder both this poem and Book II of the Psalter end now with a great Doxology. Yet we must recall (a) that *wondrous things* means actions that God alone can do, miraculous deeds that give evidence that this human king is indeed a messianic figure; (b) that God's *glory* is the manifestation to the eyes of human beings, by faith, of what God is like in himself; the word speaks of the majesty of his very being; and so his *glory* too is a *wondrous thing*; (c) that *Amen* means, quite simply, "Sure! We agree with our whole heart" (see at Psalm 2).

The compiler of the Psalter now ends his second Book at verse 20 with these words: "The prayers of David, the son of Jesse, are ended."

FURTHER READING

A. A. Anderson, *The Book of Psalms*, 2 volumes (New Century Bible) (Oliphants, 1972)

E. M. Blaiklock, *Psalms for Living*, Vol. I; *Psalms for Worship*, Vol. II (Scripture Union, 1977)

J. H. Eaton, *Psalms, Introduction and Commentary* (Torch Bible Commentaries) (SCM Press, 1967)
Kingship and the Psalms (Studies in Biblical Theology) (SCM Press, 1976)

John Goldingay, *Songs from a Strange Land* (Psalms 42-51) (Inter-Varsity Press, 1978)

John Hargreaves, *A Guide to the Psalms* (TEF Study Guide 6) (SPCK, 1973)

Derek Kidner, *Psalms* (Tyndale Old Testament Commentaries) (Inter-Varsity Press, 1973-75)

J. A. Lamb, *The Psalms in Christian Worship* (The Faith Press, 1962)

R. E. Prothero, *The Psalms in Human Life* (J. Murray, reprinted 1905)

A. B. Rhodes, *Psalms* (Layman's Bible Commentaries) (SCM, 1960, second edition 1964)

J. W. Rogerson and J. W. McKay, *Psalms* (Cambridge Bible Commentary) 3 volumes, 1977

A. Weiser, *The Psalms: A Commentary* (Old Testament Library) (SCM, 1962)